THE PROJECTS

The Projects

A New History of Public Housing

Howard A. Husock

NEW YORK UNIVERSITY PRESS
New York

NEW YORK UNIVERSITY PRESS
New York
www.nyupress.org

© 2025 by New York University
All rights reserved

Please contact the Library of Congress for Cataloging-in-Publication data.
ISBN: 9781479828432 (hardback)
ISBN: 9781479828470 (library ebook)
ISBN: 9781479828463 (consumer ebook)

This book is printed on acid-free paper, and its binding materials are chosen for strength and durability. We strive to use environmentally responsible suppliers and materials to the greatest extent possible in publishing our books.

The manufacturer's authorized representative in the EU for product safety is
Mare Nostrum Group B.V., Mauritskade 21D, 1091 GC Amsterdam, The Netherlands.
Email: gpsr@mare-nostrum.co.uk.

Manufactured in the United States of America

10 9 8 7 6 5 4 3 2 1

Also available as an ebook

For Robin

CONTENTS

Introduction — 1

1. The Birth of a Movement: Paving the Way for Public Housing — 11
2. Bringing the Idea to Life: Congress and the National Housing Act — 38
3. Cutting the Ribbon: Stories of Early Success in the Golden Age — 52
4. What Was Destroyed: The Dark Reality of Slum Clearance — 61
5. Crumbling Façades: Race, Segregation, and the Suburbs — 84
6. Abandoning the Projects: New Directions with Nixon's Moratorium — 104
7. Dealing with the Aftermath: From Distress to National Disgrace — 125
8. Fixing What's Broken: The Future of Public Housing — 144
9. The Projects Today: Five Snapshots — 160
10. Making Sense of the Projects: Looking Back and Ahead — 186

Acknowledgments — 197
Notes — 199
Selected Bibliography — 217
Index — 219
About the Author — 231

Introduction

Public housing in the United States, also known as "the projects," quickly brings to mind images of high-rise towers, stories of gang violence, and physical dilapidation. These may not be universally applicable, but they are far from unfounded. In many ways, public housing today can be thought of as a modern-day poorhouse—a residence of last resort.

Nationwide, the median public household income is just $9,044.[1] Only 15 percent of residents report income from wages—that is, from working. Not only are residents poor, but many live in poorly maintained structures. In 2019, a federal monitor was charged with overseeing the New York City Housing Authority (NYCHA), which is widely considered to be the largest and best-managed public housing system in the US, with 177,000 apartments on 335 sites.[2] The monitor went on to cite NYCHA's endemic problems with "lead-based paint hazards, heat and hot water failures, mold, elevator outages, and pests and waste."[3]

Residents face social ills, as well as physical ones. An analysis of New York police data has found that although residents of public housing make up only 4 percent of New York City's population, an estimated 20 percent of violent crime, prominently shootings, occur within one hundred feet of public housing.[4] Only 3 percent of public housing households comprise two spouses with children; 32 percent are single-parent families. (The remainder are mainly the elderly poor.)[5] It is housing not just for people in poverty but, disproportionately, racially segregated housing for the Black poor: 42 percent of public housing residents are Black, in a nation where they make up just 13 percent of the US population.[6]

Once in public housing, residents often remain for long periods. The average resident first moved in nearly seven years ago; the average "tenure" in New York City public housing is more than nineteen years. Ten percent of residents have lived in a project there for forty or more years.[7] Tens of thousands of public housing units became so "severely distressed," per federal jargon, that they were demolished. The first demolition—of the thirty-three high-rise towers constituting the Pruitt-Igoe project in St. Louis—began only nineteen years after the ribbon-cutting, when the project had won praise from the professional journal *Architectural Forum*.[8]

It was not meant or expected to be this way. Public housing's litany of social ills and management problems today obscure the public-spirited idealism bordering on the utopian that ushered public housing into American life. But such were the motivations when—as the Depression led to fundamental doubts about the private economy and its capacity to house a majority of Americans—a belief in an expanded role for a government safety net and a romance with modernist architecture and its aesthetics came together. The story of public housing's rise and often literal fall is the central story of this book, along with an assessment of its legacy and current conditions. The book seeks to be both comprehensive and critical.

Before public housing became "the projects," as even their residents would call them, the very idea of public housing was itself a project. And it was an idealistic and ambitious one at that. Those who conceived of public housing in the United States did not aim to build high-rise towers for the very poor. Their aim was to house the hardworking employed, whom they believed were being failed by private housing. But that was not all. Its early visionaries sought to change the face of cities: to replace neighborhoods they described unhesitatingly as slums and to substitute something that would be much better. They envisioned a "radiant city" of green campuses and "modern housing." Its pastoral settings were to house a third or more of US households at low rent, in buildings owned and managed by capable civil servants, rather than profit-seeking landlords they believed were cutting corners on essential maintenance and amenities.

FIGURE I.1. "Cross Out Slums," United States Housing Authority poster. (Library of Congress, 1941)

There were European precedents, including the massive, 1,250-apartment project in Vienna built in 1930, named for Karl Marx and emblematic of that city's Red Vienna period.[9] When the pressures of the Depression sparked energy and imagination about what government might undertake, what was once, for the US, a far-fetched idea of public housing became policy through federal law. It would change the face of thousands of cities and towns large and small across the US. Its stereotype as an urban high-rise notwithstanding, it was not built in just one style or one setting. Some residents have described the environs it created as idyllic; others as hellish—sometimes referring to the very same places, just at different times, as projects opened to acclaim but declined over the years.

A Chicago woman who lived in what was then the largest public housing project in the US—the Robert Taylor Homes, with twenty-eight high-rise buildings in a campus setting and home at its peak to twenty-seven thousand residents—remembered her time there from 1979 to 1999 fondly.[10] "My childhood," she recalled, "was fun. . . . We knew people in just about every building. . . . It was a family structure. . . . It was like a village in the building."[11]

The same project—demolished just forty-five years after it opened—was described quite differently in a letter to the *Chicago Tribune* in response to a public television documentary film that highlighted its crime, drug dealing, and dilapidation. "Robert Taylor is a community within a community. . . . I have found that we are a people strangely united by the devastation inflicted upon us. . . . We are a people consisting mostly of single-parent households, headed by women. We stay only because Robert Taylor offers a way to keep our families warm in the winter and together."[12] It is one thing to cut a ribbon on a new building; it was another, it turned out, to maintain and secure a Project over time.

The last remnants of the Robert Taylor Homes were cleared in 2007, but public housing is not past tense, even as its founding idealism has long been overtaken by its disappointing realities. Its effects linger; more than 1.6 million Americans continue to live in public housing projects. Newcomers still move in after long periods on long waiting lists; others have chosen to remain for decades, some their entire lives. Residents of more than thirty-two thousand households New York City public housing have lived in the projects for forty years or more.[13] Still others who came of age in that same public housing system—from Starbucks founder Howard Schulz to Supreme Court Justice Sonia

FIGURE I.2. "Eliminate Crime in the Slums through Housing," New York City Housing Authority 1936 poster. (Library of Congress, 1941)

Sotomayor—have come to understand it in a way that its originators did not intend: as a launching pad for later success.

Yet, however public housing's effects are assessed, it is the case, without doubt, that public housing complexes are atypical for the US. In a country shaped by myriad private plans and investments, public housing was powered by municipal design and federal funds. In tandem with "slum clearance" powered by government takings of private buildings that provided sites for its construction, it changed the physical face of US communities. Almost a century after those plans were hatched, their imprints remain: communities set off physically from their environs, populated by households selected on the basis of income by local authorities and federal rules, provided a home on the basis of their demonstrated need for one. Many of the original projects have been demolished, and some have been replaced by mixed-income developments—but their future success, too, remains uncertain. Rather than serving as a widely replicated model for the sort of mass subsidized housing envisioned by public housing's original advocates, these new-generation projects are meant, centrally, to correct the sins of earlier ones.[14]

The virtues and drawbacks of this system aside—although we will turn to them—this is a story of how a type of building and living unlike any other in the US took shape. It is the unlikely story of how public housing happened—how it changed communities and lives. As this is written, there remain more than thirty-three hundred local public housing authorities in the United States, most of them owners and operators of apartment complexes. One of them—the New York City Housing Authority—is the largest "landlord" in the country; it owns and must maintain some 177,000 apartments on 335 sites that are home to between 339,000 (officially) and 600,000 (a New York City Sanitation Department estimate based on refuse volume) residents.[15] It is its own big city within the nation's biggest city.

A great many other projects, however, are small complexes on the wrong side of the tracks in small southern cities towns across North Carolina, Georgia, Alabama, Mississippi, and Louisiana. Some are high-rises—or were, until the Department of Housing and Urban Development, the agency that helped finance many, judged them to be so "severely distressed" that they had to be demolished. Others are modest attached homes such as the one where Elvis Presley grew up in Memphis. Some occupy centrally located real estate in midtown Manhattan; some are on the fringes of small, southern Black Belt towns.

Even as demolitions and smaller, differentiated types of replacements and variations have thinned the ranks of the projects, there remain 886,000 public housing "units" that are home to 1.6 million Americans.[16] Many more would like to move in: in New York City, whose public housing system is the nation's largest, some 263,000 households are on its waiting list.

Such households are among the nation's poorest. Some 25 percent of households have less than $5,000 in annual income, and just 6 percent earn more than $20,000. They are overwhelmingly female-headed households—either elderly single women or young single mothers with children at home.[17]

This is a story about how this happened: how a type of building, residential living, and financial support unlike any other in the country took shape, how it rose and, in many cases, fell. It is a story central to US housing policy but transcends that topic to say much about the nation's racial politics—and housing segregation. Even more broadly, it says much about the way public policy ideas are conceived and by whom and go on to influence their potential for success and popularity—or failure and disdain. In the case of public housing, that conception occurred not at the grassroots or even primarily among elected officials but at an apex of public intellectual thought connected to political leadership. It was not demanded by voters or conceived by builders but by essayists and ambitious architects.

There is no doubt that these efforts led, for a time and for some people, to physically better housing conditions than they might otherwise have enjoyed. This book suggests, indeed insists, however, that those who made the projects possible viewed too narrowly the "slums" that they anathematized, judging them only by their worst housing—indeed, only in terms of physical housing per se. In advocating and achieving widespread demolition of neighborhoods cleared to make way for projects, they failed to take into account the social fabric—the web of institutions and relationships—found in the communities that were literally destroyed, replaced by artificial substitutes lacking them.

Virtually no significant amount of new public housing has been built in the US since 1973, when President Richard Nixon announced a moratorium that halted the highest wave of federal support for projects that had begun twenty-four years earlier, with the Housing Act of 1949, signed by President Harry Truman.[18] The contrast between statements of the two presidents on the same subject can stand as bookends for the program.

In signing the National Housing Act of 1949—which would authorize construction of eight hundred thousand public housing units, or the majority of those eventually built—Truman said this:

> This far-reaching measure opens up the prospect of decent homes in wholesome surroundings for low-income families now living in the squalor of the slums. It equips the Federal Government, for the first time, with effective means for aiding cities in the vital task of clearing slums and rebuilding blighted areas. . . . The [act] establishes as a national objective the achievement as soon as feasible of a decent home and a suitable living environment for every American family, and sets forth the policies to be followed in advancing toward that goal. I take deep satisfaction in the successful conclusion of the long fight for this legislation.[19]

In 1973, Nixon—in sharp contrast to Truman—asserted his own version of concern for the poor:

> Federal programs have produced some good housing—but they have also produced some of the worst housing in America. . . . I have seen a number of our public housing projects. Some of them are impressive, but too many are monstrous, depressing places—run down, overcrowded, crime-ridden, falling apart.
>
> The residents of these projects are often strangers to one another—with little sense of belonging. And because so many poor people are so heavily concentrated in these projects, they often feel cut off from the mainstream of American life.[20]

The drama that played out over the course of the decades between Truman and Nixon continues. This volume seeks to make sense of what happened and why.

The millions of people still living in public—and in other ways "assisted"—housing have probably never heard of Catherine Bauer, Edith Elmer Wood, or Lewis Mumford. But they live in environs spawned by the ideas of what today we would call those opinion influencers. New Yorkers who think of Robert Moses mainly as the architect of highways should know him, too, as the builder of dozens of projects. Detroit residents who know William Cobo only as the name of a long-gone sports arena could know him as the mayor, enabled by federal funds, who cleared poor Black neighborhoods to build a high-rise Project named for Frederick Douglass—its own site later to be cleared.[21] Chicagoans who might rightly celebrate the antilynching crusader and Ida B. Welles instead may know her as the namesake of a Project featured in a documentary film whose generic title—*Public Housing*—implied that its picture of pest infestation, drug addiction, and crime was one of synecdoche: the quintessential example standing for the whole.[22] Not many still remember Edward Brooke, the Black Republican senator who set rent limit rules for residents that continue in force—motivated by an effort to buffer the poor from the costs of maintaining the projects but also discouraging them from earning greater incomes and effectively starving public housing authorities of the revenue needed for maintenance and repairs.

Yet in the world of the projects—a housing universe parallel to that in which the overwhelming majority of Americans live—the efforts of all these figures remain consequential. All played key roles worth appreciating. They played roles in shaping a brand of utopianism that, in many cases, turned dystopian. This physical part of the US version of the social welfare state met and was itself profoundly influenced by the nation's unique political and social forces, not least among them race. Out of sight and out of mind for most Americans, a million-plus Americans, still today, live their lives in the aftermath of that conjunction.

The projects, in the form they predominantly took in the United States, resulted from the coincidental collision of changes: the emergence of modernist architecture, the decision by government at the local and federal levels to take a hand in both housing and altering the face of cities, and the migration of poor African Americans to those cities. Together, that coincidence of factors would shape the projects. It would be a combination that was successful at first—more successful than is generally appreciated—but proved to be difficult or impossible to sustain and limited in long-term popularity. Nonetheless, it is with us still. What follows tries to make sense of how it all happened and where it leaves us today.

This book differs from previous histories of public housing, in that it will focus less on approaches that might have or might still make public housing "work." It, rather, emphasizes the intellectual origins of the movement, including the writings of key Depression-era writers, emphasizing that there was little grassroots or political demand for public housing construction but that it was, rather, elite led. It focuses, as well, on what was lost when public housing was built—self-organized, low-income communities, particularly those of African Americans. It emphasizes that a long history of fixes to public housing's problems—its design, its concentrated poverty, and social ills—have attempted to refine the essential model, rather than consider whether it was originally misguided. It builds on my own previous book, *The Poor Side of Town: And Why We Need It*, which emphasized the value of modest, private housing for people of low income, and focuses, instead, on what, notwithstanding its early success, the author views as the misguided path of public housing—especially as it turned out to affect the poor. Most broadly, the concern of the author is for residents of the projects and their prospects for a better life.

1

The Birth of a Movement

Paving the Way for Public Housing

A good case can be made that public housing was born not in Congress or the White House but in a 1934 museum show, called the *Modern Housing Exhibition*, and its accompanying catalog, titled *America Can't Have Housing*. The exhibition was, of all places, held in New York's Museum of Modern Art. Most museum exhibits display works of the past, but the exhibit in question was about the future. It was the spearhead of a crusade; it made the economic, political, and even visual case that the federal government should finance the construction of housing for working families of modest means—not as an emergency measure but as part of the ongoing responsibilities of government. This was not an ordinary museum show.

An accompanying book written by Carol Aronovici, the chair of the committee organizing the exhibition, did not mince words in that regard:

> The purpose of the Housing Exhibition which the Museum of Modern Art has placed on display is to arouse public interest and foster a better understanding of the housing problem. . . . This book is not intended primarily as a guide to the material on exhibition. It is rather a statement of the far-reaching and varied social, financial, technological, administrative, legislative and political factors which have led to the present situation. It discusses the radical changes which must be made in our social philosophy and public policy in order to improve the housing condition of the masses of the American people.[1]

With the museum's new collection of postimpressionist paintings on one floor and renderings of housing guided by the architect Phillip Johnson on another, it linked modernism as art with the improvement of daily life for the common person, enabled by a modernist vision allied with government.

It was progressivism at its most confident. It would be only three years later that key leaders in the exhibition would go on to play a central role in writing and passing the National Housing Act of 1937, in which the United States Housing Authority, which provided the legal and financial blueprint for public housing projects, was established.

The museum show with its specific focus on the idea of public housing was not, to be sure, drawn on a blank canvas. Two years before, the same museum had, under the direction of the soon-to-be-celebrated architect Johnson, had staged an exhibit designed to promote the European "International Style" of architecture, of which the German Walter Gropius and especially the Swiss-French architect Le Corbusier were in the vanguard. Its promotion of tall city buildings based in "slender steel posts and beams, and concrete reinforced by steel," which "made possible structures of skeleton-like strength and lightness," was not limited, however, to the coming generation of skyscrapers. The same exhibition addressed, although not as it central focus, what its catalog deemed the "problem of low-rent urban housing," including "aerial photographs of 'slums and super-slums; as instructive criticisms of contemporary city planning—or lack of planning."[2]

In Europe, the stage for urban housing for people of modest means as a project for visionary architects, convinced of their role and capacity to provide uplifting mass housing, had begun to be set. Indeed, in so-called Red Vienna, the Austrian capital, municipal government—through local tax revenue—had built "social housing" housing blocks with sixty-four thousand units between 1924 and 1934.[3]

What is more, there was some similar activity in the US. In the early days of the New Deal, Franklin Roosevelt's response to the Depression included the need to use government-supported housing construction as a tool to jump-start the stalled economy. It saw the establishment of the Housing Division of the federal Public Works Administration (PWA), charged by the National Industrial Recovery Act of 1932, with helping to jump-start the Depression economy through federal support for construction projects, which would range from post offices to national park lodges. Around the time of the museum exhibit, it was already planning the aptly named First Houses in lower Manhattan, the first project of the newly established New York City Housing Authority. First Lady Eleanor Roosevelt, New York City Mayor Fiorello LaGuardia, and New York Governor Herbert Lehman would all be on hand for the occasion, which included an "abolish the slums" luncheon that followed.[4] "We hope," said Eleanor Roosevelt, "that there is dawning in this country an era when private capital will devote itself to the building of better housing and cheaper housing for vast numbers of people. But we know that the government will probably have to continue to build for the lower income group."[5] The First Lady clearly had a national program of slum clearance and public housing on her mind.

The Public Works Administration would go on to open fifty projects comprising twenty thousand apartment units in thirty cities including New York, Philadelphia, and Cleveland—and a latter-day Project in Chicago would be named for PWA head Harold Ickes.[6] Their architectural styles would include some of the high-rises later most associated with public housing—but they were a motley mix in which an older tradition of US "apartment house layout . . . collided with new ideas of housing introduced by European modernists."[7] The early New Deal focus was, it is important to note, as much on job creation for its own sake, as well as on slum clearance, a key later rationale, in authorizing these early projects. Their greatest importance, though, was their precedent: for the first time, the federal government was directly involved in financing, designing, and overseeing the construction of housing for people of modest means. Its leadership saw this as the country's housing future.

At the time of the museum exhibition, however, government building of housing had come to a halt, as the result of a 1935 federal court decision sparked by proposed slum clearance in Louisville, Kentucky, that the federal government could not constitutionally exercise the power of eminent domain to clear local properties on which to build. "Surely it is not a governmental function to construct buildings in a state for the purpose of selling or leasing them to private citizens for occupancy as homes." Explicit legislation, said a federal appeals court ruling that the Supreme Court would let stand, would have to provide a "fixed and definite guide."[8] The organizers of the housing exhibit would go on to play a key role in the drafting and passage of just such legislation.

If the precedent of federal involvement in low-income housing had been set, albeit temporarily, before the museum show, so too had a crucial corollary: the idea of clearing neighborhoods labeled as slums and replacing them not just with low-income housing but with a specific architectural type: high-rise towers designed in that European-influenced "International" style, which the museum had separately showcased in its 1932 exhibition. As early as 1930, New York City had cleared seven blocks on its Lower East Side to make way from what was to be a series of fifteen-story U-shaped towers on five of the blocks, with two set aside for parkland, designed by William Lescaze, a Swiss-born architect personally influenced by the original modernist, the Swiss-born architect Charles-Édouard Jeanneret, aka, Le Corbusier. The Christie-Forsythe project was never built, even after one thousand tenants in 375 buildings had been forced to leave their homes.[9] But the architectural seed had been planted, a blueprint example for so many projects that would go up. A 1935 PWA project in Brooklyn, Williamsburg Houses, would be again by designed by Lescaze—who helped Le Corbusier with his modernist vision he called "The Radiant City." It comprised twenty four-story buildings set in four "superblocks"—the Le Corbusier concept of what he envisioned as a city without streets.[10] The utopian architect and writer dreamt of "meditation in a new kind of dwelling, a vessel of silence and lofty solitude." It was a vision both influential and "remote from the blank and featureless spaces with which we're familiar in countless high rise housing estates."[11] Although Williamsburg Houses were not high-rise structures, they were built in the campus-style setting. It was a radical departure from historical city building—one based on government action and modernist architecture. The reformer's anathema for slums brought it to fruition.

So it was that the museum's housing exhibition—one not involving paintings at all—reflected ideas that were already born and taking physical form. Nonetheless, it must be viewed as a pivotal event in US housing history, one whose combination of vision and message affected and continues to affect the lives of millions of people. It was here that three big ideas came together, endorsed by a potent combination of leading architects, intellectuals, and elected officials. The private housing market would fail to provide adequate homes for the majority of the US population; what it would provide, except for the wealthy, was exemplified by the slums of big cities. What is more, a marriage between government and modernist architects and planners could create a new and better kind of city, one that would uplift its residents in campus-style oases of towers set in parks. Modern housing would, moreover, replace existing slum housing—requiring "slum clearance," that is, demolition of existing residential neighborhoods and on a large scale. All these elements were presented in the exhibition's book-length catalog—which previewed the arguments that would not long after carry the day in Washington.

The housing exhibit was deemed so important by the museum that an entire floor was devoted to it. Its organizers included not only Phillip Johnson but the pioneering photographer or the poor Walker Evans and the man who would reshape the face of New York City, Parks Commissioner Robert Moses. The exhibit was sponsored by some of the city's leading philanthropists, including Abby Aldrich Rockefeller (Mrs. John D.); newspaper publishers, including Arthur Ochs Sulzberger of the *New York Times* and Herbert Bayard Swope of Joseph Pulitzer's *New York World*; the first US secretary of labor and first woman cabinet member, Francis Perkins; Columbia University president Nicholas Murray Butler; and Rev. Edward Roberts Moore, head of the Catholic

Archdiocese Division of Social Action. Included, too, were New York Governor Herbert Lehman and his predecessor Al Smith. Another notable sponsor was a newly established public agency: the New York City Housing Authority.

Notably absent were any residents of low-income neighborhoods themselves. Although elected political officials were among the sponsors, there were no direct representatives of the income groups or neighborhoods that the exhibition envisioned demolishing and transforming. It would prove to be the start of a housing policy pattern, one that continued. There was, however, no element of New York's social, intellectual, political, religious, and financial elite not among those who were confident in promoting the new idea of public housing, for the city and the nation. The projects—and slum clearance to provide sites on which they would be erected—were themselves their shared project. The *New York Times* described the exhibit itself as "a series of graphic numbered panels, arranged in sequence for wall display, . . . to explain the necessity for slum clearance, the obstacles in the way and possibility of achieving modern satisfactory low-cost housing, not only in New York but throughout the nation. . . . The exhibition also will include models of housing projects and developments both here and abroad." Macy's department store donated furnishings.[12]

The exhibit also included what the *Times* described as "an old three-room flat . . . taken almost intact from a tenement recently demolished, the total floor space being 28 by 13 feet. This dark airless home of the past may be contrasted with a model three-room low-cost apartment."[13] That model would be constructed on the museum's third floor. Many years later, a similar tenement would itself become a museum, the Tenement House Museum, which would celebrate such apartments as the "urban log cabin"—starting points for striving Americans. That was not at all the theme of the museum exhibition.[14] In its "slum flat reassembled on second floor," the exhibit featured an apartment with makeshift curtain divides between sleeping areas, a kitchen with what looks like a coal cooking stove, no obvious bathroom, dirty dishes cluttered on small

FIGURE 1.1. "The Housing Exhibit of the City of New York." (Museum of Modern Art, 1934)

counters, and a bathtub in the open living area. A single hanging light provided the only illumination.[15]

It is well worth noting that although the organizers and contributors had never themselves lived in the "slums," they were quite certain that they were cesspools of immorality, depravity, and conditions that an

FIGURE 1.2. Macy's model public housing apartment. (Museum of Modern Art, 1934)

increasingly wealthy American should not tolerate. Organizer Catherine Bauer was a Vassar College graduate who had been raised in Elizabeth, New Jersey; her father was New Jersey's chief highway engineer.[16] Her key collaborator, the Columbia University faculty member Edith Elmer Wood, chaired the National Committee on Housing of the American Association of University Women. Wood was a Smith College graduate from Portsmouth, New Hampshire, who, prior to her career as a housing reformer, had written several books of romantic fiction, including *Her Provincial Cousin* (1893) and *Shoulder Straps and Sunbonnets* (1901). Both were convinced—and convincing—in their views expressed in the exhibition book that the private housing market was doomed to fail. Wood wrote that as many as two-thirds of all households would inevitably be failed by private housing developers—whose zeal for profit would make high-quality housing out of their economic reach. The wealthiest third alone would be well served, while the next two-thirds would struggle, she asserted.

> Under our old system of 100% private enterprise, the most prosperous third of our population, nearly 10,000,000 families live in comfortable modern homes. The next 10,000,000 families cannot build, buy or rent a new home. They can sometimes acquire a bargain-counter old home. They are more desirable tenants than the lowest economic third and can out-bid them in rent. They therefore have their pick of the older, shabbier, partly modern houses which the more prosperous families have discarded. Meanwhile the lowest economic third of the population occupy obsolete, inadequate, neglected shelter, damaging in varying degree to health and to self-respect.[17]

Bauer was even more strident: "There is no getting around the fact that modern housing and much of the framework of Western society, are mutually antipathetic," she wrote in her 1934 book *Modern Housing*, the template for the public housing movement.[18]

She was no outlier. A similar view was expressed by the nation's top housing official. Robert Kohn, who headed the Housing Division of the Roosevelt administration's Public Works Administration, put it this way in the museum exhibition book: "Nowhere has *laissez-faire* failed more dismally than in the field of shelter for the lower-income groups. A national housing policy will not make much progress with us until it is generally conceded that housing for these groups never has been and never will be produced for profit."[19] The social critic Lewis Mumford, another contributor to the exhibit book—and mentor to Catherine Bauer—was even more blunt in his essay. "In attempting to make [better] standards available for lower income groups hitherto housed in crowded tenements and dark hovels, it became plain that no effective work could be done as long as capitalist canons of enterprise were respected."[20]

It is no exaggeration to say that Bauer and the exhibition contributors and sponsors were engaged in a utopian crusade, motivated not by their experience building homes but by intellectual ideals that had been nurtured by Bohemian circles—first in Paris and later in Greenwich Village. While in Paris, Bauer had been exposed to the early modernist architecture movement, including what would come to be known as the "towers in the park" design, which the Swiss-born Le Corbusier had first presented in the Radiant City in 1924, before publishing the book of the same name in 1933.[21]

The utopian vision would not only imagine a complement to existing housing but would replace it. Slum clearance was central to the public housing vision. Notably, Wood and Bauer had been at work building their case for slum clearance and modern housing, even pre-Depression, even as new working-class housing was being privately built on an unprecedented scale in the form of Philadelphia row homes, Brooklyn brownstones, Chicago "two-flats," California bungalows, and New York "triple-deckers."[22] All were helping to create what the Boston sociologists Robert Wood and Albert Kennedy had called a "zone of emergence" from tenement districts. They referred to small homes, including multifamily owner-occupied structures, in neighborhoods to which immigrants moved from port-of-entry tenement districts such as Boston's North End.[23]

None of it had impressed the reformers. Edith Elmer argued in her 1919 book *Housing the Unskilled Wage Earner: America's Next Problem* that "no nation can rise higher than the level of its homes. Whether we approach the problem from the point of view of health, morals, child conservation, industrial efficiency, Americanization or good citizenship the housing problem is fundamental." The "future welfare of the country," she had written, depended on decisions regarding "future housing policy."[24] Public housing would be akin to public education—a good so essential yet so wanting that government had to step in to provide it.

As expert outsiders both calling attention to "slum" conditions and calling for their improvement, Wood and others in the exhibition stood squarely on the shoulders of reformers who had come before them. Exposés of housing conditions in low-income immigrant sections of New York City—most notably the photo essay *How the Other Half Lives: Studies among the Tenements of New York*, by the onetime police reporter Jacob Riis—had established the idea that slum housing was a physical, even a moral, scourge. His language was emotional, evocative, and, thus, memorable: "Dirt and desolation reign in the wide hallway and danger lurks on the stairs.... The wolf knocks loudly at the gate in the troubled dreams that come to this alley, echoes of the day's cares. A horde of dirty children play about the dripping hydrant."[25] Inspired by such conditions, so-called state-aided housing had been erected in European countries with governments of the both Left and Right, including in Austria, Germany, England, the Netherlands, and Belgium.[26] Unifying this history was the guiding principle that the incomes of the working poor were inadequate for them to obtain safe and sanitary housing—and nonmarket or quasi-market substitutes were needed. In the US, government involvement to provide housing specifically for people of low incomes had begun at the local level, notably in New York City. First, new buildings codes mandated so-called new law tenements with greater light and ventilation. But reformers' concerns had continued unabated. Alexander von Hoffman, an American urban planner and historian, writes, "After building regulations failed to put an end to slums, in the 1920s a group of housing reformers—primarily social workers in New York City—proposed that government sponsor housing. The campaign that began focused on the local level of government, hence the proponents referred to their program as municipal housing. In their scheme, city governments would provide tax breaks or funding to non- or limited profit housing associations, or possibly build the housing themselves."[27]

Indeed, previous efforts in New York to build housing for the poor through nonprofit, limited-dividend corporations had actually been built. A "model tenement for Negroes" built in 1854 by the New York Association for Improving the Condition of the Poor and designed by a prominent architect, the "Big Flat" quickly deteriorated because of the cost of upkeep and would be described as a "pest-hold and resort of the worst characters," before being demolished by 1888.[28] These might have served as early warning signs of the complexities of government-built housing. They did not.

The new discipline of social science had abetted the idea that poor urban neighborhoods were "slums" and a self-evident danger even to their own residents. In a two-volume 1936 study, *Slums and Housing: History, Conditions, Policy*, Harvard's James Ford, with support from the Phelps-Stokes Fund, a New York foundation, was sounding an alarm. Although not a contributor to the influential museum exhibition, Ford was listed as among the "sponsors," who, in addition to the New York elite noted earlier, included Mary Simkhovitch, the settlement house leader who, since 1931, had headed the new, nationally focused Public Housing Conference.[29] The sponsors included Ford's *Slums and Housing* patron, I. N. Phelps-Stokes, a prominent architect born into a banking and real estate fortune whose Phelps-Stokes Fund had been active in "progressive" causes—including temperance and education for African Americans through the Tuskegee Institute and other activities in housing "reform." As a member of New York's Tenement House Commission, he had authored the 1901 Tenement House Law, which had ushered in the so-called new law tenement requiring greater light and ventilation.[30] The die was clearly being cast.

Ford's sprawling 970-page work, although much informed by housing and health statistics, clearly reflects the perspective of the reformer recoiling from the neighborhood he sees—and where he could not imagine living:

> The backyards of New York slums are smaller and darker than those of other cities, with the exception of portions of Boston. A back yard of 10 or 12 feet is used in blocks where buildings are five or six stories in height. A dilapidated fence at the sides and rear, ordinarily separates a yard from its neighbors. There may be much clutter and almost invariably there is much ugliness in this area, which serves no wholesome purpose except

to provide light and air for rear windows. Clothes drying on pulley lines at many levels add to the general confusion.... For the beauty of nature and an attractive outlook the slums substitute interest in the behavior of one's neighbors and the excitement of kaleidoscopic street activities. Tenement dwellers become accustomed to this and probably derive some thrill from it, as the pillows on window ledges attest, and the many faces peering from the windows of each floor.[31]

This is what might be called the "reformer's gaze"—a perspective influenced by the values and preferences of the onlooker, not the resident, not acknowledging that what he witnessed might just as well be described as a lively and dynamic city neighborhood whose residents are striving, saving, and planning. Notably, Ford acknowledged that, in other cities, conditions differed from those of New York—singling out for praise the small row house model of Philadelphia as "providing a quality of service in the field of housing hardly equaled in any other American city."[32]

But it was New York where the housing exhibition had been staged— and where those who were shaping federal housing policy held forth. They could find, from Ford, materials that went beyond the subjective, however; he employed a trove of data to demonstrate the danger of slums and lay the groundwork for the cascade of clearance that must be understood as at least as important an element of the public housing movement as the eventual construction of the projects themselves. To his credit, Ford was careful—disputing, for instance, the conventional wisdom that "slums and bad housing are the major cause of disease, vice, and crime.[33] The advent of the smallpox vaccine, clean water, and sanitation had made for far-improved "slum" living conditions in the 1930s compared to those of the nineteenth century. But Ford was certain of the link between slums and tuberculosis, unaware of its bacterial cause, which was not yet understood.[34] He traced its spread directly to the housing and habits of the poor: "In considering the problem of tuberculosis in its relation to housing, it is necessary to bear in mind the comparative poverty of the slum dweller may mean imperfect nutrition, that the noise of tenement districts may mean imperfect sleep, that the sunlessness of the lower floors of tenement houses may mean reduced resistance . . . caused by inadequate sleep and the lack of sunshine and clean air."[35] That rates varied among ethnic groups and were high in rural Staten Island—he was critical of certain "backward races" and their habits—did not diminish Ford's ultimate conclusion favoring slum clearance. His work is a reminder that the modern housing movement was not insulated from the pseudo-social science of the era, including generalities about the habits of racial and ethnic groups. Health and mortality, he concluded, was, in part, related to "race composition." "The ever-changing racial character of slum districts should have much to do with their relative morbidity. Because of the high tuberculosis rates of Negroes and Porto Ricans, and the relatively low tuberculosis rates among Jews, the rate for any district may be increased by invasion of the former and decreased by predominance of the latter."[36]

Ford was also convinced that "bad housing" was linked to a troubled "moral life." The connection here involved notable but convoluted reasoning. Poor housing, he reasoned, would lead to a "weak or sickly body"—which, in turn, would drain residents of "practical energy" and reduce "the moral energy of individuals to resist the opportunities for evil which slum conditions so generally offer." That the affluent might not be immune from becoming ensnared in criminal schemes did not deter Ford from this sweeping conclusion.[37]

For Ford—and the museum exhibit sponsors—slums were a problem, and their clearance was the self-evident solution. There were, to be sure, related questions: What to replace them with? How to house the dislocated in the interim? Who should finance and manage the replacement housing? But all of these questions assumed that slum clearance would and should happen.

Wrote Ford, "The slum is a menace which cannot be overcome by piecemeal modernization loans or random demolitions with the owners' consent. . . . No solution will be found short of a comprehensive and intelligent policy actuated by one or more units of government, amply financed, which make the neighborhood rather than buildings the basis of operations."³⁸ Not gradual improvement over time—the goal must be "slum elimination." As for the shops, the churches and synagogues, the small businesses, street life, and so much more with which "slums" were replete, Ford was silent.

Make no mistake: the reformers wanted not only to build housing but also to change the urban environment. The cities of the future—per Catherine Bauer, Lewis Mumford, Walter Gropius, and other contributors to the exhibition book—would separate industry and commercial uses from the residential, build sun-splashed apartments in environments of relaxing green space, and call on cutting-edge architects to provide the design. "Mixed-use" projects—in which industry, retail, and residential buildings were set on traditional street layouts—were anathema. Indeed, in a chapter promoting the idea of "industrial decentralization," Ford decried the fact that employers and residences were close together, noting a survey showing that for "Manhattan residents, 31 percent required nineteen minutes or less to get from home to shop; 49 percent required twenty to thirty-nine minutes." For Ford, this was often vice, not virtue, and he wrote that "industries and workshops vary greatly in their menace to neighboring properties and residences. Some are nuisances of an extreme type; others may be in many senses a community asset."³⁹ On balance, however, industry and residences needed to be relocated on a grand scale. He added, "Obviously, if a fair percentage of the New York industries could profitably be moved to areas in outlying boroughs and their workers could simultaneously be moved to well planned residential communities near the factories, much of the congestion of population and traffic within the city could be eliminated and decent housing might be made accessible to the workers."⁴⁰ A Berlin project, in that vein, designed in part by the Bauhaus architect Walter Gropius, was chosen as the cover art for the housing exhibit book. "Siemensstadt" was the imposing collection of ultra-modernist apartment complexes built specifically to house employees of the Siemens engineering firm and comprising eighteen

FIGURE 1.3. Cover of housing exhibition catalog. (Museum of Modern Art, 1934)

thousand apartments.[41] Later designated as a UNESCO World Heritage Site, the so-called Ring Estate combined (in the section Gropius himself designed) "terraced housing with an impressive variety of expressive detailing and design."[42] The overall complex included a larger central green space.

This was beyond the mere provision of utilitarian housing. It was, rather, about building a new type of urbanscape, a city of tomorrow, in Le Corbusier's phrase—organized by government and designed by architects. It was no coincidence that Philip Johnson would go on to design such iconic modernist structures as New York's Seagram Building and his Glass House in New Canaan, Connecticut. Modern housing, for Johnson, was inextricably tied to the glass towers of modernism overall.

Gropius, in his contribution to the museum exhibit book, was clear in advocating for a vision of large apartment complexes with green space set aside as the future of workers housing—which was what the public "housers" understood themselves to be promoting. Similar design planning goals were expressed by Le Corbusier, in his vision of the Radiant City: "Everything in the Ville Radieuse would be symmetrical and standardized. At the center, a business district would be connected to separate residential and commercial zones via underground transit. Prefabricated housing towers would serve as vertical villages with their own laundromats as well as rooftop kindergartens and playgrounds. Apartments would have views out onto shared public spaces. Residents would enjoy peace and quiet, separated from industrial districts."[43]

In Le Corbusier's 1927 book *The City of Tomorrow*, he described his vision for the city as one in which "the plan must rule" and in which "there ought to be no such things as streets": "We have to create something that will replace them." That something would become known as "superblocks," where were set projects with no cross streets for stores, cars, or small homes. Le Corbusier had already designed just such a city in his 1922 plan for the Ville Contemporaine, which was to comprise sixty-story apartment buildings, all identical, surrounded by a zigzag of smaller buildings and a park. Le Corbusier asserted that "the whole urban scene is one of wasted opportunities and inefficiency." He proposes an alternative course, "which is a bold and drastic reconstruction of the entire machine." Central to his vision was that of "skyscrapers set at immense distances from one another and surrounded by large open spaces or parks."[44] Le Corbusier's ideas would fall on open ears in the public housing movement—through which it would take most concrete form in the United States.

Catherine Bauer, who would be the key to bringing Le Corbusier's vision to the US, clearly showed his influence in her exhibit paper for *America Can't Have Housing*:

> The old methods of providing shelter for people of average income or less are today so thoroughly unworkable and obsolete that any positive attempt to solve the housing problem can only be achieved by drastic measures. No back door or half-way measures will do the job any more. Modern housing means complete new communities planned entirely from the point of view of fullest usefulness and long time amenity— instead of chaotic subdivision and the erection of dwellings designed only to bring quick speculative profits. It means that rentals must be geared to the capacity to pay and not to the "market." It means that a decent dwelling is not a reward withheld for the successful, but a fundamental right to which every citizen is entitled, the provision of which becomes a responsibility of government. Almost every intelligent technician or social worker would agree with these premises. Many government officials have stated them publicly. But so far they have not even begun to be put into practice.[45]

The path toward doing so as a practical matter would be charted in the housing exhibit, as well. In Walter Gropius's advocacy for his vision of large apartment complexes with green space set aside as the future of workers housing, the Bauhaus School founder made clear, in his contribution to the exhibit, that formal city planning and new building codes would be required. To set the stage, he said, laws governing local construction would have to be changed, to ensure a sharp departure from the tenement era of low-rise density. "All zoning laws must aim at achieving light and air by limiting congested housing. For sufficient air each dwelling must have cross-ventilation and double exposure; in other words, the apartment house must be only one apartment deep," he wrote. "Sufficient lighting and equal exposure to the sun for all dwellings means opening in rows or strips of apartments and a sufficient open space between these strips. Interior courts and narrow streets which take away light and air are a crime."[46]

Building in sufficient quantity would mean large apartment complexes, not the single-family homes or small duplex or triplexes that Americans had historically preferred or at least that the private market had historically built for them. Gropius—another essential avatar of modern architecture—did not completely rule out all other forms in his contribution to the exhibit book. He just rules them out for cities. "The advantages of the one or two story single house, either free standing or in rows, are recognized throughout the world." He would go on to say, though, "It is not, however, the cure-all for the conditions in our cities. The high land values have made the single house an absurdity. Even five story tenement houses are an unsatisfactory compromise. What is then the solution? I propose after careful sociological and economic research ten to twelve story apartment houses for the thickly settled districts of our cities." Open spaces between the buildings, wrote Gropius, would create a "City of Green." Tenants would "see the sky," children would have playgrounds, and nature would "permeate" the city.[47]

It was dark irony that the contribution of Gropius, who had just fled Nazi Germany, was followed in the museum volume by the contribution of the German city planner Werner Hegemann—who specifically praised the housing vision of Adolf Hitler. The new German chancellor had, in 1926, included in what he called his "unchangeable program" a "national reform of laws governing real estate, the creation of a law permitting for public benefit the expropriation of real estate without indemnification, the abolition of ground rent and prohibition of all speculation in real estate."[48] Hegemann had no criticism for Hitler's autocratic housing vision—only for the Third Reich's slow pace of housing construction.

It is well worth pondering the fact that a seminal text making the case for US public housing, presented in one of the most prestigious cultural settings in the country and with the imprimatur of leading citizens, would have included an essay of praise for a policy of Adolf Hitler. "Hitler has done much in encouraging new marriages. They require new homes. But it may take twelve years before the sad effects on popular housing resulting from the present policy will be clearly seen."[49] The curator of the exhibit was comfortable with a powerful government hand shaping the places that ordinary citizens would live.

Editor Aronovici agreed that there was no reason to go slow. Surprisingly, she did not reference Great Britain, where the construction of houses owned by local government councils had been ongoing since the enactment, in 1900, of the Housing of the Working Classes Act.[50] But she pushed for a much faster pace of public housing legislation and construction in the US—confident that this approach could marry low cost with an aesthetically pleasing environment, made possible by modern architecture. Indeed, wrote the volume's editor, public housing would rely on architects: "the architect will have to be re-educated, if out of the 'art' of concealing, disguising and tattooing modern utilitarianism he is to find his way back to the service of building homes and communities of homes in which human beings may share in the advantages of living as civilized beings in an advanced civilization."[51]

Although Catherine Bauer was agnostic about the specific building form that public housing should take, she, too, was adamant about the reach of its planning into the details of daily life. "Housing is more than houses," she famously wrote, insisting that, as one biography of Bauer would put it, "an architect must design the entire community right from the start, including communal amenities, a primary school, shops, recreation and play spaces, possibly a café, central laundry and gardens."[52] The spontaneous, serendipitous growth of cities, historically based on thousands of private plans and preferences, was to be subsumed by a single overarching vision. None of the housing built to date by the private market for people of modest means, the non-superblocks of communities, was considered to have value. Nor were the attendant activities and organizations and enterprises of poorer communities marked for demolition.

Lewis Mumford, the polymath literary critic, historian, and sociologist, in his chapter in the exhibition catalog, titled "The Social Imperatives in Housing," sketched an even grander vision of social change and uplift, describing the modern housing vision in near-poetic and certainly utopian terms:

> To produce a completely human environment—in contrast to making patchwork improvement in physical shelter—is the objective of modern housing. Such an environment is necessary if we are to fulfill our own lives and carry on the complicated structure of our civilization. Our society cannot be run by brutes, dullards, and neurotics; it can be carried on only by healthy and well-balanced and alert people, capable of expressing themselves effectively through their work, their arts, their communal and family relationships: people who are in a state of active and sympathetic intercourse with their immediate neighbors, their fellow workers, and with the larger world around them. Our contemporary urban and rural environments are for the greater part so disordered and out of balance that they do not tend to produce such people or give them sustenance. Against all that conscious education can do, the more fundamental unconscious education of our backgrounds, our daily activities, our casual sights and responses work toward the production and the apathetic acceptance of chaos.
>
> Our problem is to create a new order in the environment at large that will encourage and carry further those germinal impulses toward order that are latent in various parts of our social heritage. Unless we build communities that enable us to function as complete human beings at higher social and cultural levels than we at present usually reach, capitalism in its decay will drag us down into a lower stage of social integration, already visible, in which "community" will be bludgeoned into us by the policeman, the soldier, and the gangster.[53]

That latter-day public housing projects can well be set to fit Mumford's dark vision is a profound irony. But Mumford, Bauer, and others were nothing if not confident in their view, notwithstanding the fact that none showed any evidence of having consulted with those who would live in this modern-era city and its dwellings. Indeed, there is reason to think that they would not approve of it. When the German architects Oskar Stonorov and Alfred Kastner prepared to design Philadelphia's Mackley Houses, an early Public Works Division Project that was envisioned as three ten-story "slab" apartment blocks, they actually conducted a survey of potential residents. (In the European, or even Soviet, approach, all were to be members of the Full Fashion Hosiery Workers Union, reflecting the connection between housing for workers and labor unions, as well as the implicit belief that a specific industry will continue in a specific locale.) But the Philadelphia study "merely reinforced Stonorov's intentions," observes the architectural historian Richard Pommer, "rather than uncovering the workers' own wishes. Thus the questioners did not ask the workers whether they wanted apartments, but simply noted that 'in general the workers did not oppose apartments; contrary to the general belief they remained open to convincing.'" This in a city of some three hundred thousand small, privately owned row houses in which apartments were virtually unknown. But as the architect Kastner would say, per Pommer, "the purpose of the survey was to sell the project despite its 'contemporary' and 'socialist' connotations." "For Stonorov," he continues, "it as a manifesto of city planning in general, not merely of housing for the hosiery workers."[54]

For these proponents of public housing, the problem—slums—implied its own solution: clearance and towers in a park. One can imagine a range of other responses to slum conditions: renovation including additional plumbing; small new and low-cost for-sale homes built on those large sites on which projects would be erected; even financial support for renters to build their own houses. But for the generation of architects and thought leaders involved in the housing exhibition, architect-designed, government-owned rental housing was the answer. The problem implied its own solution—and that was it. QED. If modernist housing design was to prevail, there remained, nonetheless, the other crucial problem that the realization of the projects faced: the political and financial challenges that construction would require.

James Ford, for his part, actually came to the conclusion that private, rather than public, management would be the better approach. Presciently, he wrote,

> In the long run the social value of any public housing project will be determined by the quality of its management. The best designed of housing developments might accomplish more harm than good if managed by scheming politicians or by grossly underpaid routine-minded public employees devoid of business training, ignorant of the needs of their tenants, or lacking in vision of social objectives. . . . Emotional turmoil and the sense of injustice, whether or not they result in mass meetings, rent strikes, and elaborate signed protests, can rob a development, and each family residing therein, of the restfulness, peace, and happiness associated with the word home.

Ford continued that "the management of projects, even when financed with public money, should not lodge with the government but . . . be delegated to competent private bodies."[55]

The housing exhibition's contributors and their allies would opt for government to both build and manage this city of tomorrow and for federal legislation that would make possible the real-world emergence of US public housing—soon to come. Ford's private approach was not to be, as the legislative structure of public housing finance, architecture, and management was to take shape rapidly following the museum exhibit. That process would be led by the key organizer of the exhibit, Catherine Bauer. It would be Bauer's role, in the museum exhibit book and subsequently in government along with Edith Elmer Wood, with whom she corresponded, to spell out the details of the "new communities" and the form that housing should take and—especially—the role of government in supporting it.

Writing in the depths of the Depression, Bauer, like Wood, emphasized the sharp slowdown in housing construction of any kind—implicitly assuming, amid economic crisis, that this might be a permanent state of affairs. "But where are the houses?" asked Bauer. "Why are 80% of the building workers still totally unemployed? Not only do the old slums remain, more crowded than ever, but there seems to be nothing but the present complete stagnation of the real estate business to prevent the erection of expensive new slums and incipient 'blighted districts" just like the old ones."[56]

To be sure, her emphasis was far from entirely misplaced in the moment. New housing starts, the Census Bureau would report in 1940, fell from 4.5 million from 1925 to 1930, to 2.3 million from 1930 to 1935.[57] The housing exhibition and the legislation that it would inspire and that Bauer would help author would take up that task of addressing Bauer's fundamental questions about the shortfall in the private housing market, which, as capitalism itself seemed to be foundering worldwide, hardly seemed wrongheaded.

But Bauer's goal, and that of many contributors to the exhibition catalog, was not merely the construction of shelter brought within the means of people of modest incomes. Bauer's *Modern Housing* was replete with photographic plates from modernist European projects, including those in fascist Germany and communist Russia. Bauer was not totalitarian but certainly shared the top-down planning impulse of those regimes, as did her housing exhibition collaborators. Indeed, so confident were the people involved in the exhibit of the success and attractiveness of publicly financed and managed housing that they feared it might attract those who did not need its help. A financial supporter of the exhibit, Abraham Goldfeld of New York's Lewenberg Foundation, in an essay titled "The Management Problem in Public Housing," wrote, "It is easy to realize that without rigid checks the publicly owned houses would soon be filled with families who could afford more expensive accommodations but who would make every effort to take advantage of any opportunity to reduce their rental budgets."[58]

Notably, Goldfeld was not naïve about the complications of the system he believed was necessary. Indeed, alone among the contributors to the housing exhibit book, he foresaw some of the problems that would ultimately plague the projects. He feared that "the occupants of the development itself are likely to come to feel themselves inmates of an institution rather than free citizens." Latter-day tenants seeking repairs in vain from a bureaucratic, underfunded owner-operator—a housing authority—would be able to relate. Goldfeld, too, noted the fundamentally different relationship between a tenant and a public housing "landlord." "Consider next the question of the financial relations of tenant and landlord in a public housing development. In cases of rent delinquency, will the city follow the practice of private landlords, dispossessing regardless of the causes of failure to pay? Or does the basic purpose of public housing imply a totally different attitude toward this problem?"[59]

When latter-day legislation (1969) reduced Housing Authority revenue by limiting rents to 25 percent of tenant income, it would have profound consequences for the maintenance of housing projects—leading directly to the first demolition of projects.[60] The foundation leader also foresaw the possibilities for financial corruption: "It is an American habit of long standing to look upon the city as a legitimate field for 'chiseling,' and we may be sure that in a public housing development the tenants, employees, and small-job contractors will not overlook the new opportunity."[61]

Such early warnings, like Ford's interest in private management, were overlooked. But latter-day municipal housing authorities would face no small number of corruption indictments for self-dealing by political appointees serving in management. As Julia Selby wrote in the *Cornell Policy Review* in 2022, "Corruption, fraud, and abuse are rife within the public housing industry today. The largest provider of public housing in the United States, the New York City Housing Authority, is no exception. Though corrupt practices have plagued the agency throughout its history, recent examples of fraud and deception display the depths of systemic and institutional issues. No-bid contracting schemes have bred bribery and waste."[62] Such complications would only reveal themselves as real-world problems over time, however.

In 1934, the intellectual winds were at the backs of public housing advocates—only to gain strength as the Depression continued and the Roosevelt administration looked for ways both to spark employment in the construction trades and to provide new housing. It would be only three years following the housing exhibition that some of its principals would play a key role in drafting the National Housing Act of 1937 and the New Deal would enable, through construction subsidies and the use of eminent domain powers for vast clearance of low-income neighborhoods and displacement of their residents, the building of public housing not just in New York but in Detroit, Boston, Cleveland—and ultimately in some three thousand municipalities across the United States.

It is important to note, keeping with Edith Elmer Wood's analysis and contrary to how the projects would later be seen, that the visionaries behind the concept of public housing did not conceive it as a program for the poor. Far from promoting housing of last resort for people of the very lowest income, they imagined a program that would serve a wide swathe of the US public, for whom housing would be a sort of municipally owned public utility.[63] The modernist architecture of "high-rise" and "superblock" projects divided from the surrounding city were not at all conceived as some sort of poorhouse—although, in time, they would come to resemble one. The projects were meant to serve the working class, intended to provide housing for employees of nearby industrial sites and businesses—whether the shipyard workers of the Brooklyn Navy Yard (Ingersoll Houses) or the Detroit autoworkers drawn into the wartime defense industry (Brewster-Douglass Projects).

It was the visionaries of the museum who laid the groundwork both for the United States' public housing movement and the legislation that would soon authorize the construction of hundreds of thousands of public housing apartments across the country, each Project owned and managed by a local housing authority.[64] The scale would be substantial.

Between 1937 and the mid-1980s, one and a half million public housing "units" would be erected—the majority (one million) between 1950 and 1976.[65]

In the exhibition catalog, Lewis Mumford had provided the blueprint. "What is modern housing?" asked Mumford.

> Modern housing is a collective effort to create habitable domestic environments within the framework of integrated communities. Such housing demands not merely an improvement of the physical structures and the communal patterns: *it demands such social and economic changes as will make it available to every income group.* In the larger processes of reconstruction, housing, sustained by public authorities and supported by public funds, is a means for overcoming gross inequalities in the distribution of wealth, for producing more vital kinds of wealth, for restoring the balance between city and country and for aiding in the rational planning of industries, cities, and regions. *The provision of sound physical shelter is only a limited aspect of an adequate program for modern housing.*[66]

The housing exhibition's contributors and their allies would take on this challenge of crafting and lobbying for the systemic changes Mumford advocated. They would bring the vision of the Museum of Modern Art to life across the United States.

2

Bringing the Idea to Life

Congress and the National Housing Act

The donors, sponsors, and writers of the Museum of Modern Art's housing exhibition would surely have been dismayed at the idea that the project they envisioned would ultimately serve just a narrow group of the very poorest Americans. Their ambition was far greater. They sought not only to improve how Americans were housed but to change how they lived and the face of cities. And they were confident in their own vision of how to do both. "Public housing, its supporters believed, would move housing reform beyond requiring landlords to install fire escapes, windows, and bathrooms on overcrowded and otherwise inadequate buildings," writes Alexander von Hoffman. "The more recent inspiration for public housing emerged from the modern idea of planning, in the broadest sense."[1] Housing was to be part of the New Deal social insurance contract, along with old-age pensions and public employment jobs. By marrying housing reform with the New Deal, public housing was brought to life.

That the conditions that originally prompted the demands for housing reform had started to change did not influence the goals of public housing's advocates. They acknowledged that, in the wake of the prosperity of the 1920s, the lowest-income neighborhoods had become less crowded and that a variety of new and better types of working-class housing had gradually developed. As Woods and Kennedy had described in the Boston context, the attached row home and other modest housing forms, in particular, had bloomed in East Coast cities including Philadelphia, New York, and Brooklyn (prior to its consolidation with Manhattan). Construction had boomed during the prosperous 1920s, and the

Lower East Side tenements had become less crowded. Indeed, between 1870 and 1940, the pre-public-housing era had seen the construction of 299,000 small, attached, single-family row houses in Philadelphia, 150,000 two-family homes in Brooklyn, 21,000 three-family homes in Boston, and 38,200 two- to four-family homes in Chicago.[2] Neighborhoods branded as slums, such as New York's Lower East Side, had begun to lose population, as residents moved out and up. As Lillian Wald of that neighborhood's Henry Street settlement house wrote, "Through the tenements there is a stream of inflowing as well as outflowing life. . . . As you neighbors have prospered, many have moved to houses where they find better quarters, less congestion, more bathtubs."[3]

Still, such progress notwithstanding, it is hard to argue that the organizers of the housing exhibition were self-evidently misguided—in the context of their times. For context, it is worth looking at the data in the US Housing Census of 1940, the first of its kind ever undertaken and a reflection of data gathered during the 1930s. In addition to data regarding housing types—single-family, two-family, large apartment buildings, and others—the Housing Census tracked the "state of repair and plumbing equipment for all dwelling units."[4] The results are, in retrospect, sobering and provided ammunition for reformers as they pushed to move quickly from theory to implementation.

According to that census, less than half—17,793,341 of 37,325,470—of all housing units had a private bath with a private flush toilet. Some 2,814,261 had running water but no private flush toilet. Finally, 6,512,727 had "no running water in dwelling unit."[5] Put another way, 18 percent of all US dwelling units had no indoor plumbing, including running water.

What is more, at the time of the exhibition, the construction industry—like the overall US economy—was at a standstill. A snapshot of housing conditions that would be captured in the census released in 1943 could well convince serious observers that the private housing market was, indeed, destined to fail. It was data such as that in the census that undergirded much of the critique—and calls for deep government involvement.

The question of how to structure government involvement in housing construction in the US system did not have an obvious answer, however. Indeed, although the *New York Times Book Review* had lavishly praised Bauer's *Modern Housing*, based on *Fortune* magazine essays published even prior to the housing exhibition, as a brilliant "criticism of civilization as well as houses," the *Times* reviewer went on to write that, although "she had stated a problem most effectively, she had by no means solved it."[6]

Contributors to the exhibition were clear on one thing as they approached a housing solution, however: it would require government direction. Notably, the leaders of this modern housing / public housing movement would come from both the Left and Right. Bauer was known (affectionately) as "Communist Catherine" by Frank Lloyd Wright. Philip Johnson would notoriously become known as an admirer of Adolf Hitler, an attendee at a Nuremberg Nazi rally, and a supporter of the American antisemitic radio priest Father Coughlin. Walter Hegemann, the German émigré who had praised Hitler's housing policies, would correspond with Edith Elmer Wood while she served in government, from his office in New Rochelle, New York.[7]

No changes as extreme as those envisioned by Adolf Hitler—such as outright expropriation of land—were endorsed by Wood, Bauer, or other contributors to the exhibition, nor were they included in the national housing legislation that Bauer herself would soon author. The exhibition and, later, the legislation would instead propose a complex form of federal financing, coupled with ongoing local government ownership and control, that would adapt the European public housing ideal to the US political context—and set the stage for both success and failure.

Catalog editor Aronovici spelled out what would, in the decades to follow, become the federal government's essential approach: providing the administrative vehicle and subsidies to close the gap between the rent that people of modest means could afford and that which would be required to obtain housing of a higher standard. "This task will only be achieved by new systems of building and finance economy which would harmonize with the rent paying resources of lower income families. Because of the high cost and low productivity of labor, because of the increasing cost of materials encouraged by the New Deal, and heavy tax burdens, low-cost housing is at present impossible. Money must be made available at a rate of interest and amortization low enough to meet the difference between the cost of building and the rental resources of those who must be housed."[8]

Writing based on the early British experience, Robinson Newcomb presciently elaborated on an approach that was shortly to be realized in the United States: "If the rent which can be secured will not pay a proper return on the properties, some new method for providing these properties must be found. The method will depend on the political, social and economical conditions prevailing. *It may be outside the profit system*, or it may be a reduction in construction costs or a combination of the two."[9]

The approach sketched by Aronovici would take specific form just three years following the exhibition, in the details of the landmark National Housing Act of 1937. It would be championed, not surprisingly, by an elected official from New York, where the intellectual seeds of the public housing movement had sprouted. New York Senator Robert Wagner—already famed for sponsoring the National Labor Relations Act, recognizing the rights of labor unions to collectively bargain—would, with help from *Modern Housing* author Catherine Bauer, draft the Housing Act. Bauer would then be named to serve as the director of information and research at the newly established United States Housing Authority.

In promoting the idea of a permanent United States Housing Authority, Senator Wagner clearly channeled Catherine Bauer, Edith Elmer Wood, and Carol Aronovici and their contributions to the housing exhibition. Bauer herself would play a central role in shaping the 1937 Housing Act, the foundation of overall federal involvement in housing markets. The archives of her papers include a 1935 telegram from Secretary of the Interior Ickes saying, "I would be glad if you personally attend and participate in the discussion" in a "conference of all persons and associations interested in an open discussion of the Administration on the next housing act in the Interior Department auditorium."[10] Over the course or 1936 and 1937, as the National Housing Act was being drafted and debated, Bauer corresponded frequently with Leon Keyserling, who would become the first head of the US Housing Authority. On August 18, 1936, he wrote to her of "perfecting the New Deal." He urged her to continue to play a role in pushing for housing legislation, which had previously failed. "How, after such an effort, can one have the heart to try again, to gild the City? But no! With an equal sense of dedication to a great cause, with a willingness to spend all in the effort, a work of equal note may yet be done. Napoleon was the second child but he carried the Revolution forward."[11] Bauer and Keyserling were clearly close, as their correspondence included personal as well as policy matters.

So, too, was Bauer's vision apparent in the language of Senator Wagner, who would, in 1937, get the housing bill over the congressional finish line—and set the stage for Bauer herself to help implement it. "Nothing quickens the imagination and fires the intellect more than the thought of bringing space and sanitation into the dreary lives of those who now inhabit the slums," Wagner told the Senate in August 1935. A Wagner biographer would take special note of its ambitiousness—at a time when President Roosevelt had become committed to reducing federal spending and balancing the budget. (Roosevelt himself was on the record as taking the view that "families should have individual homes of their own, however modest.") The "Wagner housing bill," as reporters soon began calling it, was certainly considered a recovery measure. But it was also something more—another step in Wagner's lifelong effort to orient American liberalism toward the problems of the nation's urban-industrial population.[12]

The National Housing Act of 1937 would, indeed, make public housing more than a temporary recovery effort. By establishing the United States Housing Authority, it created the mechanism to extend federal financing to projects across the country; the Authority would back the borrowings of hundreds, later thousands, of local housing authorities—exactly the kind of financing envisioned in the housing exhibition.[13] By the eve of World War II, some 136,000 public housing rental apartments had been built. Momentum was slowed by the diversion of US resources to the war effort and arms production—but the same legislation would, as amended in 1949, authorize no fewer than 800,000 public housing units across the country. (New York, public housing's heartland, had actually continued construction during the war.)

The original bill had not been without controversy and sharp debate.[14] Senator Carter Glass of Virginia, who opposed it, had framed Northeastern cities as its primary beneficiaries. "Upon what recognized theory of Government [did] it become the business of the national government to tax the American people to clear up slums in specified parts of the country?" he asked.[15] But the Housing Act of 1949, the original bill's progeny, reflected bipartisan consensus, in part because the original legislation called for no more than 10 percent of federal Housing Authority funds to be directed toward any one state—ensuring what would be extensive construction in the South, including in smaller cities, providing an infusion of federal funds into the nation's poorest region.

The Housing Act worked around the problems of the Public Works Administration through the expedient of US federalism: decentralizing the siting and management of projects through local housing authorities across the US, overseen by locally appointed (not elected) boards, in keeping with the expert-driven model of the housing exhibition. The new federal Housing Authority would use the borrowing capacity of the federal government to subsidize public housing construction cost, thus driving down rents indirectly. The local housing authorities would own and manage them, and local governments would make the decisions as to where they would be built. By working through state and local government, and with direction from consultants including Edith Elmer Wood, they could use the power of eminent domain to condemn entire neighborhoods, clearing them for projects. Significantly, although the construction quality of the structures themselves was intended to surpass what the private market would provide for low-income tenants, their rents—crucially, as it would turn out—were mainly expected to cover the upkeep and operating costs of the new projects. Such was the language of the law. Ongoing operating subsidies for local housing authorities and tenants were not envisioned, at first. According to the 1937 Housing Act, "The Authority shall fix the rentals at the amounts necessary to *pay all management, operation, and maintenance costs*, together with payments, if any, in lieu of taxes, plus such additional amounts as the Authority shall determine are consistent with maintaining the low-rent character of such project."[16] Living in the projects was not, in other words, to be rent-free, nor was it meant to be limited to the very poorest. The local housing authorities were meant to be public versions of private real estate management, drawing enough rent revenue to maintain the structures.

All this, nonetheless, left open a crucial question: Where would the projects be built? The Housing Act had an answer, one that would change the face of US cities. It authorized not only the construction of new government-supported housing but extensive "slum clearance" to make way for it. It was not enough to build projects; the "slums" were assumed to be so without value that they had to be cleared and their residents moved out. As the 1937 Housing Act stated, "the Authority may make loans to public-housing agencies to assist the development, acquisition, or administration of low-rent-housing or slum-clearance projects by such agencies."[17] The dual focus of the housing exhibition—to build housing for the poor that would be "safe and sanitary" and to remake cities through the demolition of existing poor neighborhoods—would be incorporated into the landmark legislation, clearly reflecting Bauer and Wood's values.

The approach of the previous Public Works Administration–built housing projects, which the courts had halted in 1935, had shown how slum neighborhoods designated for clearance would be identified. Housing experts focused on specific physical conditions and would work as consultants to do the job. PWA consultants had, indeed, already included Edith Elmer Wood. Hired in 1933 as a consultant to the Department of Interior's Public Works Administration Housing Division, she had traveled the country identifying sites for the fifty-some projects that the department would build before being stopped by the courts. Her opinion had clearly been viewed as important. A November 1933 letter to her from a Housing Division official, credited her for the decision to direct $6 million (a significant sum at the time) "to carry on the slum clearance project. It has become evident that your report to the Housing Division was more than favorable."[18] Indeed, her personal papers at Columbia University bulge with travel receipts for trips to Knoxville, Birmingham, Toledo, Memphis, Atlantic City, and many more. This emissary from Cape May Point, New Jersey, and Manhattan's Gramercy Park (correspondence to each is found in her papers) would arrive in town and decide, on behalf of Washington and in concert with local officials, which neighborhoods were irredeemable slums and should be cleared for projects.[19]

Implicit in the approach of the National Housing Act were numerous paths not taken. It was assumed that the working class and poor preferred to live in "modern" housing of the type contemplated; it was assumed that the projects should be both owned and operated by government, not private management; it was assumed that there was no value worth preserving in neighborhoods—on the Lower East Side, in Detroit, in Cleveland, in St. Louis, in Chicago, in San Francisco—that were to be demolished and cleared, displacing both households and local businesses. It was assumed that the new housing should be rental, rather than in some way owned by residents individually or cooperatively. There was no thought given to the possibility that, by competing with privately owned low-rent housing, public housing might make poor neighborhoods even shabbier by drawing rental income away from private landlords. All these assumptions would prove to have consequences.

Complications would not, moreover, be slow to develop. Indeed, the people contemplating not just the theory but the practical realities of public housing were not unaware that things might not go according to plan. There was concern, for instance, that Project quality would be so high that it might attract the well-off, for whom it was not intended. Abraham Goldfeld, of New York's Lewenberg Foundation, which had itself built and managed its own "model tenements" (limited-dividend, philanthropically financed low-income housing), expressed concern about just such a scenario in his contribution to the exhibition catalog. In "The Management Problem of Public Housing," Goldfeld wrote, "American municipal government being what it is, the pressure from political personages for the admission of unqualified 'friends' is likely to be all but irresistible. In a word, unless the utmost precautions are taken, those for whom the buildings are designed will be the last to stand the chance of occupying them."[20] Just such a scenario would later be described in Michael Patrick MacDonald's memoir about growing up in a South Boston housing project: "After Seamus was born, the Boston Housing Authority broke down one of our walls for us, adding a second apartment. Only three families in Old Colony has a 'breakthrough' apartment. Ma had pulled a few strings with the local politicians."[21]

More broadly, the utopian idealism of the modern "housers," a group with little experience in government, was about to be transformed, one might even say distorted, as it encountered the US political system. The 1937 act would notably take steps not just to house the poor but also to ensure that they would not be housed in housing of which others might be envious. As if responding directly to Abraham Goldfeld's concern about the affluent being attracted to the new projects, the act imposed a specific cost ceiling on how much could be spent on public housing construction.

> No contract for any loan, annual contribution, or capital grant made pursuant to this Act shall be entered into by the Authority with respect to any project hereafter initiated costing more than $4,000 per family-dwelling-unit or more than $1,000 per room (excluding land, demolition, and non-dwelling facilities); except that in any city the population of which exceeds 500,000 any such contract may be entered into with respect to

a project hereafter initiated costing not to exceed $5,000 per family-dwelling-unit or not to exceed $1,250 per room (excluding land, demolition, and non-dwelling facilities), if in the opinion of the Authority such higher family-dwelling-unit cost or cost per room is justified by reason of higher costs of labor and materials and other construction costs.

With respect to housing projects on which construction is hereafter initiated, the Authority shall make loans, grants, and annual contributions only for such low-rent-housing projects as it finds are to be undertaken in such a manner (a) that such projects will not be of elaborate or expensive design or materials, and economy will be promoted both in construction and administration, and (b) that the average construction cost of the dwelling units (excluding land, demolition, and non-dwelling facilities) in any such project is not greater than the average construction cost of dwelling units currently produced by private enterprise, in the locality or metropolitan area concerned, under the legal building requirements applicable to the proposed site, and under labor standards not lower than those prescribed in this Act.[22]

The utopian dreams of the housing exhibition—which for some of the principals would include swimming pools and canals at public housing sites—were to be reined in. Cost control was emphasized. This was, in other words, to be utilitarian housing—built by union labor, in keeping with Senator Wagner's championing the latter—even if doing so increased the construction costs about which the act was concerned. It was all a long way from the soaring rhetoric of Radiant City. But the subtle implications of the multitude of directives detailed in the 1937 legislation would not detract from the initial rush of enthusiasm as the first ribbons were cut for public housing projects.

The local zeal for the gut renovation of New York's very first project, the former tenement rechristened as First Houses, was reflected by the fact that the bonds sold to finance them were themselves purchased by two of the city's wealthiest citizens, John Jacob Astor and Bernard Baruch. Eleanor Roosevelt, who had spoken at that project's

FIGURE 2.1. Eleanor Roosevelt at the Detroit Brewster Houses ground-breaking. (Walter P. Reuther Library, Archives of Labor and Urban Affairs, Wayne State University)

ribbon-cutting, would be present, as well, at the ground-breaking in Detroit for the Brewster Houses, one of the first public housing complexes reserved for African Americans, opened in 1938 with 701 units. Its segregation was framed as benevolence, in that Blacks were not excluded from the new program. Later, its six-story apartment buildings would be supplemented by fourteen-story tower buildings named for Frederick Douglass—as if to imply, like projects in New York named for Langston Hughes and James Weldon Johnson, that these would be permanently reserved for African Americans.

The modern housing envisioned by the housing exhibition came to fruition, not even five years after it had been mounted—thanks both to the federal financing and to its authorization of "slum clearance." The poor and working class were to make way for projects, whether they wanted to do so or not. In Detroit, the new housing was built on what had been two Black residential and commercial neighborhoods, Black Bottom and Paradise Valley, whose clearance sparked "significant amount of opposition from black families who did not want to move into new housing—and did not want to have their homes taken from them."[23] Such opposition was, however, no match for the combined momentum powering the twin goals of slum clearance and modern housing.

Brewster-Douglass would ultimately become an eyesore, itself demolished and its site left vacant. But that fate was decades off. Public housing, in its early years—especially in the post–World War II era, when a second round of federal support was enacted in 1949, entered something like a golden age, when many projects were, indeed, safe and sanitary, when an upwardly mobile blue-collar population found them attractive. In Detroit, that included the future music superstars Diana Ross and Smokey Robinson. In New York, it included the future

FIGURE 2.2. Slum clearance in New York. (Library of Congress)

Supreme Court justice Sonia Sotomayor. In Chicago, the future Massachusetts governor Deval Patrick grew up in the high-rise Robert Taylor Homes. One cannot know, of course, whether these American success stories would have happened absent the advent of public housing. But there are many much-less-well-known former residents who look back nostalgically on their childhoods in the projects. Nor was it misguided, at least for many years, to describe the vast New York City system of 325 projects housing one in every fifteen city residents as public housing that worked.[24]

From the 1940s into the 1970s, projects of a wide variety—from big-city high-rises to small-town garden apartments—would be built across the country, sited, managed, and owned by some three thousand local public housing authorities. The modern "housers" may have focused on transforming cities, but as their utopian idealism encountered the US federalist system, municipalities big and small would all get a share of assistance. In Alabama alone, there would be housing projects in more than one hundred cities and towns. As it would prove to be with federal grants generally, funding, as a political matter, must be distributed across the entire country—in the case of public housing, in places distant from its policy origins.

In many ways, the vision of the 1934 Museum of Modern Art housing exhibition was realized in the United States. Indeed, in 1937, when Secretary of the Interior Harold Ickes convened a group of housing experts to discuss how to implement the National Housing Act of 1937—which would make public housing a permanent feature of US government—he invited the housing exhibition participants or sponsors Catherine Bauer, Edith Elmer Wood, Mary Simkhovitch, Nathan Straus (who would become the head of the US Housing Authority), and Langdon Post, who would head the New York City Housing Authority.[25] Over the course of decades, however, public housing would be both transformed and transmuted by American preferences and government, in ways they never anticipated, leading to a version of public housing that was distinct and,

FIGURE 2.3. President Truman signs the National Housing Act. Image courtesy of the *New York Times* Overseas Service. Harry S. Truman Library and Museum.

in many ways, at odds with its founding conception. What is more, that original vision would be followed and superseded by adjustments, alternatives, and variations, continuing to be developed and refined, not by putative beneficiaries themselves but chiefly by policy makers and social scientists, and continuing to take shape to the present day.

3

Cutting the Ribbon

Stories of Early Success in the Golden Age

The case for building the projects had built slowly. But when it took hold, construction occurred with dramatic speed. By 1950, not only had the 1949 bill jump-started slum clearance and construction of public housing, but this second, larger generation of projects—including many of the iconic high-rises such as those that would dot the South Side of Chicago—were opening their rental offices. What is more, they were a hit, popular not only with the legislators who helped make them possible but also with their new tenants themselves. The early reviews were strongly positive, including those about projects that would later become synonymous with danger and dilapidation. Many, though not all, followed the towers-in-the-park design envisioned by the Museum of Modern Art housing exhibition—but it was nonetheless standard even for low-rise projects to be set off, in a campus, from a surrounding neighborhood, to eschew both cross streets and the mix of commercial and residential buildings and uses that characterized traditional city neighborhoods.

What can only be called fond memories of this golden age have been captured by extensive tenant oral histories, including those at a National Public Housing Museum in Chicago. Stories laced with a fond nostalgia about that of one of the nation's largest public housing systems—that of Chicago—are typical enough that they have been collected in a book tellingly titled *When Public Housing Was Paradise: Building Community in Chicago*. The author, J. D. Fuerst, observes about the oral histories he collected what he calls a nostalgia for "the almost bucolic world of public housing in the 1940s and the 1950s," where, as he summarizes,

FIGURE 3.1. Robert Taylor Homes when new, Chicago. (Wikimedia Commons)

the housing complexes were like "extended communities," where tenants assumed the responsibility for "cleaning hallways and porches and other common areas."[1]

Fuerst's interviews include one with Bertrand Ellis, a retired bank executive who had lived with his parents in Chicago's Ida B. Welles project, from 1941 to 1955. The project, named for a legendary antilynching crusader, was later captured as a drug-infested, racially segregated dystopia by the filmmaker Frederick Wiseman.

It did not start out that way, though. "Life in Ida B. Welles was a wonderful experience for us," said Ellis. "Three buildings formed a triangle and in the middle of that triangle was a playground. We grew up playing football, baseball, hockey. . . . We were poor kids in a poor neighborhood but we didn't know we were poor, really. We have everything kids could want."[2]

Another onetime tenant similarly recalled Cabrini-Green, the Chicago project, combining row houses with twenty-three high-rise towers, bordered but not crossed by local streets. "You know, when I hear people say, wow, the projects are so tough and this and that, oh, that didn't happen until later. It was a wonderful place to live, and I remember mixed races in the projects. We would have basketball tournaments and programs, and we would have a place called the Lower North Center in the Cabrini-Green Projects where young people could go participate in activities, . . . play basketball, do arts and crafts, take little field trips, and there were activities when I was growing up in the Cabrini-Green."[3]

So, too, were there once fond memories of the soon-to-be-notorious Pruitt-Igoe, the high-rise complex of thirty-three eleven-story buildings in St. Louis that replaced the frame houses of the Desoto-Carr neighborhood: "It was a big beautiful place, like a big hotel resort," recalled Ruby Russell, an early tenant of the high-rise towers and campus grounds. "It was like an oasis in the desert. All this newness. I never thought I would live in that kind of surrounding."[4]

The Brewster-Douglass Projects, Detroit, five city blocks long and three city blocks wide, including six fifteen-story high-rise towers, was where Mary Wilson met Diana Ross and Florence Ballard and formed the famous Motown group The Supremes. "Moving into the projects as a child was like moving into a wonderland for me," Wilson would later recall in an interview.[5]

Pomonok Houses, located in New York City's borough of Queens, opened in 1941 and was composed of twenty-two seven-story and thirteen three-story buildings on fifty-two acres.[6] "I loved Pomonok as a kid, compared to the slums of the Lower East Side I came from," said former resident Daniel Ross in the 2014 documentary *Pomonok Dreams*. "There was central heating, elevators, a garbage incinerator, windows in every room."[7]

Of all of the aforementioned projects, Pomonok is the only one that had not been demolished by 2024. But they all opened and operated in an era where the projects were considered desirable places to live. What, then, were the preconditions for what the historian Nicholas Dagen Bloom has called public housing that worked? There can actually be said to have been a formula. It included tenants who could pay the rent and a management at pains to provide the services and maintenance that paying tenants expected. Conditions for admission were demanding, as well.

Notwithstanding the fact that government, through the United States Housing Authority, would subsidize the cost of project construction, household rents, as per the Museum of Modern Art housing exhibition, were meant to cover the ongoing costs of operations and even maintenance. The implications of that policy in public housing's early years were far-reaching. To ensure revenue, housing authorities rented to households that could afford the required rent. That meant employed, working-class tenants—not those of lowest income on what was then termed "relief" or welfare.

In New York City, where the twin processes of vast tenement neighborhood demolition and new project construction were in full swing in the immediate post–World War II era, that meant "full background checks," including twenty-one specific factors that favored married couples with employed heads of households. As the city housing authority itself put it, "the Authority adopted as a policy for all projects that occupancy be limited to normal types of families and that unwed women with out of wedlock children be denied admission." The factors used to exclude tenants also included "irregular work history" and "poor housekeeping."[8]

Public housing, in other words, was not seen by the nation's largest housing authority as lowest-income housing. The assumption was that poorer families would be less likely to maintain their households (even a minimum number of furniture items was one of the aforementioned twenty-one factors). But the need for reliable levels of rent revenue, as much as any discrimination based on values or moral standards, must be seen as crucial. Washington was not going to subsidize the projects once they were up and running. Indeed, Treasury Secretary Henry Morgenthau in the Roosevelt administration had pushed for the idea that all operate on a "pay as you go basis"—rather than being built through federally backed borrowing. They would, once in operation in these early years, more closely resemble the management of private real estate.

In turn, housing authorities themselves knew they had to keep the premises well maintained or risk losing vital good-paying tenants. In New York, individual project buildings had specific "porters" assigned to oversee building maintenance and respond to complaints. "They came for repairs right away. They used to shine the bannisters."[9] Such is what happens when rent collection matters, buildings are relatively new, and rent revenue is reliable.

New York was exceptional in such ways, certainly in its scale and the extent of its role in the city's housing supply. But the golden age could also be explained elsewhere by some simple facts of housing life. Providing new apartments with modern kitchens and appliances at rents below what the private market was asking was bound to attract tenants willing to pay the price being asked. The very fact that the projects were new was a key part of their golden age. What is more, in the early 1950s, the wave of single-family home construction in expanding US suburbs was only just getting under way; there were fewer competitors for households with members holding well-paying jobs.

The projects—new, shining, and inexpensive—actually had a comparative advantage in the housing market of the time. Housing authorities, in the golden age, could afford (literally) to be choosy about their tenants. A combination of new buildings, carefully selected tenants, and hands-on management made for the golden age of public housing. Bloom credits the New York City Housing Authority with fulfilling these factors for success; for example, he contrasts New York's civil-service-chosen employees with more politically influenced hiring in Chicago and St. Louis. But New York was not alone in having a management closely concerned with maintenance and even housekeeping. Consider the following excerpt from a memoir of Lauderdale Courts in Memphis, where the teenage Elvis Presley lived with his parents from 1949 to 1952: "Communal life in the courts included monthly inspections by the Memphis Housing Authority staff. Elvis got written up for leaving a cereal bowl on the table. He was late for school. There was a report like, 'Needs help in cleaning up.' Then they would come back and give you a cleaning lesson."[10]

Indeed, had that set of conditions—booming public housing construction and limited private alternatives—continued, projects might have remained well maintained and popular. This had, after all, been the housing exhibition vision: housing as a public utility for a large swathe of the population. It was a vision that proved not to take hold, however, or to prove sustainable in those cities that built projects at large scale (although superior management, long the case in New York City, did fend off decay for longer than in other cities).

In fact, it had not even been a vision uniformly shared by the elected officials who had first sponsored the federal housing legislation that made the projects possible. Nor, as it turned out, was it the role for public housing that golden age tenants themselves embraced. It became common for tenants to express the view (though how widespread it was cannot be determined) that their tenure in the projects was intended by government not as long-term, working or lower-middle-class housing but as a launching pad for upward mobility—an idea that would come to be commonly held but was nowhere mentioned in the housing exhibition or by legislative proponents such as Robert Wagner or even Republican Robert Taft. Yet it appears repeatedly in oral histories.

In *Pomonok Dreams*, a documentary that reunites former tenants of the housing project, Audrey Jacob recalled her time there as "an age of hope." "People thought they were going to have a better way of life especially for their children," says Joel Klein, the film's coproducer. He adds that Pomonok "was a place that cultivated a lot of successful people," with the documentary including former tenants who go on to identify themselves as doctors, lawyers, pharmacists, judges, airline pilots, research scientists, meteorologists, and members of other professions.[11]

Ken Black, a boyhood friend of Elvis Presley in Lauderdale Courts—and the brother of Bill Black, Presley's bass player—later became a member of the Lauderdale alumni group "Poor Boys Done Good," which would meet every Thursday for coffee at in East Memphis to reminisce about the project.[12] Similarly, the Chicago Housing Authority (CHA) itself points to a number of notable residents, including the former Massachusetts governor Deval Patrick, the baseball star Kirby Puckett, the actor Mr. T, and the singers Jerry Butler and Curtis Mayfield. Lastly, the New York City Housing Authority points to Supreme Court Justice Sonia Sotomayor, Goldman Sachs chief executive Lloyd Blankfein, Starbucks CEO Howard Schulz, and comedian Whoopi Goldberg as former project residents who were able to use public housing as a launching pad.[13]

While this message of "up and out" may have ultimately been embraced, it has never been explicit in the goals or theoretical foundation of the projects. If anything, from the very start, the idea that public housing was a program for the working poor was in tension—even for Robert Wagner and Robert Taft—with the idea that it should serve the poorest Americans.

For example, Senator Wagner himself was uncomfortable with government-subsidized housing that did not serve people of lowest income. In keeping with Edith Elmer Wood's view about the limits of the private housing market, Wagner had made clear, in his comments regarding the 1937 bill, that he believed there is a portion of the population that simply could not be expected to have the means to pay even modest rents—and that they should not be faulted for their limited means or limited in access to public housing. The need for public housing, said Wagner, "embodies recognition on the part of a socially awakened people that the distribution of our national income has not been entirely equitable, and that partially-subsidized housing, like free schools, free roads, and free parks, is the next step that we must take to forge a better order."[14] The scale of Wagner's ambition to house even the very poorest was made clear when he was asked by Republican Senator Arthur Vandenberg of Michigan if there was "a figure available indicating the sum of the total of the low-cost housing need." Wagner responded, "Yes there is but I would not dare mention it."[15] Wagner would presumably be shocked by the future trajectory of the projects—as they often came to be housing of last resort, dominated by the very poorest.

In other words, the golden age would come to an end, to be overtaken by the dilapidation and "concentration of poverty" for which the projects would become known. In part, as we will see, those changes resulted from a departure of a key element of the golden age: tenants who both were willing to live in the projects and could pay rents commensurate with maintenance needs. One could have imagined a radically different alternative—one logically in keeping with the vision of the original modern housers: cities in which public housing constituted almost all the available housing. Such a scenario has actually been realized—in the Asian city-state of Singapore. There, the combination of slum housing and disastrous fires led to the establishment of the Housing Development Board, which, since 1960, has built and maintained fully 80 percent of the island nation's housing.

As a Bloomberg news report has observed, "In the movie 'Crazy Rich Asians,' the main characters move between opulent mansions and colonial-era hotels in Singapore. But the reality is the vast majority of families live in modestly-sized apartments built by the government—concentrated, high-rise housing estates that elsewhere in the world might, to some, conjure images of low-income urban blight. Yet here, the concrete suburbs are well-maintained by the state and their basic, functional flats are lovingly renovated by the owners, often with the help of professional interior designers using the finest materials."[16] Thus, it is in Singapore that the Radiant City / *Modern Housing* vision can be said to have been realized, although with a capitalist twist: "HDB flats" are owned by their resident households—and sold on an open market, often increasing in value. In that, it differs from the housing blocks that were built throughout the Soviet era, in Russia, eastern Europe, or Vienna.

Merely describing the Singapore system makes it obvious that such a housing market could never have become the norm in the US. Singapore, for instance, has no suburbs; its residents cannot commute from neighboring Malaysia, a nation that expelled Singapore from its government in 1965. Public housing is Singapore's norm, not its exception. It employs strict management methods, some of which—such as separating ethnic groups by floor—would strike Americans as objectionable.

Even from the early days of public housing in the US, during the golden age of the projects, the view about the role of public housing by its tenants was distinct from the Wagner / Wood / Bauer / Museum of Modern Art view of the way the housing world works. The first generation of public housing tenants viewed the project not as a long-term home in a failed housing market but, rather, a starting point—the first stop, albeit a pleasant one, on their route to social and economic upward mobility. They saw the projects to be a starting point for their own, and especially their children's, upward mobility—a path that would lead out of the projects. This meant that for the original formula and vision to be sustained—that in which employed families paid enough in rent to maintain the properties—their successors would have to be younger versions of themselves.

But such households would find alternatives to the projects—which themselves would become places far different from those that Robert Wagner dreamed of.

4

What Was Destroyed

The Dark Reality of Slum Clearance

It might have been possible to erect public housing without demolishing some existing neighborhoods considered to be slums. But that had never been the plan—either in the Museum of Modern Art's housing exhibition or in the federal legislation it inspired. After all, slum clearance was specifically cited in the National Housing Act. An August 1938 internal New York City Housing Authority memorandum made that plain through numbers reflecting the pace of "slum" demolition that it sought funding to do.

> Consultation of the record indicates that during 45 months of operation from March, 1934 through November, 1937, the project demolished approximately 110,000,000 cubic feet. This is an average of slightly less than 2,500,000 cubic feet per month for the period.
>
> I have been advised this date by the Director of Demolition that his Division is in a position to make application to your Administration for the demolition of 5,000,000 cubic feet per month. This is approximately 60 old law tenements.[1]

The dry language of the memo concealed, of course, the fact that thousands of low-income tenants were being left without homes, even as projects were yet to be built on cleared sites. Building owners would have received compensation, to be sure, but not tenants. Nor would owners be compensated for the potential future appreciation of their properties.

NYCHA records do, in fact, reflect owners' objections, including to the characterization of one tenement as substandard. In 1934, the attorney representing the owner of a building on Cherry Street on the city's Lower East Side wrote to the Housing Authority, "On March 16 last, I attended a meeting at your office of owners of so-called 'slum properties.'" The attorney wrote, "we would be throwing away some three or four thousand dollars of value of the house if it were torn down" to make way for the modernist Rutgers Town development.[2] This owner may have been simply holding out for greater compensation, rather than defending the condition of the building, although his including the term "slum" within quotation marks is suggestive. Unrecorded completely, however, in the archives of the nation's fastest-growing and largest public housing authority are the views of those residents being displaced from their homes.

There is no doubt of the confidence of public officials that they were engaged in an important action, even a crusade, to clear cities of slums. But there is good evidence, as well, that residents of "slum" districts were not convinced that they were being done a favor—or that the quality of life in their neighborhoods merited their clearance.

The NYCHA archives include a paper submitted to the authority by the New York writer Helen Harrison, "We Live Again," intended for magazine publication. This extended celebration of the establishment of the authority—"a truly significant departure from the deplorable conditions existing for 100 years"—included, as well, an emotional justification for slum clearance. What are identified as thirteen slum districts in New York "breed tuberculosis, crime, juvenile delinquency, immorality and a general breakdown of social morale." Harrison captures both the concern and the fear that these districts engendered among New York social elites. They included such leaders as the first Housing Authority chairman, Langdon Post, whom she takes care to identify as "from an old New York family, who left private school at seventeen to join the Army during the World war and was deemed the man best suited to head the Authority." He and others, per Harrison, "do not think that slums are solely a menace to their own community. They are equally a vital hazard to the districts contiguous to them and insidiously pollute those farther away." "Slums breed criminals as surely as they breed disease," she wrote, noting in particular that "the role the foreign-born plays in the drama of delinquency is disproportionate."[3]

Such neighborhoods—without any redeeming value apparently—were to be swept away, justifiably, per project advocates, replaced by public housing described with breathless idealism. "The Government is now to give to its people such advantages of environment as its citizens might demand for the East Indian lascar or the Chinese coolie. A chance, that is, to forget the long entombed years somewhat endured by those breathing dead—a chance to truly live again!"[4]

But what was viewed as an unquestionable, self-evident improvement was, on closer examination, a policy that failed to acknowledge trade-offs—if the projects brought gains, they also brought losses: whole neighborhoods that were simply disappeared.

There is little record of how residents of "slum" neighborhoods, overwhelmingly new immigrants and non-English speakers, viewed the pending demolition of their residences, their streets, their stores, or the businesses at which they were employed. The federal census, however, provides a snapshot of the lives of those who lived in areas designated with the black mark for demolition. There one can find a listing of residents and the work they did—including for the same block of Cherry Street about which Samuel Herriman had objected to its being characterized as a "slum"—and which he believed was of greater value than judged by the newly established Housing Authority.

Apartments on Cherry Street in 1930 were undoubtedly crowded and dark, as per the housing reform movement: bathrooms may have been shared; rent was paid, in part, in some households, by taking in lodgers. One can be sure that those who contributed to the Museum of Modern Art housing exhibition or the early leaders of the New York Housing Authority would have been aghast at the idea of living there themselves, an emotion that could well have helped motivate their movement. But a snapshot of Cherry Street could just as well be described in far more positive terms: as teeming with hardworking immigrants, some with their own businesses, making their way up in America as new immigrants. Federal census records tell the story. On Charles Herriman's "slum" block on the Lower East Side's Cherry Street lived Max Kolokowsky, a plumber and his wife, Betty, a "milliner"; Charles Disalvo, a chauffeur; Louis Krieger, a tailor; Ben Schaeffer, a bookkeeper. Adolph Lucas was an electrician; George Vicari owned his own store. On Cherry Street, one could have found a butcher, a longshoreman, a clerk, and a peddler. Immigrants, virtually all married couples with children, had come from Russia, Poland, Italy, and Ireland. There were blocks on which all spoke only Yiddish. Most would have relied on customers from crowded streets. Theirs was an unplanned, chaotic, and spontaneous place, certainly one with flaws. Yet it is hard to be at all certain that residents and business owners would, if asked, through translators, have agreed to be relocated to a high-rise tower set in a "park" without any cross streets at all and without any stores or businesses. They were certainly not surveyed as to their opinion.[5]

Vastly underappreciated, as well, was the fact that "tenement" neighborhoods were not static—they were, in fact, being steadily improved and upgraded by local owner-developers and architects. That is the theme of a remarkable 2019 book by Zachary J. Violette. In *The Decorated Tenement*, he contrasts the social and even moral goals of housing reformers with the gradually improving living conditions in actual buildings. Reformers, he notes, "sometimes couched their arguments in religious terms, seeing tenements as a treacherous deviation from a divinely inspired social order. William P. Patterson, a leader in the Methodist Episcopal Church, was perhaps the most unabashed," saying, "The tenement is an impediment to God's plan for a home." Violette notes that Jacob Riis—the author of *How the Other Half Lived* who did more than anyone else to frame Lower East Side living conditions as a scandal—believed that a "shanty is better than a flat in a cheap tenement any day." Violette sees the reformer's fanaticism in such assertions, upon closer examination of the "new tenements that were going up in the 1880s and 1890s." (These were even earlier than and later complemented by the so-called new law tenements of New York's Tenement House Law of 1901.) Tenants in buildings described by Violette—some "decorated" with exterior architectural flourishes—"had a whole host of things that many in the working class had never had access to before: a kitchen with a range, a hot water boiler, and a sink with running water and sewer connection; a dumbwaiter easing the vertical lugging of goods and fuel, a flush toilet, albeit likely down the hall and shared with a number of other families; a separate parlor, wallpapered with folding blinds, a faux-marble mantel, and fancy lambrequins, even if the room was rented out at night or doubled as a bedroom; gas lighting, maybe a dining room; a marble lobby with colored glass, painted frescoes, and tile floors in a building whose façade employed widely understood visual symbols of respect and propriety."[6]

What is more, finds Violette, such improvements were the work of "immigrant builders and architects" themselves, replete with aesthetic touches that he clearly believes worthy of celebration, not demolition, including, in an 1889 Madison Street tenement built by Peter Herter and his brothers, "terra-cotta and carved stone ornament executed in an eclectic Moorish Revival mode . . . with fine arabesque riveted moldings and cushion capitals. . . . Elongated bearded satyrs in heavy relief marked the keystones. . . . The columns of the portico and niches, panels and even the recurring Star of David motif at the apex of each opening were nearly identical to those on the nearby Eldridge Street synagogue, the signal landmark of the area's new Russian Jewish community, designed by the Herter Brothers three years earlier."[7]

These and other intricate plans, investments, and improvements constituted what Catherine Bauer, Edith Elmer Wood, and others who were distant from these places denigrated as slums without redeeming value. With the coming of the projects, Bauer et al. would be the ones choosing the architects, the locations, and the modernist housing style. It is hard to see the process as anything else but one of elites—of different social class and even religion—deciding how the working class was meant to live.

The modus operandi of minimalist community involvement that made possible the construction of the projects can be seen in a memo from New York City's legendary master builder Robert Moses—who, in addition to building bridges, roads, and parks, was deeply involved in slum clearance. Among his many posts, Moses served as "chairman, Committee on Slum Clearance Plans." In April 1952, in a letter to New York's then-powerful Board of Estimate, which approved city contracts, Moses discussed pending plans for the "North Harlem Slum Clearance Projects." Under the terms of the National Housing Act, wrote Moses, "we have been advised by the Housing and Home Finance Agency, acting for the United States of America, that they are prepared to enter into a contract providing a grant to the City of New York for the North Harlem Slum Clearance Project." All that remained before proceeding was a public hearing "before authorizing acquisition of title." Moses wrote on April 15; the hearing would be held on May 8. "We will transmit, under separate cover, . . . resolutions . . . approving the contracts and authorizing the Mayor and Comptroller to execute."[8]

Slum clearance, whether in Harlem, on Cherry Street, or in sites across the US, would, in other words, be a fait accompli, once set in motion. The writer Martin Anderson would later describe the process as the work of the "federal bulldozer." Anderson cites, as an example, a 1961 notice posted on Boston residential buildings in the Scollay Square area, which was set to be demolished to make way for that city's Government Center complex of city, state, and federal buildings. "The building in which you now live is located in an area which has been taken by the Boston Redevelopment Authority according to law. . . . The buildings will be demolished after the families have been relocated. . . . Plans presently being prepared."[9] This particular notice was not related to the construction of public housing; the 1949 Housing Act authorized such demolition and clearance for a range of commercial and residential purposes that local authorities judged to be in the public interest. Indeed, slum clearance did not necessarily lead to neighborhood residents being housed in projects erected on the sites that were cleared—as with the Pomonok Houses, built on the site of a country club.

The scale of the use of federal urban-renewal funds for what was deemed slum clearance was, however, indeed, great. A National Bureau of Economic Research paper found, in sum, that "Approved projects had cleared (or intended to clear) over 400,000 housing units, forcing the relocation of over 300,000 families, *just over half of whom were non-white*. The proposed clearance areas included nearly 57,000 total acres (90 square miles), of which about 35 percent was proposed for residential redevelopment, 27 percent for streets and public rights-of-way, 15 percent for industrial use, 13 percent for commercial use, and 11 percent for public or 'semi-public' use."[10]

A review of the evaluation process to determine which neighborhoods should be demolished makes it difficult to avoid the conclusion that the decisions were, to some extent, subjective or even questionable, dating to the earliest era of public housing. A 1935 report, for instance, by the Joint Committee on Housing in Baltimore, a local group choosing sites for Public Works Administration housing projects, selected six separate areas chosen "on the basis of nine basic factors." These included little objective information about the quality of the homes, other than "nearly all the buildings are at least 90 years old" in one area. Evaluation of the physical quality of residences was vague: "The physical condition of dwellings which place them below a minimum standard for satisfaction"; "Health and sanitary conditions below the general standard of the city as a whole." Those criteria that were more specific reflected interests other than those of the neighborhood residents: "A declining tax return for the city"; "Proximity to better areas, allowing improvements to be protected against bad environment." In other words, one might say that low-income neighborhoods merited demolition to protect against their encroachment on higher-income areas. The same evaluation left no doubt that it would target Black neighborhoods specifically for demolition. "This is emphatically a colored area. In the heart of the negro [sic] belt of Baltimore. It is old mansions converted to rooming houses. . . .

It should be noted that a large number of domestic workers in private homes are drawn from these areas, that a great deal of laundry work is done within them." One might have viewed this as a community of dispersed ownership marked by the sense of community provided by rooming houses. But no. Another mark against it was that there were "several families occupying the same dwelling" and that "the white evacuation of the neighborhood has led to the usual conversion of white houses into colored tenements." What is more, the "city as a whole" was making "inefficient use of this area. Potentially the area is the most in need of development for benefit to the city as a whole."[11]

Such was the cold and distant judgment cast by outside eyes on the "heart" of Black Baltimore. As slum clearance rolled on, however, and its nature became clear, resistance to the replacement of "slums" with projects did begin to emerge. Put another way, citizens began to question the determination that the communities in which they lived had so little value that they deserved to be demolished and their homes replaced by projects. So it was in the Hill District, a historically African American neighborhood of Pittsburgh.

The Hill, in particular the so-called Lower Hill, was known in Pittsburgh for the rude character of some of its housing, including residences without indoor plumbing. At first, that blunted opposition. "Initially, the prospect of improvement won the approval of some of the neighborhood's elites, but these projects, all intended for a primarily white audience that lived beyond the borders of the Hill, coupled with an inadequate relocation effort, quickly ignited grassroots resistance. Neighborhood activists objected to renewal plans and to official definitions of Hill District blight, which implicated not only buildings but *also the African American population that lived, worked, and shopped in them, as factors contributing to urban decline.*"[12] In other words, the Hill was blighted because it was Black.

There is no doubt that public housing did, in some ways, seem to offer a better future. In the city's African American newspaper, the *Pittsburgh Courier*, the columnist Paul Jones expressed hope that those who were living in the "dingy, crowded back streets of the lower Hill" would be eligible for better public housing. "The street won't be their children's only playground. Wintry blasts will no longer make the inside of the house as cheerless as the outside." Public housing would replace the absentee landlord—and for the better. Indeed, public housing had already come to the Hill in the form of Bedford Dwellings, 420 units set in midrise brick buildings on slightly more than eighteen acres and at the time still relatively new and desirable.[13]

But Jones, nonetheless, found much that gave him concern, as well. He made clear that the clearance plans had simply not accounted for the Hill's many community institutions and civil society. Judging a neighborhood narrowly on the basis of the character of its housing did not convince him that it should be demolished. "What about the churches, schools, business neighborhood associations, civic groups? All these are part of the whole problem of uprooting the lives of many people, whose patterns of living have been labeled, 'not desirable, not acceptable, not endurable.'"[14] The projects by their nature—government owned and managed, including no private ownership but only rentals, excluding retail and commercial businesses—would not foster the spontaneous community of dispersed ownership.

That the Hill was rich in these uncounted ways is without doubt, boasting a radio station, a newspaper, and an array of jazz clubs, including the Crawford Grill. But it was, in other words, taken for granted, from the time of the housing exhibition and onward through the march of federal housing legislation, that "slums" were to be judged only by their apparent and superficial physical condition —and not by what their residents were crafting through their own plans, rather than those of city planners.

Housing was the sole prism through which a complex community was viewed—and judged. So it was, as well, in cities not associated with public housing, such as Roanoke, Virginia. There, the historically African American Gainsboro neighborhood was cleared for a highway, civic center, and two public housing projects. A self-taught artist, David

Ramey Jr., whose work has come to be celebrated, captures in ink and colored pencil the homes, shops, churches, and social clubs—the rich social capital—of a neighborhood literally on the other side of the Norfolk and Western tracks from Roanoke's white downtown, before it joined so many Black neighborhoods in being branded a slum and sacrificed to bulldozers. His drawings provide detailed portrayals of people Ramey knew in movie-still-like action: Dr. Brooks of the Brooks Drug Store on Henry Street, the owners of Louise and Lillian's beauty salon, Big Nick of Weeby's Groceries, and more. Shadow and reflection play across the pastels.[15]

Even the urban-renewal opponent Martin Anderson did not consider the nonmonetary value of community institutions, emphasizing, instead, the extent to which government subsidies spurred promised private investment—or fell short (as he concluded). But there was another important, quite tangible type of asset held by Hill residents that could easily have been accounted for: the extent to which they had wealth in the form of home ownership. "Slums" may, per conventional wisdom, be viewed as having been universally owned by absentee landlords. Indeed, to the extent that that may have been true in immigrant New York—an apartment-based city—that assumption tended to drive project construction elsewhere. But there were many African Americans in Pittsburgh, concentrated in the Hill District, who owned their own homes. The 1940 federal Census of Housing, the first of its kind, reported that there were 13,539 nonwhite tenants in Pittsburgh—but also 1964 nonwhite owner-occupants of their own homes. In other words, these were families who were building wealth through ownership of homes and land. Clearance meant not only that their homes were taken at whatever compensation level was deemed appropriate at the time but also that future appreciation of the land was denied the owners. Those who, in later years, would be concerned about the gap in wealth between white and Black Americans should not fail to note this loss of Black-owned property. The same census, what is more, reported that a large number of all owner-occupied homes—54.6 percent—were two- to four-family structures, including 4.5 percent with ground-floor businesses. Moreover, 26 percent of the city's entire tenant population lived in just such structures. By no means were all owners living outside their own neighborhoods; owners and renters, in other words, were sharing the same premises. This, too, creates social fabric. It can also mean that owners have an incentive to maintain their properties. The 1940 Housing Census reports further that 1,575 of 1,793 homes owned by nonwhites and for which the census had data were "dwelling units not needing major repairs."[16]

This panorama of small homes and businesses fills the work of the *Pittsburgh Courier* photographer Teenie Harris, whose newspaper work has come to be celebrated and housed in Pittsburgh's Carnegie Museum of Art. An iconic photograph, *Herron Avenue at Intersection of Milwaukee Street, Hill District, c. 1945–1949*, shows cobblestoned streets lined with small brick buildings replete with ground-floor businesses and second-floor residences. A two-story family home is pictured in Harris's *Houses at 6 and 8 Watt Street, Hill District, March–May, 1959*. Both are found in a volume of his work, a heartbreaking collection of images of a gone community that fell in large part to housing reform's wrecking ball.[17]

This is not to suggest that there was no crowding or other housing issues in the Hill. The 1940 census reported that 26 percent of nonwhite tenants had to share a toilet with another household—and that 192 had no running water. (Notably, there were 951 white tenant households that lacked running water, as well.)[18]

The goal here is to paint a more nuanced picture of the pre-project "slums." Was demolition the only approach to improving physical conditions? Should other factors have been weighted? Indeed, other voices in the *Courier* acknowledged poor living conditions but placed blame for them on city government, in particular for the danger of crime and disease. In John R. Clark's "Wylie Ave." column in the *Courier*, he routinely blamed the Hill's problems on lax law enforcement on the part of city and county police. In a warning to the city and to concerned Hill

FIGURE 4.1. Herron Avenue at Milwaukie Street, Hill District, Pittsburgh. (Carnegie Museum of Art, Pittsburgh; Teenie Harris Archives)

residents, Clark stated that the crime currently situated in "bottoms" and "pretty girl 'houses'" would move to the new housing projects and to other neighborhoods if enforcement did not improve. Reform, not redevelopment, was the solution.[19]

It is a profound irony, indeed, that exactly those institutions and patterns of living about which Paul Jones eloquently expressed concern would, once they had been replaced by projects and a Civic Arena, become celebrated as the backdrop to the work of one of America's greatest playwrights, August Wilson—all of whose plays but one are set in the Hill, where he came of age. It is where the jitneys of Wilson's *Jitney* picked up riders; the site of Seth and Bertha Holly's fictional boardinghouse on Webster Avenue, in *Joe Turner's Come and Gone*; the Bedford Avenue house in *Fences*. In an irony upon irony, Wilson's success led to his own childhood home being preserved and placed on the National Register of Historic Places—even as its context was physically erased. It is part of a tourist map for devotees of Wilson's work who are drawn to Pittsburgh to see its roots.[20]

In writing about the importance of the Hill to August Wilson's work—in an article about those few locations still standing decades

FIGURE 4.2. Hill District house with picket fence. (Carnegie Museum of Art, Pittsburgh; Teenie Harris Archives)

FIGURE 4.3. Hill District residents playing checkers. (Carnegie Museum of Art, Pittsburgh; Teenie Harris Archives)

after urban renewal—the *New York Times* observed that "the seminal elements of Wilson's plays pay homage to the people of the Hill District."[21]

Sites in Wilson's work were caught in the tide of urban renewal demolition: In the summer of 1956 alone, some thirteen hundred structures were razed, displacing about fifteen hundred families (more than eight thousand residents), the great majority of whom were Black.[22] Between 1950 and 1990, the Hill lost 71 percent of its residents (more than thirty-eight thousand individuals) and about four hundred businesses, leaving the neighborhood hollowed out.[23] Five of the twenty-seven Pittsburgh Housing Authority projects that still stand, as of this writing, can be found in the Hill District.[24]

The fate of the Hill District was far from unique. In Detroit, the same fate awaited the predominantly African American neighborhood of

Black Bottom. It, too, had been a community of concentrated Black institutions. Migration transformed Hastings and St. Antoine Streets into the city's major African American community of Black-owned businesses, social institutions, and nightclubs, nationally famous for its music scene in Paradise Valley. Hastings Street is also where Aretha Franklin's father, the Reverend C. L. Franklin, first opened his New Bethel Baptist Church. Businesses included ten restaurants, eight grocers, seventeen physicians, and six drugstores, Barthwell Drugs being one of the well-known enterprises.[25] In Detroit census tracts that were 60 percent or more Black, 28 percent of homes were owner-occupied, with small multifamily homes and the renting of rooms to lodgers making the number of residences in which the owner lived with tenants even higher.[26] A photograph in Ford's *Slums and Housing* shows the preclearance Black Bottom dotted with hundreds of small homes and stores. It was taken by the federal Public Works Administration as part of its public housing planning process.[27] The neighborhood would be cleared to make way for the Brewster Homes Project, later the Brewster-Douglass Houses, which included six fourteen-story high-rise towers. These, in turn, would later be deemed distressed and themselves demolished.

In St. Louis, the predominantly Black Desoto-Carr and Mill Valley neighborhoods, which would make way for their own projects, were characterized, as well, by a modest but not insignificant extent of owner-occupied housing; census data, pre-public housing, shows that, in census tracts that were more than 60 percent Black, 15 percent of housing was owner-occupied.[28] As in other communities designated as blighted, Mill Valley included significant employers, including the Standard-Tilton (Flour) Milling Company and the Dinks Parish Laundry. The Berea Presbyterian Church was the "first African-American Presbyterian church west of the Mississippi River. . . . Berea was a community hub of the Mill Creek Valley, offering sports teams along with typical religious activities."[29] Yet, as a St. Louis Public Schools history of the neighborhood's Vashon High School puts it, "The students, alumni and particularly the residents of the Mill Creek Valley area were unaware that . . .

their neighborhood had been targeted for obliteration."³⁰ Desoto-Carr and Mill Valley would make way for the quintessential modern housing project, the thirty-three eleven-story towers set on fifty-seven acres known as Pruitt-Igoe. Designed by the modernist architect Minoru Yamasaki, it was praised by *Architectural Forum* as a successful example of "slum surgery" and praised, when it opened in 1954, as the "best high apartment of the year."³¹ The project would stand for less than twenty years before its dramatic "implosion."

Indeed, in the debate about whether African Americans should be awarded financial reparations in recognition for slavery and other past injustices, the topics of urban renewal's neighborhood demolition and replacement public housing have come to renewed attention. In San Francisco, the fate of the once-predominantly-Black and culturally vibrant Fillmore District, as described in a 2023 *New York Times* story, reminds of the stories of Pittsburgh, Detroit, and Chicago:

> Standing at the stoop of her childhood home—a slim but stately Victorian shaded by an evergreen pear tree—Lynette Mackey pulled up a photo of a family gathering from nearly 50 years ago. The men were all in suits, the women in skirts. Ms. Mackey, a teenager in red bell bottoms, stretched her arms wide and had a beaming smile. Soon after that time, in the 1960s and 1970s, Ms. Mackey watched the slow erasure of Black culture from the Fillmore District, once celebrated as "the Harlem of the West." The jazz clubs that drew the likes of Billie Holiday and Duke Ellington disappeared, and so, too, did the soul food restaurants.
>
> By the mid-1970s, many of her friends were gone as well, pushed out by city officials who seized homes in the name of what they called "urban renewal." Then, finally, her family lost the house they had purchased in the 1940s after migrating from Texas. In many cases, the old Victorian homes were torn down and replaced with housing projects, but the city kept Ms. Mackey's home standing, and it has since been renovated into government-subsidized apartments. Her grandfather

suffered a heart attack while fighting to save their home. "He died saying, 'I'm not going to sell this house,'" she said.[32]

It is important to note that "slum clearance" of working-class neighborhoods for projects was not limited to African American communities. This was particularly true in and around Boston, where, in the heyday of public housing construction, the Black population was relatively small and a significant poor white population in such enclaves as the South Boston and Charlestown neighborhoods of the city was present. Major public housing projects were built in both and especially in Charlestown—a historic neighborhood surrounding the Bunker Hill battlefield site—where large-scale demolition (of the Point neighborhood) took place to clear the way for public housing named for the neighborhood's most famous attraction. "The current area of the Projects in Charlestown was identified and hence began the construction. About 90 houses were razed by the City of Boston to make way for the Projects, which began in 1939."[33]

The affluent inner-ring Boston suburb of Brookline made use of the Housing Act of 1949 to clear what it considered its undesirable poor side of town, a low-income Irish American neighborhood known as the Farm. Like other such areas deemed "slums," it was notable for its concentration of small, owner-occupied multifamily houses—in its case, the prototypical New England frame three-family. Its 121 homes comprised 348 individual units. In other words, here again, owners and tenants shared the same premises. The importance of maintenance to retain tenants was clear to low-income landlords; the potential for ownership was clear to low-income tenants.[34] Here, too, the neighborhood was marked by retail and commercial uses: corner stores, a commercial laundry, an auto repair shop. The Farm, like Black Bottom and the Hill, would be cleared to make way for public housing, as well as a luxury high-rise known as the Brook House.[35]

The same story of urban "renewal," clearance, and construction of projects or highways played out repeatedly, especially since the 1949

Housing Act supercharged the process by providing authorization and funding not just for construction but for clearance. In Buffalo, the "Italian colony" on Lake Erie was replaced by the Marine Drive project; in Lowell, Massachusetts, the "three-decker" houses, streets, and shops of French-speaking "Little Canada" were replaced by a highway "Connector."

But African American neighborhoods clearly drew special opprobrium and were, as per the previously cited research, disproportionately demolished. Indeed, in at least one instance in working-class white South Boston, local resistance to clearance proved successful, probably reflecting greater political power than that of Blacks. "The result of a long contentious period of development, Old Harbor Village was originally intended as a slum clearance project for nearby land. When public outcry over the use of eminent domain and the fair price for the real estate stalled the initial project, it was moved to this vacant site."[36]

The disproportionate extent of slum clearance to make way for Black public housing has, belatedly, begun to get public attention. In Cincinnati, it included the Kenyon-Barr community. A 2017 photo essay in *Cincinnati Magazine*, in an issue titled "Lost City," described the demolished "slum" this way:

> Since the 1920s, the West End—and Kenyon-Barr in particular—had been the heart of the Black community in Cincinnati. What remains of Kenyon-Barr today is 2,700 photographs in the Cincinnati Museum Center's archives, a survey conducted prior to demolition. Each photo is numbered and dated, the same signboard held by a rotating cast of city employees. The photos are, wittingly or not, heartbreaking, even haunting: people and potted plants filling residential windows, corner markets busy with shoppers, billboards and businesses, rowhouses upon rowhouses—a vivid street life, frozen in time address by address, as architecturally significant as any street in Over-the-Rhine.[37] They are imbued with an ominous sense of what's to come: the willful, wholesale demolition of a 400-acre neighborhood. And not just the structures but the community—the social, political, and cultural network—that filled them.[38]

The clearance of Kenyon-Barr and the adjoining Lower West End area led to two of the outcomes cheer-led by James Ford and Catherine Bauer. The Laurel Homes and Lincoln Court public housing projects were constructed on what would be called Ezzard Charles Drive.[39] And clearance would replace housing with "Queensgate" (Cincinnati is the "Queen City"), a distinct new industrial area—as per James Ford's "industrial decentralization" vision—served by an interstate highway that would bite through what remained of the district.

> City documents also remain in the library's local history stacks. There are two slim planning volumes, plus a thick final report tied up neatly in a red box, a water-stained relic of a fundamentally flawed remake of the city's urban landscape (those shiny renderings of a bustling Queensgate never quite came to be). The phrase "slum clearance" comes up a number of times. As a talking point, it makes sense: Who wouldn't want to clean up unhealthy living conditions? To be sure, a majority of the units were in need of repair: they'd been subdivided and neglected by landlords for years, and structural and sanitation improvements were daunting.
>
> But the term *slum* vastly oversimplifies the neighborhood and falsely suggests there was no alternative. . . . The photos depict a much more nuanced reality. As does the city's list of "Units of Use," which included: 10,295 dwelling units, 137 food stores, 118 bars and restaurants, 86 barber shops and beauty parlors, 80 churches and missions, 24 dry cleaners, and 6 funeral homes. Of 11,535 total units, only 171 were vacant lots.[40]

The author's emphasis in describing Kenyon-Barr's streets replete with "rowhouses upon rowhouses" must not be passed over. From Philadelphia to Chicago, Boston to Detroit, Baltimore to St. Louis, poor neighborhoods were not generally characterized by the multistory tenement structures typical of New York. This is not a minor matter, for it was the condition of New York that cast an outsized influence on housing "reform." Indeed, James Ford's *Slums and Housing* was subtitled *With Special Reference to New York*. From the time of Jacob Riis in the 1890s into the era of the New Deal and federal housing legislation, New York can be said to have set the tone. But, as Ford himself noted, New York was an exception. Philadelphia, he noted, served the working class well with its hundreds of thousands of row houses. "Slum housing of the New York type, with its dark rooms and intensively crowded land, is unknown in Philadelphia." In Detroit, "a young city," Ford noted that "more than half its families live in single-family homes, and over 40 percent own their own houses." In Cleveland, "more than 36 percent of the homes are occupied by their owners," and thanks to a 1915 housing ordinance, they provide "light, air and sunshine." Even in its "slums," "only one third of 1 per cent lacked running water and . . . 39 percent [were] not provided with a private indoor water-closet." In St. Louis, Ford described slums as "the crowding of industrial quarters with two or more house per lot, which makes many rooms gloomy." In Chicago, "city lots are deeper than those of New York," and "instead of one many-storied building on such a lot, two and even three frame buildings of not over three stories in height have usually been erected."[41]

It is understatement to say that the perspective of residents of these neighborhoods deemed to be blighted was little considered, as the impact of the National Housing Act—and especially its 1949 provisions authorizing the use of federal funds for neighborhood clearance—swept across US cities. It was assumed that cities and towns would be improved as a result. The lives of residents, not just in relation to their housing but as whole persons in communities, simply did not figure. Although Jacob Riis, the journalist-photographer who first sparked public outrage about slums in his book *How the Other Half Lives* wrote of New York's Lower East Side in the 1890s, that broader picture is well captured by a recent critical biography of him: "In fact there was more to the slums than abject poverty. Hundreds of families lived relatively normal lives. They worked, although usually under deplorable conditions, paid rent, fed their children and had hopes and dreams for their children. For a large number of immigrants [and one must include Black immigrants from the South to the North] life in the tenements was an improvement over their old lives, offering a more dignified existence." What is more, "poverty was not a life sentence."[42] Put another way, the modern housing movement took its inspiration from a snapshot of specific neighborhoods at a specific moment and presumed that conditions were permanent—and intolerable.

The retrospective views of some of those who were affected tell a different story, however. In Detroit, a funeral home owner who had operated in Black Bottom lamented its demolition in an oral history: "When I came to town, the people I lived with went to Bethel A.M.E. Church, which was located on Hastings and Napoleon. It's all torn away now.... Negro businesses are just gone."[43] In Brookline, onetime Farm resident Frank Moroney observes, in some wonder, "They could have fixed it up. They didn't have to tear it all down."[44]

A more detailed, blow-by-blow narrative of the effect of clearance to make way for projects is provided by a little-known account—detailed and personal—of the sense of loss and dislocation experienced by those whose neighborhoods were cleared for projects: *The World of Patience Gomes*, written by a Vista volunteer who lived in the affected community, just as the dramas of urban renewal and its replacement by public housing were playing out. It tells the story of the demise of the Fulton neighborhood of Richmond, Virginia, an African American neighborhood of fifty blocks near the James River, home to twenty-five hundred residents and seven hundred households. Although some houses and small tenements were in poor repair, "most houses were well-maintained, surrounded by neat yards and white picket fences."[45] The modest homes, slated to be taken by urban renewal, had been seen both as measures of accomplishment by the descendants of slaves who had moved to Fulton from rural Virginia and as vehicles for the accumulation of wealth. "Fulton had detached houses and duplexes which could be purchased for a few dollars down. These appealed to upward-moving men and women whose families had striven to acquire farmland in the country." The houses "of Fulton had been proof that hard work and virtuous living—not political power or government money—bring success in this world. The houses were a statement of the essential morality of the universe, a statement which the housing authority bluntly and decisively rebutted."[46]

From the residents', and especially the home owners', point of view, they had "made striking economic gains" and "took pride in their independence from white society." The means of achieving that involved community institutions in which the book's central character, Patience Gomes, participated. She and her husband, Frank, a railway worker, "belonged to the Rising Mt. Zion Baptist Church . . . and attended regularly. [She] supported church groups such as the Candlestick Club (which raised money for church projects and looked after those who were sick or in need)."[47]

But all this was not part of the calculus of the Richmond Housing Authority. "Housing Authority employees thought they were planning on behalf of the city rather than conspiring against the people of Fulton. To their minds, the facts fully justified clearance. Against the anger of Fulton residents, they stood their ground. Fulton was a poor residential site; the houses were dilapidated; the street grid obsolete. . . . Clearance was the logical course." The neighborhood "was scaled to people not cars. It incorporated dozens of convenience stores, restaurants, social clubs, a school, a supermarket, churches, playgrounds, retail stores and a factory. People walked a few blocks to get what they needed. As they walked they talked to neighbors who sat on front porches. Streets were safe because they were watched."[48]

Community opposition emerged, including that of a local resident who became a local leader; he went so far as to tell the *Richmond Times-Dispatch*, "I pledge myself to you now that, as long as I have breath to breathe, those bulldozers will not come into Fulton." But come they did: "Before long, the houses, stores, churches, trees, sidewalks would be broken apart, loaded into dump trucks, and hauled away." The author asserts that "half the old people who moved would die from the strain. . . . The old people [had] depended on this neighborhood and could not live without it."[49]

FIGURE 4.4. Atlanta before public housing. (Atlanta History Center)

None of these dimensions was part of the thinking of the people in the housing exhibition who set in motion the slow-moving policy tsunami that would sweep away Fulton, the Hill, Black Bottom, the Farm, Desoto-Carr, and hundreds of communities across the US, white and Black. Those who took it upon themselves to plan the residential lives of the poor and working class and to remake the face of large swathes of US cities were deeply uncurious about the true, lived reality of "slums." They proceeded on the basis that vibrant communities, perhaps because the planners could not imagine living there themselves, were abject and needed to be gone. Yet, as Brookline's Frank Moroney said, "They didn't have to tear it all down." The fact that so many African American neighborhoods in particular were cleared for "urban renewal," often to be replaced by projects, leads to a theme that is unavoidable when discussing US public housing: how it came to be disproportionately Black and poor—and what that has meant.

5

Crumbling Façades

Race, Segregation, and the Suburbs

African Americans are underrepresented in many fields in American life. They are not underrepresented in public housing. In a country in which Blacks make up some 13 percent of the population, they are 48 percent of the public housing population.[1] Historically, that figure has been even higher—it stood at 53 percent in 1989.[2] What is more, many individual projects are even more predominantly African American. In New York City, whose public housing system of 177,000 apartments represents 19 percent of the national total, five developments are 83 percent Black or more. The Rutland Towers of Brooklyn's East Flatbush neighborhood are 94 percent Black.[3] The same holds true for a great many small public housing projects throughout the US South: in Mobile, Alabama, Blacks make up fully 96 percent of all public housing residents. For Charleston, South Carolina, that figure is 91 percent.[4]

It is fair to say that none of the people involved in the Museum of Modern Art exhibition intended such an outcome; indeed, neither the exhibition nor its accompanying book mentions race specifically; the terms "Negro" or "colored" or "Black" do not appear at all. Nor do they appear in the text of the National Housing Act of 1937. Yet not only did public housing become disproportionately black, but the projects became widely associated in the public mind with Black poverty. An all-Black Chicago project, the Ida B. Welles Houses (ironically named for the antilynching crusader), was the setting for a film produced for public television by Frederick Wiseman, widely considered the premier US

FIGURE 5.1. Black Bottom in Detroit before urban renewal. (Burton Collection, Detroit Historical Society)

documentary filmmaker. It was simply titled *Public Housing*, implying that this high-rise complex, portrayed as a nexus of crime and poverty, was an example representative of the whole. Virtually no white character, other than police, appear in the film at all. The implications of the racial makeup of US public housing are, in other words, a key part of its story. It is well worth inquiring how it came to pass.

Racial segregation in US housing is well understood to have limited the accumulation of wealth and the overall quality of life of African Americans. This makes it all the more ironic that the racial segregation of US public housing can be said to have its roots, in part, in benevolence. It is a story that can be said to have started in September 1935, when First Lady Eleanor Roosevelt herself felt that the ground-breaking for the Brewster Homes Projects in Detroit was important enough that she should attend. It was to be the first federally subsidized public housing for African Americans. Indeed, it would be exclusively Black. The

Michigan Advance, Detroit's black community newspaper, would later recount the event in celebratory tones:

> A street pageant festival was held in Detroit to celebrate the building of the Brewster Homes, the nation's first federally funded housing project designed for African Americans.
>
> On that day, four vehicles motored from city hall downtown to the Hastings-Benton Street area located on the city's lower east side. Passengers included city Mayor Frank Couzens, local legislative members, and one special guest: first lady Eleanor Roosevelt.
>
> They arrived at 651 Benton Street in the heart of the city's growing Black community. . . . A makeshift platform awaited the dignitaries. One of the city's most respected clergy leaders, the Rev. William Peck, pastor of Bethel A.M.E. Church and founder of the Booker T. Washington Business Association, was among many there to greet them. The city of Detroit and the Detroit Housing Commission, co-hosts of the event, called the program "Demolition Ceremony and Public Reception for Mrs. Franklin D. Roosevelt." Construction followed in later weeks, but first land had to be cleared to make room for the new development.[5]

As elsewhere, that meant demolition of the existing homes, in this case the brick row homes of Detroit's Black Bottom neighborhood. As the account reflects, the fact that this was to be a racially segregated project was not a concern; rather, dignitaries, including Mrs. Roosevelt, were celebrating the fact that Washington was willing to provide safe, sanitary new apartments for African Americans at all. Martin Meyerson and Edward Banfield, in their classic account of the early history of public housing siting in Chicago, put it this way: "their demands did not go much beyond that; they did not for example, make an issue of the fact that most public housing projects in northern cities were segregated."[6] Thus, public housing segregation began as incidental to a Progressive push that Blacks not be excluded entirely from a program regarded as clearly beneficial for all those it would include. At the same time, the fact was, as well, that public housing was being built to replace neighborhoods deemed to be "blighted"—and that, in itself, would have racial implications. There is reason to believe that just the very fact of a neighborhood being predominantly Black led to its being deemed blighted, in Chicago as in Pittsburgh's Hill District. The Chicago Planning Commission, charged with designating those parts of the city deemed blighted in the early 1950s, was, to be sure, meant to be guided by a series of very specific criteria, including the number of structures designated as "substandard," "unfit for use," or occupied by more than one and a half persons per room. As Meyerson and Banfield observed, however, "despite its seeming clarity, the definition of blight left a good deal to interpretation," noting that, in Chicago, "it was once charged—but not proved—that when in doubt the Plan Commission classified blocks blighted if they were occupied by Negroes."[7]

That this was akin to official policy is made clear in a 1942 public statement issued by the federal Public Housing Authority Office of Race Relations, titled "The Negro in Public War Housing." Presented to the authority's "Race Relations Conference," it looked back with implied pride at the fact that, during the period in which early public housing was being built through the federal Public Works Administration, "7,500 Negro families became tenants in more than one-third of the 21,322 units developed in 48 projects in the continental United States.... The degree to which accommodations have been made available to Negroes, despite the existing obstacles, accents the story of the struggle for decent housing." It went on to note that at the time it was issued, "36,800 of the 106,050 units now open for occupancy are or will be tenanted by Negro families; another 10,950 units planned for Negro occupancy are among the 37,000 now under construction." Clearly, this was to be racially segregated housing, as would have been expected in the Jim Crow South, where hundreds of small city projects were being built. But not only were projects being explicitly set aside for Blacks; they were replacing historically Black neighborhoods that were being cleared. That story was told in bureaucratic understatement:

> Generally, in terms of occupancy, the public housing program recognized the housing needs of Negroes on an equitable basis. This program, however, provided no natural outlets for the overcrowded but rigidly constricted Negro neighborhoods. Site selection was essentially the responsibility of local housing authorities, which planned, constructed, managed, and actually owned the developments. The emphasis on slum clearance generally made possible the restriction of developments to areas traditionally occupied by Negroes. In some instances, this served to block the natural expansion of these areas. Since there were so many such areas for project sites, very few cities reached the point of having to decide what to do about Negro families who needed housing when there was no "Negro slum areas" available for a "Negro" project.[8]

Translated, this is the story of the destruction of Black neighborhoods without regard for their social fabric of churches, owner-occupied homes, locally owned stores, and social clubs. All this was to be, as in the account of Richmond in *The World of Patience Gomes*, discussed in chapter 4, shoehorned into institutionalized life. The potential for gradual racial integration—as civil rights laws changed and some Black residents acquired the wealth to move up and out—was forestalled. Indeed, the potential acquisition of wealth through the sale of homes or land, as Black neighborhoods became more valuable for new real estate development, was rendered impossible through eminent domain takings at a government-dictated price.

That public housing would be a vehicle to continue to confine Blacks in historically "Negro" neighborhoods was made clear in 1936 when Edith Elmer Wood, very much an advocate of improving housing for Blacks, recommended that a public housing project in Atlantic City, New Jersey, be built outside a historically Black neighborhood. There was local enthusiasm for the idea expressed in a letter from the city's NAACP to

Eleanor Roosevelt herself. Yet Wood's recommendation was, atypically for her, rejected. In explaining the decision, Robert Kohn—a fellow contributor to the museum housing exhibition serving as director of housing for the Federal Emergency Administration of Public Works, predecessor to the Public Works Administration—assured Wood that the "project was not arbitrarily rejected. . . . The Special Board, which passes on Public Works loans, is getting more and more particular about projects proposed for vacant land. . . . Can not this group which is interested in this housing project in Atlantic City come closer in to the city and acquire a few blocks of present time slum or blighted areas for which they could design a project?"[9] This is a close as a New Deal official would come to saying that Blacks should know their place—at least, geographically.

There is clear evidence that Black communities were not pleased about public housing segregation. In a February 10, 1937, letter marked "personal-confidential," C. E. Pynchon of the Public Works Administration wrote to Wood (at a Morningside Drive address in New York City) regarding "a situation [that] has arisen" on which he would value her "view-point":

> In several cities where Housing Projects are located, we are faced with demands by negro [sic] citizen groups that citizens of their race have equal consideration in selection of tenants. In other words, integration of white and negro tenants in the same project. They raises the question that there is racial discrimination in our present policy.
> At Stamford, Connecticut, over fifty negro families have filed applica tions for residence in a project planned for low-income white families. . . . I find the method of approach a rather difficult problem. Apparently the negro groups feel that separate projects for white and negroes only will not satisfy them. We have done this in some places, Cleveland being one of them, but now they are taking the stand in that city that all federally financed housing projects should be open to any citizen white or negro. . . . I find that the Resettlement Administration on its rural program is confronted with the same thing but so far they have done nothing about it.[10]

Wood's papers do not include her reply, if any. But subsequent actions by local housing authorities make clear that no such open housing policy was adopted. Indeed, in Atlanta, two of the earliest projects were, in keeping with Jim Crow laws of the era, explicitly segregated: Techwood Houses for whites, University Houses for Blacks. Techwood Houses was, notably, the first project opened in the US, when, in 1935, the electricity was turned on by President Franklin Roosevelt himself.[11]

Thus was the road paved toward both the disproportionate presence of Blacks in public housing through the race-influenced demolition of Black neighborhoods—mistakenly viewed as uniformly blighted—and the racial segregation of public housing generally.

The public housing erected in the nation's most well-known Black community, New York's Harlem, reflected the same pattern. Black neighborhoods were deemed blighted; once they were cleared, replacement housing would be provided on the sites or nearby. In Harlem, the racially segregated character of the new towers in parks was reflected by project names such as the James Weldon Johnson Houses, named for the prominent African American poet and author of "Lift Every Voice and Sing," often referred to as the "Negro national anthem." In time, New York projects would be named for Langston Hughes and Marcus Garvey, as well.

None of this could have transpired, however, were it not for the fact of the Great Migration—the movement of Blacks from the Deep South to Northern cities. It was, it might be said, a coincidence of that movement and housing policy that was an underlying factor in the disproportionate presence of Blacks in the projects. Previous waves of ethnic migration had moved through cities prior to the advent of public housing. The numbers are notable. Between 1920 and 1950, the Black population of Detroit increased from forty thousand to three hundred thousand.[12]

A powerful combination of factors was in play: the arrival of Blacks in major cities where public housing would be built at large scale; the tendency to designate Black neighborhoods as blighted because they were Black; the benevolence, as it were, of 1930s Progressives. If "slums" were to be cleared, replacement housing would have to be provided. If Black neighborhoods were more likely to be designated as slums, their residents were more likely to be directed to the projects. That, however, raised a crucial—and contentious—question: Where should projects be sited?

In New York, the nation's largest system, racial segregation was far from universal. Indeed, some projects, such as the Pomonok Houses, built on a previously nonresidential site, were racially integrated. "The black population was spread much more evenly among the growing number of postwar federal and state projects compared to the prewar pattern, not only in contrast to private housing in New York City but most public housing elsewhere. . . . The city projects, often in all white neighborhoods, had been tenanted with an appreciable black population."[13]

But in New York—and elsewhere—the combination of designating Black neighborhoods for clearance and the pressure to relocate those who were losing their homes often led to a different outcome. In 1956, Charles Abrams, the head of New York's State Commission Against Discrimination, charged that the city Housing Authority was "building racial ghettoes" in Harlem. Abrams was no opponent of public housing: two decades previously, he had expressed the view that neither housing conditions nor costs could be "remedied by the ordinary operation of private enterprise." Abrams pointed out that "14 public housing projects are 85 percent or more minority occupied in previously minority neighborhoods."[14] As a leader of the New York chapter of the Congress for Racial Equality put it, "Since New York City housing is predominantly segregated, merely placing people in projects in the neighborhoods in which they have been living perpetuates and seals segregation in official mortar and brick."[15] As Nicholas Bloom writes, "Condemnation of land for Moses' redevelopment placed a heavy burden on fragile housed minorities and tended to speed up racial change in NYCHA development because site tenants gained an edge in admissions. By 1956, for instance, at least 40 percent of slum clearance site tenants and 50 percent of public housing site clearance tenants were black or Puerto Rican."[16]

Such was the public housing construction default. Indeed, even when projects replaced a low-income racially integrated neighborhood, racial division could be created. In Atlanta, that city's first public housing projects—Techwood Homes—replaced a low-income neighborhood known as the Flats, whose population had been significantly African American. Techwood, however, would be for whites only—by rule of its pre–National Housing Act funder, the Public Works Administration. A "sister" project, University Homes, would be reserved for Blacks, although many Black residents of the Flats would not find housing there either.

> While Techwood Homes did provide affordable, clean, modern living for 604 white families, its construction also meant the clearance of the Flats, which displaced 1,611 families. Twenty-eight percent of the Flats community had been African American, and because public housing was segregated by national policy, only white residents were permitted in Techwood Homes. Some quickly found refuge in the all-Black University Homes public housing project on the west side of Atlanta, but many African Americans from the Flats were never rehoused. Furthermore, income qualifiers for public housing meant that many former Flats inhabitants, white and Black, *were too poor for public housing.*[17]

In Detroit, "where racial segregation was an important part of the issue, a 14,350-unit public housing program planned in 1949 was very much reduced, especially in vacant land sites, by an opponent of public housing who was elected mayor."[18]

Race-related reasons did not explain all local opposition to public housing: the fiscal impact on local budgets figured, as did the prospective taking of property by a newly established housing authority. Nor can one rule out the possibility that smaller jurisdiction did not want to expend funds or grant a property tax exemption for housing that was likely to be occupied by Blacks. For whatever reasons, however, the fact remains that between 1949 and 1954, "in at least 70 communities

FIGURE 5.2. David Ramey drawing of historic Gainsboro. (Taubman Museum of Art, Roanoke, VA)

(most of them small ones) opponents of public housing brought the issue before the electorate in referenda . . . [and] public housing lost in five cities for every three in which it won."[19] It is fair to say, moreover, that public housing, with some exceptions, from its earliest days and onward, tended to reinforce or even extend the racial isolation of African Americans. "Middle and upper income groups were generally unwilling to permit the movement of lower class or minority groups into new neighborhoods. In the northern industrial cities especially, the question of where public housing was to be located was closely connected with the question of whether the residential segregation of Negroes was to be maintained. Race appeared again and again in the deliberations of those who supported public housing and those who opposed it."[20]

It was a pattern that played out most famously in Chicago, as that city's Housing Authority struggled, in the early 1950s, to identify sites on which to rehouse Blacks who would be displaced from their homes on the city's South Side. The contentious struggle roiled the city's politics— and has been recounted in dramatic detail in two of the most important accounts of public housing siting, Martin Meyerson and Edward Banfield's *Politics, Planning and the Public Interest: The Case of Public*

Housing in Chicago and the tellingly titled *Making the Second Ghetto: Race and Housing in Chicago, 1940-1960* by Arnold Hirsch.

The race-saturated struggle over where to build the Chicago projects brought together a modern housing true believer who would have been at home in the 1934 housing exhibition. Edith Wood of the Chicago Housing Authority (not to be confused with Edith Elmer Wood) was not only a crusader against slum housing but an advocate of its Le Corbusier–style tower replacements. "Her reflection brought her to the conclusion that the best course of action . . . was entirely to rebuild blighted areas into protected residential areas." She expressed "an unalterable determination to relocate all transit and traffic in such a way that the blighted areas are divided into superblocks averaging, let us say, about 80 acres, through which no street car or other public transit passes, through which no traffic goes, so designed that entrance to the interior streets discourages traffic."[21]

Like Catherine Bauer and James Ford, it never occurred to the CHA's Wood—armed with the power to clear whole neighborhoods and replace them—that "blighted" areas had any value. She was undeterred, in fact, by organized opposition to public housing that emerged in Chicago's Black community, including "a slogan that appeared on posters in many shop windows in the Negro district: 'Slum clearance is Negro clearance.'" Opposition included that of Black property owners—some accused of profiteering from crowded conditions but nonetheless building wealth. One leading Black minister asserted that "public housing would be run by whites; Negroes (he maintained) would not be fairly treated except by landlords of their own race."[22] This makes an important point, as per Detroit and elsewhere: there was local property ownership in the "slums." There was concern, as well, that the modern housing attachment to reducing housing "density" would inevitably lead to an overall reduction in the amount of housing—in effect forcing Blacks into the projects, if they were fortunate enough to get in.

Wood of the Chicago Housing Authority was having none of it, however, as she made clear in a 1945 speech. "Poor people can be housed in physically bad houses which have a malevolent effect on the community or in good houses which have a benevolent effect." Public housing would not only have to correct for overcrowding and poor maintenance but also have to be the means of "head-on facing of the problem of the cultural level of the slum dweller. This means that there shall be instituted an educational program for slum dwellers through every available medium in relation to their living habits."[23] Wood focused particularly on what she viewed as the inevitable tendency of the poor to toss garbage wantonly in the streets. The goal, she continued, should be "a series of residential neighborhoods so attractive as to compare favorably with the suburbs."[24] Such was the vision that led to the construction of projects whose names alone would become synonymous with crime and despair—Robert Taylor, Stateway Gardens, Ida B. Welles, and Cabrini-Green—before they were themselves reduced by bulldozers to piles of bricks.

Having so denigrated the population that the Housing Authority was to serve, Wood ought not to have been surprised by the opposition that organized in regard to the locations of the forty thousand project units on seven sites that the CHA planned to build in the early 1950s—"a vast and sudden expansion of public housing."[25] Crucially, not only was new housing to be built, but it was to be dispersed and not confined to formerly "slum" areas. That required "building on vacant land."[26]

So it was that the table was set for struggle—one that deeply involved race. "The question of where public housing was to be located was closely connected with the question of whether the residential segregation of Negroes was to be maintained? Race appeared again and again in the deliberations of those who supported public housing and those who opposed it."[27] To build outside Chicago's South Side "Black Belt," some public housing would have to be built in outlying "conservation" areas, adjacent to white residential communities, which organized against it.

That racial animus and fear were among the driving elements of such opposition was clear. One realtor and mortgage banker among the opposition leaders put it this way: "Here in our community [Roseland] we have always had a reasonable number of colored who have come and used... our parks and shops. The Negroes we have had in our community have owned their own homes. We get along with them all right. But CHA has shoved Negroes into neighborhoods where there weren't any Negroes. Our people do not support... public housing."[28]

But the opposition, on close examination, went beyond the racial to involve social status and social class. A key opponent, a truck driver named George Strech, chaired the Southwest Neighborhood Council, a group representing twenty property owners' associations. Strech, referring to those projects built in the first phase of public housing, criticized them as unsightly. "The houses are not taken care of properly. Garbage is thrown all over, mops are hanging out the window." Referring to the residents, he said, "If these people would work and save they could have a house of their own." But Strech—even at a time well before the civil rights movement and when more open racism was far less unacceptable, felt constrained to distance himself from race as the chief reason for opposition:

> You know, a lot of people say it's the colored we don't want, but the kind of whites who live in public housing are just as bad. It's not the colored alone it's a whole class of people who are like that. I talked to a colored woman who spoke against the site at Lake Park and 43rd [in a Black neighborhood]. She called me to ask if we could give her any help. I asked her what her reasons were for being against public housing, and she said, "We're high class n——s and we don't want any low-class n——s living next to us."[29]

Public housing, in practice, had come a long way from the vision of an approach meant to house the working and lower middle class broadly—as in the 1934 housing exhibition. It was being understood otherwise—as an affront and threat to the hard-won social gains of blue-collar families by introducing low-income households into their neighborhoods.

It is, of course, important to ask how else the condition of Chicago's Black community was to be improved. For the proponents of public housing in Chicago—including all of the city's major newspapers and its leading merchants—no alternative seemed available to relieve housing conditions experienced by the city's African Americans. But there were roads not followed that might have been. Government might have been directed to repairs and renovations of "slums."

One answer, surprisingly suggested by Meyerson and Banfield, in what reads today like "might have been" alternative history, was for government to play a far more limited role: perhaps offer support to renovate and repair the worst structures but otherwise to allow for the likelihood of a gradual improvement that the booming postwar economy would make possible—and that would come to include the gradual introduction of better-off African Americans even into neighborhoods on the barricades of public housing resistance. Their vision of a future that was much at odds with the assumptions both of the housing exhibition and of Chicago's proponents of the need for clearance of Black neighborhoods merits revisiting.

"It may be that the attitude of the people in the 'conservation' areas toward the Negro was mainly 'race' prejudice.... However, we suggest that there were important attitudinal components based on class rather than on race." Meyerson and Banfield went so far as to assert that sheer "dislike of people of different skin color" was "declining from year to year." It was their hope that "a fundamental improvement in race relations might be in the offing, for the national income was so high and was increasing at such a rate that lower class people, Negro and white, would very rapidly be assimilated to the standards of the middle class. If, indeed, color was no longer the principal basis of objection to the negro, he might prove to be only the latest of a succession of slum dwellers to be assimilated into Chicago's life.... There were some grounds for hope that the long-term experience of the Negro would not be essentially different from that of other minorities who by now made their way out of the slums."[30] Some twenty-five years later, a similar sentiment would be expressed by Daniel Patrick Moynihan, in his role as a domestic policy adviser to President Richard Nixon. Moynihan urged that instead of projects, the fate of the minority poor—and US race relations broadly—would be better left to "benign neglect."[31]

Instead, seen through the prism of Chicago, public housing not only gutted the economic and cultural life of Black communities but served to stir racial animus by failing to take account of the social class anxieties of whites who understood their own hold on middle-class life to be threatened by people of lower status.

For trends to have been different, however, it would have been imperative for Blacks, like whites, to have access to the financial means of upward mobility—particularly the assured opportunity to buy a home outside the "slum"/ghetto. This was not yet the case; the federal Fair Housing Act would not be enacted until 1968. The era's *Underwriting Manual* of the Federal Housing Administration (FHA) clearly countenanced race discrimination. "If a mixture of user groups is found to exist it must be determined whether the mixture will render the neighborhood less desirable to present and prospective occupants.... Protective covenants are essential to the sound development of proposed residential areas since they regulate the use of the land and provide a basis for the development of harmonious, attractive neighborhoods suitable and desirable to the user groups forming the potential market."[32]

As it happened, only two of the seven sites identified for public housing by the Chicago Housing Authority won the required approval from the mayor and City Council. Both were high-rise towers on the South Side Lake Michigan shoreline and would later adjoin a major highway. "Most significantly, whites in outlying neighborhoods were able to shape the Chicago Housing Authority and transform that agency from one that tinkered with the status quo into one that served as a bulwark of segregation."[33] In what Arnold Hirsch described as the "second ghetto," nothing prevented households from using the advantage of low rent to save—and strive. Such are the families who expressed a positive recollection of their (limited) time in the projects for the city's Public Housing Museum. But in many ways, the second ghetto—in effect a city-directed racial segregation—was worse than the first. In the projects, there were, by design, no locally owned business or commercial streets. No extra income could be (legally) realized by renting a room to someone who might otherwise be without shelter. "The peddler who required an inexpensive and conveniently located barn for his horse and wagon would have no place in a housing project. Neither would the old Italian who made his living by selling sausages from a sidewalk cart." It could mean "the loss of a valued cultural heritage."[34] Renting was the only option; ownership, even of a dilapidated house that one hoped someday to improve, was not on offer.

Lost in the telling of this history is its path-dependency: that is, there were ways other than slum clearance and public housing construction that could have been employed in pursuit of the "public interest." "Instead of building new projects, the Authority might have repaired old structures or rented them to needy families; or it might have built new housing in a highly decentralized fashion, developing small vacant sites with a few units each. These were two possibilities; there were, of course, many others."[35] In effect, the Housing Authority, imbued with the modern housing approach, was effectively ensuring maximal opposition—both by its insistence of the vast scale of tower blocks and by making clear their views that "slum-dwellers" and their bad habits that would need to be ameliorated. The lack of interest or faith in gradualism can be said to haunt housing policy to this day.

It was certainly not desirable to have all the public housing projects in one section of the city and for them to be racially segregated. But the siting saga might have been different if Black neighborhoods had not been deemed most in need of demolition—leading to the need to rehouse their residents—and if lower-income whites continued to see public housing as desirable, as they did in New York's Pomonok Houses, at least for a time. The latter, it is worth noting, included not only a mix of white ethnic groups that had once lived in separate immigrant neighborhoods but also African Americans—though, of course, screened by income and employment status, as were all new tenants.

But at the same time that construction of the projects was under way at a large scale—350,000 new units in eleven hundred communities between 1949 and 1953—a much different mass housing approach would dwarf it and have its own racial implications. This one was government supported but private. There is no getting around the fact that even as public housing was in its ostensible heyday, the aspirations and assumptions of the housing exhibition and its key figures, such as Catherine Bauer, proved to have limited appeal in the US—even in the Roosevelt administration during which the National Housing Act became law. Indeed, the far more dominant response to the problem of housing affordability for people of modest means took the form of the advent, in 1934, of the Federal Housing Administration and the Homeowners Loan Corporation. In keeping with Roosevelt's own avowed preference for small, owner-occupied homes, for what he called a "nation of homeowners," these set the US on a path toward widespread, thirty-year home mortgages insured by the federal government and requiring relatively limited down payments.[36] These "amortized" loans—in which the principal amount borrowed would be gradually reduced over decades—replaced so-called balloon mortgages, which required a large final payment after only five years of ownership.

The language of the "Home Renovation and Modernization" section of the law was technical: "The Administrator is authorized and empowered, upon such terms and conditions as he may prescribe, to insure banks, trust companies, personal finance companies, mortgage companies, building and loan associations, installment lending companies, and other such financial institutions . . . against losses which they may sustain as a result of loans and advances of credit, and purchases of obligations representing loans and advances of credit, made by them subsequent to the date of enactment of this Act." Translated, that meant that a national system of small banks that would be protected against loss could broadly finance home mortgages.[37] The barrier to home ownership that Edith Elmer Wood took as a fact of life would be lowered for millions of Americans. Private home ownership, not government ownership and management of rental housing, would become and remain the dominant housing policy of the US, established in sharp contrast to the dreams of the modern housers.

Even before public housing became law in 1937, the New Deal had, in effect, ensured that it would be a sideshow in US housing life. Indeed, by 1950, for the first time, more Americans would be home owners than renters.[38] The FHA—and related government-chartered mortgage finance entities such as the Federal National Mortgage Association (Fannie Mae)—would become the key financing vehicles for the movement of Americans from cities to the emerging suburbs of the post–World War II era. The government was responding, as one FHA official would put it, to the clear American preference for "low-density" living—not modern housing.[39]

This system operating in parallel to the growth of the projects, however, must be implicated in the disproportionate presence of African Americans in public housing. "Between 1950 and 1970, America's suburban population nearly doubled to seventy-four million. Eighty-three percent of all population growth occurred in suburban places."[40] But it was government-backed growth that occurred under a financing regime guided by strict racial guidelines. Writing at the time, Charles Abrams, a staunch advocate for interracial housing, including in the projects, put it this way:

> The official manual of the FHA during this period read like a chapter from Hitler's Nuremberg laws. In the twenty-five years preceding the end of the Second World War, no less than seventy-five percent of the new home developments were built in peripheral sections. But these neighborhoods are almost exclusively for whites. Often the political fate of public officials depends on their ability to keep out minorities. . . . The FHA and the Home Loan Bank Board . . . openly advocated racial segregation of

minorities, the barring of "inharmonious groups" from new neighborhoods, restrictive covenants and other exclusion devices.⁴¹

Such covenants were struck down by the Supreme Court in 1948, but the die had been cast.⁴² Indeed, as Richard Rothstein has written, in the tellingly titled "Public Housing: Government-Sponsored Segregation," "Although the Supreme Court ruled in 1948 that racial restrictions were legally unenforceable, the FHA and VA continued to insure such mortgages." This was not a minor matter, he notes. "By 1950, the federal agencies were insuring half of all new mortgages nationwide."⁴³

It is simplistic, but not inaccurate, to say that government policy amounted to home ownership for whites and public housing for Blacks. Nonetheless, this account overlooks the role of the modern housing movement, sparked by the 1934 housing exhibition, not just in building the projects but in clearing away "blight"—and the extent to which that meant the demolition of African American neighborhoods filled with small home owners, locally owned businesses, churches, and mutual-aid charitable associations. This demolition would wipe out Black assets and wealth, just as public housing would, as Rothstein rightly points out, provide no means to accumulate it through home equity, contributing to the persistent gap in wealth between whites and Blacks in the US. So-called slum clearance to make way for public housing in the first place played its own role in destroying and hindering the economic advance of African Americans. Public housing, in other words, deserves to be criticized not only for fostering segregation but also for being tied, at its origin, to declaring Black neighborhoods to be blighted and marked for demolition.

Again, the counterfactual pondered by Meyerson and Banfield is well worth keeping in mind. In that history that did not happen, a growing national economy would—as it did for many Americans—lift Blacks' income. The "ghetto" slums would have slowly emptied, just as New York's Lower East Side did in the first quarter of the twentieth century. Ideally, "fair housing" laws barring discrimination would have made it possible for Blacks to buy homes wherever they could afford. But even under the draconian FHA rules, they stood to move—and many did—to neighborhoods immediately adjacent to Black neighborhoods.

Black institutions would not have been bulldozed. Such gradualism would have been a vehicle for creating and preserving wealth in a way the projects could never be. The projects had no interest, however, in such gradualism. They were part of the vision of a wholesale makeover of US cities and US housing—one that never really took hold broadly but nonetheless became and remains the reality for millions of Americans.

If the combination of "blight" clearance and race discrimination in government financing programs together explain why the projects became disproportionately Black, it does not explain another major element of the fate of public housing. They became not only Black but poor, the locus of what would be called "concentrated poverty." They became something that the original modern housing visionaries could never have imagined: a new—and worse—version of the slums they sought to replace. The reasons for that were many, each important, as we will see in chapter 6. But as public housing became—not entirely but certainly in the public mind—a new version of the nineteenth-century poorhouse, the groundwork was laid for a dramatic denouement: the end of new project construction.

6

Abandoning the Projects

New Directions with Nixon's Moratorium

On September 19, 1973, President Richard Nixon sent a special message to the Congress. Its sole and specific focus—unusual for any president—was housing policy. Thirty-six years after Franklin Roosevelt signed the first National Housing Act, Nixon, in his "Special Message to the Congress Proposing Legislation and Outlining Administrative Actions to Deal with Federal Housing," would point the country in a dramatically different direction than that charted in the New Deal.

Nixon, in fact, specifically acknowledged the New Deal and its impact on housing. "Since 1937, the Federal Government has tried to help low income families by providing housing for them," he said. "Over the years, nearly $90 billion of the taxpayers' money has been spent or committed for public housing projects and other subsidized housing programs." Nor would all of the message be inconsistent with Roosevelt's views. Indeed, Nixon devoted a large portion of the text to the need for the federal government to ensure credit for those who would be home buyers, by reinforcing the system established in the New Deal. But Nixon would signal a sharp departure in Washington's view of public housing projects. In a section subtitled "The Failure of Federal Housing Programs," Nixon painted public housing as one of those failures, characterizing some projects as "monstrous, depressing places—run-down, overcrowded, crime-ridden, falling apart." Probably channeling his domestic policy adviser the accomplished social scientist Daniel Moynihan, Nixon, in language verging on the poetic, not only described deficient physical conditions but implicitly acknowledged what had been lost through slum clearance. "The residents of these projects ae often strangers to one another—with little sense of belonging. And because so many poor people are so heavily concentrated in these projects, they often feel cut off from the mainstream of American life." Nixon asserted that a fork in the road had been reached: "Leaders of all political persuasions and from all levels of government have given a great deal of thought in recent years to the problem of low-income housing. Many of them agree that the federally subsidized housing approach has failed."[1] The special message affirmed Nixon's landmark decision of the previous January: to impose, by administrative action, a moratorium on all new federally subsidized housing project construction. His proposal was the result of a study, and he announced at that same time that he would submit policy recommendations to Congress in September to replace housing programs stopped by the moratorium.[2]

Although criticized, including at congressional hearings, the Nixon moratorium and new housing subsidy proposals did, indeed, roughly signal the end of the public housing construction era in the United States. It would not mark the end of all housing subsidies or of subsidized housing construction, which were to take new forms, including a major departure charted by Nixon. But the signal nature of Nixon's message and new policy demand analysis that goes beyond their specific proposals. They suggest this question: How, in less than four decades since the Museum of Modern Art housing exhibit and the National Housing Act of 1937, and only twenty-five years since the vast expansion of public housing support and slum clearance funding of 1949, had a president come to the conclusion that it was both good politics and good policy to turn his back on the projects?

The evident proximate precipitant—indeed, the cited rationale—for Nixon's decision was what remains the most dramatic moment in public housing history: the physical implosion into clouds of dust of the quintessence of modern housing, the Pruitt-Igoe Project in St. Louis. Indeed,

Nixon specifically referred to that demolition in his remarks—even citing the sociologist Lee Rainwater's study of the project in his message.

> A particularly dramatic example of the failure of Federal housing projects is the Pruitt-Igoe project in St. Louis. It was nominated for all sorts of awards when it was built 17 years ago. It was supposed to house some 2,700 families—but it simply didn't work. In fact, a study of this project was published two years ago with the appropriate subtitle: "Life in a Federal Slum."
>
> Last month, we agreed to tear down this Federal slum, every unit of it. Almost everyone thought it was the best thing we could do.
>
> Pruitt-Igoe is only one example of an all too common problem. All across America, the Federal Government has become the biggest slumlord in history.[3]

Nixon's reference to Rainwater's book-length study—*Behind Ghetto Walls: Black Families in a Federal Slum*—was not misplaced. The Harvard sociologist described what had once appeared to be the premier version of slum replacement this way: "Pruitt-Igoe houses families for which our society seems to have no other place. The original tenants were drawn very heavily from several land clearance areas in the inner city. Although there were originally some white tenants, all of the white tenants have moved out and the population is all Negro. Only those Negroes who are desperate for housing are willing to live in Pruitt-Igoe—over half the households are headed by women, over half derive their principal income from public assistance of one kind or another; and many families are so large they cannot find housing elsewhere."[4] Transcripts of resident interviews recounted the sordid conditions of daily life. "There's too much broken glass and trash outside. The elevators are dangerous. The elevators don't stop at every floor, so many people have to walk up or down to get to their apartments. There are mice and cockroaches in the building." Common behavior was said to include "holding up someone and robbing them," "teenagers yelling curse words at adults,"

FIGURE 6.1. Pruitt-Igoe implosion in St. Louis. (Wikimedia Commons)

"breaking windows," "boys and girls having sexual relations with a lot of different boys or girls."[5] Residents, moreover, had a sense of history: "They were trying to better poor people [but] they tore down one slum and built another; put all kinds of people together; made a filthy place. They were trying to get rid of the slum, but they didn't accomplish too much. Inside the apartment they did, but not outside."[6]

It is important to note that, although public housing had become synonymous with Black poverty, there were predominantly white projects replete with similar malaise. Boston's Michael Patrick MacDonald, in his memoir, *All Souls: A Family Story from Southie*, describes life in the early 1970' in South Boston's Old Colony project, which had once been idealized for its "low-rise buildings and treed courtyards supposedly bringing suburban advantages to low-income city dwellers." MacDonald, in contrast, describes a housing project in which organized crime, led by the infamous Boston gangster James "Whitey" Bulger," found willing recruits, including two of MacDonald's brothers, both of whom died young. Writes MacDonald,

> Ours was one of the worst buildings in Old Colony for trying to sleep on the humid nights. Not only were the lights on all night for the cockroaches, but the Duggans were always up late breaking things and beating each other. Moe Duggan, one of the few fathers I ever saw in Old Colony, came home drunk and beat on all six kids....
>
> ... Whenever I came home late, I was scared to walk into the dark hallway with all the broken lights. I might turn a corner and get bitten by the rats that were moving in, or someone being chased might mistake me for a cop and shoot me.[7]

The question of what had gone wrong at Pruitt-Igoe—and with public housing—prompts some easy but superficial answers. The modernist design that had, indeed, been judged prize-worthy—thirty-three-story buildings isolated from stores and industry—came under scrutiny, notably for such innovations as its "stop-skipping elevators," which were actually meant to encourage community when residents met on stairways. The lack of ongoing maintenance and repairs would matter in any apartment complex, high-rise or not.

But the problems ran deeper. Indeed, the essential model of US public housing had run afoul of reality. The assumptions behind the original public housing legislation had proved unsustainable as the United States—its housing preferences and migration patterns—had changed around the projects.

Recall that federal financial support was originally meant to enable initial construction. Rental income, paid by tenants to the local housing authority, would be the lifeblood of upkeep. It was exactly that which gradually dried up at Pruitt-Igoe and, in subsequent years, at projects across the country, as many veered toward a condition that Congress would later term "severely distressed." The modern housing vision of government owned and managed housing as a sort of public utility for intact working-class or lower-middle-class households with regular income from jobs had briefly been realized in that "golden age." But, thanks to the combination of private home building, federal mortgage subsidies, and interstate highways, Americans had an obvious housing choice in expanding suburbia. Catherine Bauer had confidently asserted that "the premises underlying the most successful and forward-pointing housing developments are not the premises of capitalism, of inviolate private property, of entrenched nationalism, of class distinction."[8] Federally insured single-family housing may not have been laissez-fair capitalism—but it was much closer to it than were the projects.

The extent of movement to the suburbs over the life span of Pruitt-Igoe during the 1950s and 1960s cannot be overstated. As Kenneth Jackson has noted in his discussion of the post–World War II rise of the US suburb, between 1934 and 1960, some 12,166 mortgages were taken out by home buyers in the city of St. Louis. In contrast, a staggering 63,772 were provided to new buyers in outlying St. Louis County. With help from the same federal government that had supported the construction of Pruitt-Igoe, the potential employed, rent-paying tenants for public housing were fleeing the city—and the cities in general. Jackson details similar outflow figures for New York (87,183 mortgages in suburban Nassau County, compared to just 15,483 in Brooklyn) and metro Washington (44,432 mortgages in suburban Maryland and Virginia counties, compared to just 8,038 in the District of Columbia).[9] "This same result," concedes Jackson, "might have occurred in the absence of all federal intervention. But the simple fact is that the various government policies toward housing [had] the same effect from Los Angeles to Boston."[10] As Jackson notes, "by the end of 1972, the FHA had helped 11 million Americans buy homes," and the "number of owner-occupied dwellings rose from 44 to 63 percent."[11]

There is no doubt that those federal policies worked, as previously discussed, to the overt and indefensible disadvantage of African Americans, who were, as Jackson put it, quoting the urbanist Jane Jacobs, "credit blacklisted." Indeed, as of 1960, only 5 percent of African Americans in major US metropolitan areas lived in suburbs. But, government barriers notwithstanding, that was changing, as well.

The employed Black families who would much later look back fondly on Chicago housing projects' golden age used it as a launching pad for their upward mobility, rather than remaining to pay rent. A good example is Deval Patrick, who rose from the Robert Taylor Homes to become governor of Massachusetts, just as the future Supreme Court justice Sonia Sotomayor and the comedian Whoopi Goldberg had moved up and out from New York City public housing. Such families were no longer interested in living in public housing.

By the last four decades of the twentieth century, the Black presence in suburbs saw exponential growth. Between 1960 and 2000, more than nine million African Americans moved to the suburbs. In 1980, 24 percent of the Black population in standard metropolitan areas resided in suburbs. By 1990, it was 30 percent, and by 2000, it was 35 percent. Most of this growth came as a result of the rise of a significant Black middle class that could afford to purchase homes in suburban areas and was no longer prevented from doing so by law and custom. According to Quinton McDonald, Black suburbanization "was also driven by 'Black Flight' in the 1980s as African Americans left crime-ridden central cities because of growing drug use and related gang violence."[12] They also clearly understood that public housing offered no opportunity to accumulate wealth—not when government, not the household, was the owner.

The lack of a tenant base capable of paying adequate rent would prove to be the ultimate and key factor that pulled the cornerstone out from under Pruitt-Igoe—and many other public housing projects. In 1969, the St. Louis Housing Authority, owner-operator of eight thousand public housing units, under fire for substandard conditions of all sorts, including rodents, bed bugs, broken windows, and no heat, was itself teetering toward bankruptcy. According to its 1968 budget, the St. Louis Housing Authority had a $54.16 allowance per unit, but operating costs totaled $57.38 per unit. This gap, stretched out over time and across the city's approximately eight thousand units, resulted in progressive underfunding and widespread deterioration of the housing units. The Housing Authority's deficit was compounded by increasing vacancy rates, themselves brought on in part by the deteriorating conditions of the units.

Not illogically—but counterproductively—the Housing Authority moved to raise rents. Between 1965 and 1967, rent increases for public housing in St. Louis had ranged from 16 percent to 32 percent, depending on the project and the room count.[13] The increase led some one thousand public housing tenants from across the city—including Pruitt-Igoe—to declare a rent strike. The Housing Authority moved to evict seventy-three tenants from the complex. "As a result, many tenants moved out, renting private units or often even purchasing homes with saved up funds. Vacancy rates in the complexes spiked."[14] Thus was a downward spiral sparked; just four years later, the thirty-three eleven-story towers had literally disappeared in a cloud of dust, and the president of the United States had cited it as proof positive of the negative results of the modern housing movement.

Nor did Pruitt-Igoe's implosion—and the public housing moratorium it inspired—halt its aftereffects. Crucial to accelerating the physical decline of projects across the country was legislation inspired by the St. Louis public housing rent increases and related rent strike. That same year saw the passage of the Housing and Urban Development Act of 1969, as amended by Senator Edward Brooke of Massachusetts, a Republican and the first Black member of the Senate since Reconstruction. The "Brooke Amendment" moved to buffer public housing tenants from rising rents by amending the 1937 law "to provide that rent in public housing projects may not exceed 25% of a tenant's income."[15] The effect was legally to apply a tourniquet to the flow of adequate rental income for public housing authorities that were already struggling to pay their bills. At the same time, this new regime would have the effect of driving out higher-income households that the housing authorities so badly needed; they would have to pay higher rents for deteriorating housing. Were their incomes to rise, so, too, would their rents.

This new policy penalized employed tenants and paved the way for an increase in the tenant population receiving unemployment benefits and other forms of government assistance. Once scrupulously careful about admitting tenants, local housing authorities became less discriminating and relaxed screening procedures. Families less frequently used public housing as a springboard because upward mobility became less common among the new breed of residents. Instead, families remained without time limit. Children spent all their formative years in the projects, and intergenerational public housing families became commonplace. Department of Housing and Urban Development (HUD) data indicate that the average public housing household has resided in a project for eleven and a half years.[16] For too many Americans, residents and onlookers alike, public housing had metamorphosed into a dumping ground for society's unfortunates and an absolute last resort for anyone who could not possibly do better elsewhere.[17] Moreover, it had become culturally unthinkable to screen new tenants on the basis of marriage status or, for that matter, housekeeping habits, as was the case in the early days of New York City public housing.

Indeed, the change in the population of public housing residents may have been self-reinforcing—as the projects became poor, they may have encouraged the formation of the single-parent, low-income families that dominated them. As Richard Disney and Guannan Luo have observed regarding a similar evolution in public—or "council"— housing in England and Wales, "As the criteria for council house priority shifted from slum clearance and rehousing to family 'need,' there were strong incentives for families to assume the characteristics (lack of job, large number of children, partnership dissolution) that increased eligibility."[18]

Thus did events create the logic of the Pruitt-Igoe implosion. But across the country, the projects still stood—effectively leftovers from an old idea whose physical form remained. Nor was it inevitable that what would become known as their "concentration of poverty" dictated disrepair. The federal government—indeed, government at any level—could have stepped in to fill the revenue gaps for local housing authorities, conceding that the original idea that public housing could be self-sustaining had been overtaken by events. Indeed, the 1970s did see the advent of "operating assistance" for public housing authorities, as part of the budget of the new federal Department of Housing and Urban Development, established as part of the Johnson administration's Great Society antipoverty efforts. But, as budget figures demonstrate, there was little appetite for such spending. From a modest start of some $22 million in 1976—for the nation's thirty-three hundred housing authorities—such assistance declined steadily to some $10 million in 2003.[19]

The projects were an old, new idea, orphaned as they aged. They had morphed into poorhouses, unable to command the political support and the funds they needed. Of all people, Catherine Bauer had seen it coming. Writing for *Architectural Forum* in May 1957—a time when public housing construction was in its heyday—Bauer wrote a sort of obituary for it. In contrast to so much of the New Deal of which the 1937 Housing Act she had written was part, the projects she had championed had simply not, she acknowledged, taken root in the US:

> Low-rent public housing has not followed the normal pattern for reform movements in modern democratic countries. Every social experiment starts off as an abstract idea, frequently in an atmosphere of violent theoretical debate. But after it has been tried out for a while, one of two things usually happens. Either it dies off, an acknowledged failure, or it "takes" and is accepted as an integral part of the ordinary scheme of things. The original theories, meantime, become modified and adapted to actual conditions. In the U.S., public attitudes about social security, collective bargaining, and national economic controls have all followed the classic steps outlined years ago by George Bernard Shaw: 1) it's impossible; 2) it's against the Bible; 3) it's too expensive; and 4) we knew it all the time. . . . But public housing, after more than two decades, still drags along in a kind of limbo, continuously controversial, not dead but never more than half alive.

> No obituary is yet in order for the U.S. Housing Act of 1937 "as successively [but only in minor respects] amended." It is more a case of premature ossification. The bare bones of oversimplified New Deal theory have never been decently covered with the solid flesh of present-day reality. Even among public housing's most tireless defenders, many would welcome a fresh start if they did not fear that in the process any program at all might get lost.[20]

Bauer continued, acknowledging but minimizing the impact of organized private-sector housing opposition, which had mounted during the early 1950s:

> If the public housing program in its present form had managed to achieve real popularity with the general run of ordinary citizens and their leaders, and above all with the people who live in slums and blighted areas, the real estate opposition would by now have lost its political force. The idea of public housing would be taken for granted, like old age pensions or FHA mortgage insurance.
> But this has not happened.[21]

Ultimately, Bauer, the original modern houser, cuts her previous vision to the quick: "Life in the usual public housing project just is not the way most American families want to live. Nor does it reflect our accepted values as to the way people should live."[22]

Such was part of the run-up to the Nixon moratorium, which can be said to have gained steam even as public housing was being built. The moratorium had not, in other words, been as sharp a policy departure as it might have seemed. Both support for the projects had ebbed and new forms of housing subsidies and perspectives on slums had been emerging.

No sustained support, noted Bauer, from local civic groups had emerged, while other organized interests pushed back. Indeed, opposition to public housing construction by the private real estate industry had been sparked by the large increase in construction plans in the 1949 Housing Act and had persisted, not without effect. In 1952, following the election of a Republican president for the first time since 1928, the real estate industry had made its concerns clear:

> A post-election statement of policy adopted by the National Association of Real Estate Boards at its 1952 convention, Miami, Nov. 10–15, declared public housing to be "contrary to the best interests of the country and its people." A resolution by the delegates asked a comprehensive investigation by the new Congress of all public housing projects to determine full production costs, management costs, and tax-revenue losses. Another resolution called for immediate liquidation of the public housing program and sale of the properties to private owners. The convention was told by Rep. Cole (R., Kan.) in an address, Nov. 12, that public housing had been "sold to the American people in the guise of slum clearance by power-hungry planners."[23]

Then, in 1954, the Eisenhower administration had signaled the sort of pullback that Nixon would later formalize, through an Advisory Committee on Government Housing Policies and programs that expressed a view much at odds with that of the original vision of the modern housing movement—instead predicated on the idea that public housing should, indeed, be the province of the poorest:

> It is the sincere hope of our subcommittee that, over the long term, a solution of the problem of housing for low-income families will be found both in the ability of private enterprise to reach a lower and lower income group and by raising of substandard incomes through greater productivity of our people. We recognize, however, that even then there will be a hard core of low-income families—the aged, the broken families, the incapacitated—who may represent a continuing housing problem for whom public housing assistance may be needed if they are to live in keeping with our accepted American standard of living.[24]

It was just such a "hard core of low income families" who composed the population of Pruitt-Igoe—and the nation did not like what it saw. There is little doubt that the shadow of Pruitt-Igoe—as well as the highrise "second ghetto" of Chicago—had darkened enthusiasm for public housing. But it was also the case that government had moved on to new approaches. The fact that subsidized housing would, as a practical matter, be meant for the very poor—not a cross-section of working Americans—changed the nature of what would be proposed.

The utopianism of the modern housing movement had faded away. Indeed, even before Nixon signaled an end to new public housing project construction, the Lyndon Johnson administration—dedicated to expanding the role of government to assist the poor at a scale not seen since the New Deal—had acknowledged that subsidized housing was not only meant for the poorest but should be part of an effort to restore the neighborhoods in which people of lowest income—particularly poor African Americans—lived in what became known in the 1960s as the "inner city." The goal of slum clearance, and replacement with the uplifting environment of the projects, had been abandoned in favor of what had been eschewed by the Housing Act of 1949: rebuilding the "slums." The vehicle for doing so was a new cabinet-level federal agency, the Department of Housing and Urban Development.

Although HUD had a broad mandate to improve urban life generally, there was no doubt where its chief focus lay. "The first challenge," Lyndon Johnson stated, was "to attack the problem of rebuilding the slums."[25] It was the era of what the economist John Kenneth Galbraith had called the "Affluent Society," when the US economy was viewed not only as a powerful but also perhaps even as an unstoppable engine of economic growth—an engine that was said to be leaving a few groups behind. The most prominent group was African Americans, the awareness of whose situation was heightened by the 1964 and 1965 summer riots in the Watts section of Los Angeles and New York's Harlem.

A sense of national crisis emerged and was dramatically reflected in works with such breathless titles such as *Cities in a Race with Time*.[26]

It would be HUD's mission not only to respond to what the sociologist Kenneth Clark termed the "dark ghetto"—in other words, poor, Black, urban neighborhoods—but, at the same time, to "save" cities. In that context, HUD's mission was designed by its early leaders, including Robert Weaver, the former head of the Housing and Home Finance Agency, who became the first HUD secretary (and, in keeping with HUD's focus on Black neighborhoods, the first Black cabinet secretary in any department), and Robert Wood, the former head of the Massachusetts Institute of Technology's Political Science Department, who became undersecretary. Wood told the National Association of Social Workers in 1966, "The impacted urban ghetto has, in a comparatively short period of time, become the most explosive social problem of our day."[27] This was the essence of HUD: a massive intervention in poor Black neighborhoods to renovate the buildings there, despite the fact that the incomes of residents themselves, at least as judged in the moment, could not support rents that would pay for such improvements. Thus, "ghetto" housing would be subsidized: it would remain inexpensive and would also be "decent and sanitary," in the language of the National Housing Act of 1937.

But why was that necessary? What was wrong with new urbanites using older housing—even not upgraded as per HUD—until they could afford better? To understand HUD's intervention, one must look at the nation's essentially pessimistic and, arguably, patronizing view of the prospects of the Black poor, which was directing subsidies to a new form of projects—older buildings that would remain privately owned but whose renovation and monthly rents would be government supported.

The idealism of modern housing had envisioned communities of working families. In practice, many Americans had viewed the projects as way stations, as they had been for Elvis Presley's neighbors, the poor boys who had "made good," or the Pomonok households in Queens. The view of HUD's founding fathers was not simply that society could not wait until the rising tide of affluence lifted Blacks as it had others; it was far more pessimistic. Although Wood acknowledged that previous groups of urban newcomers had followed what he repeatedly called the "long tenement trail to relative affluence and acceptance in American society," he did not believe that Blacks would follow in their footsteps. "The historic role of the city has deteriorated badly," observed Wood. "In some city neighborhoods, blight and poverty have gone hand-in-hand for generations, and the slum is no longer a way station." Moreover, said Wood, "the bus has stopped running to the suburbs and the urban poor are increasingly insulated from the larger society."[28] It is crucial to note that, in retrospect, we have learned that Wood's assertion was exactly the opposite of what was occurring. At the very moment when the designers of HUD were asserting that the process of upward economic mobility would not lift Blacks out of poverty, Black movement to the suburbs, heretofore impeded by discrimination, was beginning to increase. HUD, however, had set out to make the ghetto comfortable, through both continuing the construction of new public housing—the pipeline for which would continue to be filled until the Nixon moratorium—and the advent of slum rebuilding.

It was a dramatic change from the slum clearance of the 1949 act, but it shared, in a crucial way, the assumption that African American communities should be understood to be slums, that the efforts of their residents would not, over time, lead to improvements. The Johnson administration, through its Great Society initiatives, reflected a view of the Black community so dim that it believed it had to provide a version of civil society and social institutions for it; the Model Cities programs would create community groups directed by paid employees, in contrast to the array of associations that had once been found in Pittsburgh's Hill District or Detroit's Black Bottom, now long gone.

One cannot discount the role played in the development of this policy and subsequent legislation not only by arguably well-intentioned but misguided social reformers such as Robert Wood but also by self-interested developers—the private owners of the new, subsidized quasi-public housing. Just as the original public housing program was inspired, in part, by Franklin Roosevelt's debt to construction unions and hard-pressed Depression-era builders, so were HUD rehabilitation subsidy programs influenced by a range of financial interests. In Boston, for instance, the CEO of the parent company to Boston Gas headed up a syndicate of investors to renovate more than two thousand apartments in the city's Roxbury ghetto, all of which were, in that heavily subsidized process, converted from traditional New England oil heat to natural gas. CEO Eli Goldston was neither the first nor the last to assert that his firm is "doing well by doing good."

It would be a socially conservative Democrat, Nixon's domestic policy adviser Daniel Patrick Moynihan, who would dare to enunciate, in a 1969 memo, a radically different view of how African American and other low-income communities should be viewed. In direct contrast to Robert Wood, Moynihan argued that the best approach for government to take toward the inner city was "benign neglect." Although Moynihan referred to race in general and not the issue of "ghetto" conditions in particular, the onetime Harvard social scientist was endorsing the sort of improvement over time—gradualism—that housing policy had rejected since the 1937 act. In January 1970, he wrote Nixon the following: "The time may have come when the issue of race could benefit from a period of 'benign neglect.' The subject has been too much talked about. The forum has been too much taken over to hysterics, paranoids, and boodlers on all sides. We may need a period in which Negro progress continues and racial rhetoric fades."[29] Moynihan's broader view of the situation of African Americans differed notably from that which had guided Robert Wood and the establishment of HUD. For Moynihan, the way up and out of the ghetto was very much extant:

> In quantitative terms, which are reliable, the American Negro is making extraordinary progress.... The 1960s saw the great breakthrough for blacks. A third (32%) of all families of Negro and other races earned $8000 or more in 1968 compared, in constant dollars, with 15% in 1960.... Young Negro families are achieving income parity with young white families. Outside the South, young husband-wife Negro families

have 99% the income of whites! For families headed by a male age 25 to 34 the proportion was 87 percent. Thus it may be this ancient gap is finally closing. Income reflects employment, and this changed dramatically in the 1960's. Blacks continued to have twice the unemployment rates of whites, but these were down for both groups. In 1969 the rate for married men of Negro and other races was only 2.5 percent. . . . Black occupations improved dramatically. The number of professional and technical employees doubled in the period 1960–68. This was two and a half times the increase for whites. In 1969 Negro and other races provide 10 percent of the other-than-college teachers. This is roughly their proportion of the population.[30]

If all this could be taken as a rationale for pulling back from housing subsidies generally, Nixon, although eschewing new projects, did not reject a core assumption of the Museum of Modern Art housing exhibit: that government must intervene to ensure adequate housing for people of lower incomes. Instead, he set in motion, first as an experiment, then as policy, a dramatically different approach toward that goal, one that not only drew back from "bricks and mortar" construction (as such housing subsidy would come to be called) but also eschewed interest in so-called place-based subsidy—slum rebuilding. Instead, Nixon would move toward a "tenant-based" approach. In 1974, the same administration that had initiated the "food stamp" program that supplemented low-income household buying power at the supermarket would provide what might be termed housing stamps—so-called certificates that low-income families could use to rent housing in the private market. In 1983, these would be renamed as "housing vouchers" by the Reagan administration, which would expand the program. In time, the program, originally linked to a new section of the National Housing Act (Section 8), would become known as the Housing Choice Voucher program and overtake public housing with regard to the number of Americans it would serve. Its original rationale was based clearly on its being a contrast to new projects. Nixon, in proposing what he began in 1973 as the Experimental Housing Allowance Program, in a message to Congress described housing allowances as "the most promising way to achieve decent housing for all our families at an acceptable cost."[31]

Nixon clearly understood tenant-based housing help as a policy rejoinder to the projects, which, even as they had hit a policy wall, continued to cast a shadow—and even to retain advocates within his own administration. Indeed, his HUD secretary, former Michigan governor George Romney, had pushed for construction of new public housing projects outside the inner cities, in suburban areas.[32] It was a position reminiscent of that of the Chicago Housing Authority in the early 1950s, when it sought to site new projects in outlying, predominantly white sections of that city. Nixon was having none of it. Although known, politically, for a "southern strategy" that targeted white voters dismayed by Democratic courtship of Blacks, Nixon framed his housing policy, at least publicly, in a high-minded policy context:

> But the quality of Federally-assisted housing is by no means the only problem. Our present approach is also highly inequitable. Rather than treating those in equal circumstances equally, it arbitrarily selects only a few low income families to live in federally supported housing, while ignoring others. Moreover, the few often get a new home, while many other families—including those who pay the taxes to support these programs—must make do with inferior older housing. And since recipients often lose their eligibility for public housing when they exceed a certain income level, the present approach can actually reward dependence and discourage self-reliance.
>
> The present approach is also very wasteful, for it concentrates on the most expensive means of housing the poor, new buildings, and ignores the potential for using good existing housing. Government involvement adds additional waste; our recent study shows that it costs between 15 and

40 percent more for the Government to provide housing for people than for people to acquire that same housing themselves on the private market.

One of the most disturbing aspects of the current approach is the fact that families are offered subsidized housing on a "take it or leave it" basis—losing their basic right to choose the house they will live in and the place they will live. Too often they are simply warehoused together wherever the Government puts them. They are treated as a class apart, with little freedom to make their own decisions.[33]

As in public housing projects as they evolved, tenants would pay a fixed percentage of rent in a private apartment (at first 25 percent, later 30 percent), with the remainder paid through the new Section 8 (Housing Choice Voucher) program. Ironically, the voucher funds would be distributed by local public housing authorities—a function drastically different from that envisioned for them by the modern housing movement.

The voucher program, which, at the time this is written, serves some 1.3 million US households, would, like the projects it succeeded, lead to its own concerns. As a later HUD assistant secretary, John Weicher, would write, "The most basic concern about tenant-based housing assistance is that certificates and vouchers do not result in better housing for their recipients. This is claimed to be true not just for some recipients, as in the case of the worst public housing and privately-owned projects, but for most. An important corollary . . . is that tenant-based assistance merely drives up rents, particularly for those who received subsidies, but also for other low-income households that are not receiving any assistance." Weicher, further, discussed two "opposite concerns. . . . The first is that [voucher holders] will be unable to find private rental housing because of discrimination in the market. The second is that they will be all too successful in finding private housing, and in moving from inner-city minority to suburban white communities, they will destabilize neighborhoods and create new concentrations of the poor."[34]

Such concerns, which emerged as the US struggled to find a housing policy in keeping with the 1937 act but did not involve new projects, do raise the question of whether the problems that emerged in Pruitt-Igoe and elsewhere should not have simply signaled a withdrawal of government from "low-income housing" altogether. Indeed, a stillborn Nixon administration initiative might have moved the US in just such a direction. Its Family Assistance Plan was as close as the US would move to an income floor, or guaranteed income. "Nixon's plan envisioned a welfare system that ventured not only to fix welfare dependency and rising costs for government, but also aimed to combat rising inequality within the welfare system and afford income assistance as a basic, universal right."[35] The plan, dubbed "Nixon's Good Deed," won approval in both 1970 and 1971 in the House of Representatives, only to die in the Senate.[36]

There is no way to be certain that Nixon would not have moved toward housing vouchers had the Family Assistance Plan become law. But the failure of the latter was followed by the enactment of the former. An income supplement that simply left it up to low-income households how to apportion their assistance might logically, however, have ended the story of the projects and their aftermath. (This is to advocate neither a guaranteed annual income nor a universal entitlement to a housing voucher but rather to point out that these are logical policy options.)

But a Family Assistance Plan was not to be. Indeed, housing assistance in a variety of forms would continue even after the advent of an income supplement for all those who were employed but still judged to be impoverished: the Earned Income Tax Credit. It would not replace the many varieties of "targeted" public assistance, including those for food and housing.

Nor did Nixon's public housing moratorium signal an end to the still-unfolding story of the projects. As of 2023, nearly nine hundred thousand public housing units would continue to be owned and operated by thousands of local public housing authorities, across the fifty states and even extending to Puerto Rico and the US Virgin Islands. They would

FIGURE 6.2. Robert Taylor Homes at the time of demolition. (Library of Congress)

both face daunting management challenges and inspire a new burst of utopian thinking, envisioning a new and better formula for projects that would physically and philosophically reshape them. But crucially, the shadow of the projects hung over what has gone after them. Their key selling points would include their being different—not being like the projects, which had gone from breakthrough to blighted.

7

Dealing with the Aftermath

From Distress to National Disgrace

In 1992, four decades after President Truman's push for public housing and twenty years after Richard Nixon's decision to turn away from it, a commission established by the US Congress issued what might have been called a "State of the Projects" report. In it, the bipartisan group, along with housing authority officials from across the country, coined a new and disturbing term for tens of thousands of public housing apartments: "severely distressed." The sobering term became part of the title for the report's introduction: "Severely Distressed Public Housing—A National Disgrace."

The Commission on Severely Distressed Public Housing found that at least eighty-six thousand units in projects across the country, residents were "living in despair" in "physically deteriorated buildings," routinely exposed to "the presence of criminal activity." Many more units, it continued, were on a similar "downward spiral." "Public housing," the commission wrote, "is becoming the housing of last resort for low-income families and very low-income families, families that need the most support services to become part of the community."[1] It was the next watershed in the history of the projects—an acknowledgment both that "conditions are extremely difficult to manage" and that public housing had effectively become an American poorhouse. What had been intended as safe and sanitary housing for the working class had officially been described as places of residents "generally needing high levels of social and support services." Most of the "non-elderly" households were headed by single women with children; the rent structure—in which "earned income" led to a higher rent than public assistance—worked such that one could be employed and be left with less monthly income than neighbors living on welfare payments. Residents in some systems paid almost no rent at all—a far cry from the original principle of rent-supported maintenance. Management was often distant and overextended, rather than being present "on-site"; a single property manager, said the report, could be responsible for the maintenance of upward of two thousand apartments. The hands of management could be tied up in red tape.[2]

There are many congressional reports that cause brief stirs but little long-term impact. The Commission on Severely Distressed Public Housing was not one of them. It would prove to be the most important blueprint for the future of US public housing since the 1934 Museum of Modern Art exhibit companion book. The commission's National Action Plan would have dramatic effects—including "units to be demolished or disposed of as part of a comprehensive treatment program for severely distressed public housing." Local public housing authorities should, said the report, be permitted a choice between "revitalization" and "replacement" of projects.[3]

So it would be. By 2018, some 250,000 US public housing units had, in fact, been demolished. Pruitt-Igoe had foreshadowed a clearance wave that would include public housing in Chicago, New Orleans, Atlanta, Baltimore, Columbus, Philadelphia, and Tucson. Observed the *New York Times*, "Just about every American city got into the action."[4] In Chicago alone, between 1995 to 2010, the housing authority demolished over 21,000 units of public housing.

As powerful as was the logic of demolition—and the signal from the national commission that it had become an acceptable, even preferable approach to the projects—the wave of clearance held its own surprise. Just as long-ago slum residents objected to the advent of the projects, there were those public housing residents who opposed demolition, who felt they were losing homes and community.

Among them was a fifty-eight-year-old former resident of Chicago's Cabrini-Green project. Annie Ricks, profiled in the *New York Times*, had been moved to Wentworth Gardens, one of the few Chicago Housing

Authority projects still standing by 2018. Her apartment in a Cabrini-Green high-rise, where she had lived for twenty-one years, had been torn down, and she had been mandated for relocation. A physically better apartment did not, she told the *Times*, assuage a sense of loss from having been uprooted involuntarily.

> She often made the trip to visit her friends at the remaining strip of rowhouses at Cabrini-Green. She went to the jazz concerts held in the nearby park. Like many relocated families, she felt safer in the vestiges of the old neighborhood. When Raqkown, Ricks's youngest, left his high school most days, he traveled to the field house at Cabrini. The principal at the neighborhood elementary school said two-thirds of his students were former Cabrini families who took the bus and train long distances to get there. Several Cabrini-Green Facebook pages formed, people reporting job opportunities and business ventures, sharing words of inspiration and announcements of deaths in the Cabrini family. Oftentimes a post showed a photo of one of the disappeared high-rises—"Who can say what building this is?"—leading to long threads of competing memories.[5]

This is not to say that the predemolition Cabrini-Green should have remained standing or that the Chicago Housing Authority did not do what it could to prepare tenants for change. But, for some residents, that change was too great. The victim of a home invasion in her new project, Ricks moved with one of her children into one the remaining row houses left in the Cabrini complex—and soon after died.

Cabrini-Green (named for the Catholic saint Mother Frances Cabrini) had been one of the most notoriously dilapidated and crime-ridden projects in the US. Like dominoes stacked against one another until one tipped, the projects that had inspired bitter debate in the Chicago of the 1950s fell: Robert Taylor, Ida B. Wells, Stateway Gardens, and Cabrini-Green. Thousands of units followed the precedent of Pruitt-Igoe. One can say it would have been both unconscionable and impractical to let projects like Cabrini—neither safe nor sanitary—remain standing.

Nonetheless, just as it had once been built according to blueprints drawn by legislators and architects, so would it be demolished based on a new blueprint that was not drawn by residents, who were whipsawed by policy change. This is not to say that the residents should have been in charge of the projects' future but, rather, that, as with the history of the projects, they were, given the scale of public investment and complexity of the undertaking, inevitably buffeted by larger policy forces.

It was a change that took two essential forms. Chicago, the nation's second-largest public housing system after New York's, would embrace dramatic expansion of the private housing voucher program started by Richard Nixon. And both it and cities around the country would also turn in a surprising new direction, as well—one that reflected a new surge of the utopianism that had inspired the projects in the first place. Both would provide new versions of what had come to be called "affordable housing." Both would take their place in a questionable tradition of what might be called artificially directed residential patterns. Moreover, the long shadow of the projects continued to influence US housing policy, as the virtues of new approaches to housing assistance are consistently promoted by contrasting them with "traditional" public housing. Even more broadly, the core assertion of Catherine Bauer and Edith Elmer Wood—that the private housing market would inevitably fail the poor—continued to guide policy intervention, unchallenged. The assumption was reflected both by the new experiments in mixed-income replacement housing for older projects and by the steady growth of the housing voucher program.

As judged by scale alone, the combination of demolition of older projects and the expansion of housing vouchers was dramatic. In 1989, 1.36 million households lived in public housing projects, while 1.06 million relied on a housing voucher.[6] By 2023, HUD reported that only 886,000 public housing units remained, far fewer than the 2.75 million "housing choice voucher" units.[7] It was the contrast between projects and vouchers that clearly helped to sell the latter to both Democrats and Republicans. Vouchers' bipartisan appeal lay in their promise of reaching more households as lower cost. As the former HUD official John Weicher has observed, "Cost is the most striking difference between the programs." Referring to both public housing and subsidized renovation or construction run by private managers, Weicher found "vouchers less expensive than either of the large older subsidy programs, which is one important reason why neither of these subsidy programs is now a source of incremental assistance. If they were to be revived, . . . each would cost 50 to 100 percent more than vouchers on a per unit basis."[8]

In other words, the shadow of the projects continued to matter, even as their towers turned to dust. But their lingering aftereffects involved more than the contrast between the projects and those who would, as in Chicago, find themselves "vouchered out" from them. The projects had, in part, because they favored the poorest households in their selection process, created "concentrations of poverty" by inadvertently encouraging poor, single-parent families, with poor life prospects, to form in the first place. "Vouchering out" would disperse those households throughout lower-income, working-class communities, where some people viewed them as problematic new neighbors.

In 2003, an independent monitor of the Chicago Housing Authority's first years of relocations offered a bleak assessment: "The result has been that the vertical ghettos from which the families are being moved are being replaced with horizontal ghettos, located in well defined, highly segregated neighborhoods. The families that were dispersed from Chicago's demolished public housing have been blamed for the city's recent surge in gun violence, as well as for crime in the suburbs, the greater Midwest and even parts of the South."[9]

In my own reporting and interviewing, I found that the new neighbors of those who were vouchered out to middle-class, predominantly African American suburbs south of Chicago viewed them as a threat to what they viewed as their own hard-won upward mobility:

> In south suburban Chicago, with one of the highest concentrations of voucher holders in the country, middle-class African-American residents

complain that they thought they'd left the ghetto behind—only to find that the federal government is subsidizing it to follow them. Vikkey Perez of Richton Park, Illinois, owner of Nubian Beauty Supply, fears that the small signs of disorder that have come with voucher tenants—the unmown lawns and shopping carts left in the street—could undermine the neighborhood. "Their life-style," she says, "doesn't blend with our suburban life-style." Kevin Moore, a hospital administrator and homeowner in nearby Hazelcrest, complains that children in voucher homes go unsupervised. Boom boxes play late at night. "I felt like I was back on the West Side," he says, referring to the Chicago ghetto where he grew up. "You have to remember how to act tough."[10]

Writing in *The Atlantic* in 2008, the journalist Hannah Rosin reported that the dispersion of families from projects felled by wrecking balls had led to higher crime rates in the neighborhoods to which they were relocated. Her focus was on Memphis and on a police lieutenant and a social scientist, his wife, who had worked together to see whether they could "connect the dots" between neighborhoods in which crime was increasing and those to which onetime projects residents had been moved. They found, Rosin reported, "The match was near-perfect. On the merged map, dense violent-crime areas are shaded dark blue, and Section 8 addresses are represented by little red dots. All of the dark-blue areas are covered in little red dots, like bursts of gunfire. The rest of the city has almost no dots." Rosin recounted upsetting stories, from the point of view of the police lieutenant, Doug Barnes:

> As we drove around his beat, this new suburban warfare was not so easy to make out. We passed by the city zoo and Rhodes College, a serene-looking campus on a hill. We passed by plenty of quiet streets lined with ranch houses, not fancy but not falling down, either. Then Barnes began to narrate, street by street, getting more animated and bitter by the block.
> Here was the perfectly pleasant-looking Maplewood Avenue, where the old azaleas were just starting to bloom and the local cops were trying

to weed out the Chicago drug connection. Farther down the avenue, two households flew American flags, and a third was known for manufacturing "cheese," a particularly potent form of powdered heroin. The Hollywood branch of the local library, long famous for its children's room, was now also renowned for the time thugs stole $1,800 there from a Girl Scout who'd been collecting cookie funds. Finally we came to a tidy brick complex called Goodwill Village, where Barnes had recently chased down some gang members who'd been taking turns having sex with a new female recruit. As we closed in on midnight, Barnes's beat began to feel like the setting of a David Lynch movie, where every backyard and cul-de-sac could double as a place to hide a body.[11]

There is no social science consensus about this description of collateral damage from the projects and their demolition. A New York University study specifically sought to test Rosin's assertion and made a subtle and not all that reassuring distinction about the program, that "voucher use in a neighborhood tends to increase in tracts that have seen increases in crime, suggesting that voucher holders tend to move into neighborhoods where crime is elevated."[12] The cash value of housing vouchers is often such that households have limited options as to where they may find housing that they can afford and property owners willing to accept them. Or they may exacerbate an already rising crime problem.

Justified or not, the new neighbors of those who are vouchered out might look askance at them, leading to discomfort on the part of former public housing tenants. "Annie Ricks's oldest daughter, Kenosha, left Cabrini-Green when she was in her 20s and moved with her family to a block on the West Side. 'I've been out here almost a decade, and I know three or four of my neighbors,' she told me recently. 'They from the projects,' people say."[13] Although Hannah Rosin's reporting was controversial, the idea of voucher "hot spots," whether problematic or not, has become accepted.[14]

One does not have to generalize in negative ways about the character of onetime project families to note how the projects and their rules and culture have continued to redound in US housing markets and communities. There is no doubt that vouchers, as a project substitute judged on a purely financial basis, provide assistance that impoverished families may desperately need—especially when they have lived without any assistance at all. Concludes former HUD official Weicher, "With vouchers, lower-income households that have been spending most of their income to live in decent housing can reduce their rent burden to manageable proportions."[15] Just as in the projects, voucher tenants pay only 30 percent of their total rent (an increase from the Brooke Amendment's original 25 percent).[16]

Nonetheless, in an effort to find an improved alternative to the projects, vouchers perpetuate some of their concerning factors. The households that had been formed in part in response to the availability of project apartments for low-income, single-parent households find, as the national commission worried, that they are punished by a higher rent if they increase their earnings. This is the legacy of the Pruitt-Igoe rent strike and the Brooke Amendment limit on projects rents. The work disincentive that concerned the commission continues. One must ask whether any tenant in a privately owned building would ever sign a lease with this sort "escalator clause": the more you earn, the more rent you pay.

It is also the case that the policies shaped by the projects, as they evolved, continue even as the original rationale of the modern housing market has been overtaken by time. The Catherine Bauer and Edith Elmer Wood belief that, absent massive government intervention, the poor would be housed in abject conditions has not held up. As Weicher notes, "Relatively few housing units, even among the least expensive segment of the housing stock, are in fact physically inadequate, so that most households that receive subsidies were living in decent housing to begin with."[17] There is simply so much more housing in the US a century after the Depression that even the least of it is a far cry from New York's long-ago tenements.

That does not mean, however, that the projects do not retain their influence, even as the rationale for housing assistance has shifted from that of "safe and sanitary" to "affordability." The households that may have been incentivized to form remain vulnerable to financial risk; the rules for tenants continue even as the projects have fallen; the dispersion of the "vouchered out" has, at the least, created complications and concerns. Even when the old projects are gone, they are with us, if only as foils.

Perhaps most surprisingly, the old projects became the inspiration for new versions of themselves, indeed for a new utopianism not dissimilar in idealism and sense of vision as that of the original modern housers—a new utopianism that combined architecture with social uplift. This new version began, surprisingly, in one of the worst public housing projects still standing in the early 1980s, a project that was not dissimilar from Pruitt-Igoe and that seemed destined for the same fate. The Columbia Point housing project in the Dorchester section of Boston was the largest in New England. *Architect* magazine described it, with an acknowledgment of its design debt to modern housing and Le Corbusier, as "27 nearly identical three- and seven-story apartment buildings, deployed on super-blocks à la Ville Radieuse (Radiant City). The architecture followed the no-frills style of public housing of that era: utilitarian, flat-roof boxes. Although the project functioned reasonably well at first, by the 1970s, thanks to the absence of screening, lax management, and general neglect, it had become a no-man's land of crack houses, street crime, and lawlessness. By 1979, things were so bad that three-quarters of the 1,504 housing units were boarded up and vacant."[18]

Because, like so much public housing, Columbia Point's population was virtually all African American, its dramatic history included, as well, the fact that it had figured notoriously in the 1974 Boston school desegregation "busing" federal court order and protests: its children had been, prior to that order, sent to predominantly Black schools in the city's Roxbury section, notwithstanding Columbia Point's geographic

FIGURE 7.1. Columbia Point housing project aerial view, Boston. Photograph by Spencer Grant (ca. 1969–1986). Digital Commonwealth.

proximity to predominantly white schools in neighboring South Boston. That decision regarding so-called feeder patterns helped lead to the court decision that Boston school officials had, like Jim Crow southerners, engaged in "de jure segregation."[19]

Columbia Point was regarded as the greatest problem facing Harry Spence, a court-appointed receiver of the Boston Housing Authority who had minced no words in describing the problems of the nation's fourth-largest system, which he had been charged with turning around. As negotiations over how to deal with Columbia Point's dangerous dilapidation stalled, Spence went so far as to force the issue by threatening to place tenants who were languishing on the Housing Authority's waiting list in the admittedly dangerous project.

As Jane Roessner described in a history of Columbia Point, "Spence decided that a preemptive move was necessary to halt the abandonment, physical as well as institutional, of Columbia Point. He informed the city that unless it undertook an immediate, good-faith redevelopment effort, he would begin 'reoccupying the project,' notwithstanding conditions there": that is, notwithstanding an absence of "fundamental services for health and safety." He was, however, prepared to carry out the threat in order to "halt the charade" that steps were being taken toward improvement.[20]

The ploy led to a breakthrough: Columbia Point, like Pruitt-Igoe, would be demolished but not with a vacant lot left behind. Instead, it would be replaced by a new—and new kind of—development. Harbor Point might have been called the "un-project." It would be built and managed not by the Housing Authority but by a private development firm. There would be no high-rises, only three-story town houses organized like a suburban housing development, including small interior streets of the kind Le Corbusier disdained. Crucially, there would be no "concentration of poverty"; two-thirds of the residences would be "market rate," with the revenue from their sales and rents helping to subsidize the cost of those units that would be set aside for the small number of remaining former residents of Columbia Point. A crucial part of the un-project: all the townhouses would look the same from the outside, whether set aside for the poor or sold to the better-off. Utilitarian, modernist project design, associated with concentration of poverty, would not characterize neotraditionalist Harbor Point townhouses.

The plan for Harbor Point was the work of Joan E. Goody of Boston-based Goody, Clancy & Associates. She sympathized with the demands of the public housing occupants. "They wanted to live in a 'normal' neighborhood," she wrote in a 1993 article in *Places* magazine, "one that didn't look or work like a project, one that felt safe for walking around and letting their children out to play."[21] Harbor Point would look to Boston like a suburb in the city. There would even be some commercial component, in the form of a nearby strip mall that would be renovated.

Although novel in many ways, Harbor Point would hark back, too, to the early history of New York City public housing, by screening tenants and enforcing "rules of behavior: no pets, no repairing or washing cars on site, no consumption of alcoholic beverages in public areas, no loud noises after 11 p.m. In addition, car access is restricted to residents and guests; the streets are publicly owned, they are maintained—and patrolled—privately."[22] In its own way, it would be a gated community. The difference between Columbia Point and its successor was both dazzling and influential. In the Museum of Modern Art tradition, architecture critics were impressed. Not only was Harbor Point a pleasant new development on the waterfront, adjacent to the nearby I. M. Pei–designed John F. Kennedy Presidential Library and University of Massachusetts, Boston, but its design, including individual front doors of which the architect Oscar Newman, a proponent of "defensible space" as a means to minimize crime, would have approved, "nurtures pride and identity," as the *Boston Globe* architecture critic Robert Campbell was quoted as saying in a 1990 appreciation.[23]

Harbor Point was taken to be not just a dramatic improvement in design over what it replaced but a new model for projects that could actually work—that is, to house the poor through a financial approach that provided enough revenue to maintain the buildings and would avoid the dreaded concentration of poverty with what were assumed to be its inevitable social ills.

The new assumptions and resulting changes in approach would have an impact far beyond Boston. They would lead to an ambitious new project construction program that would prove to have national impact. Known as Housing Opportunities for People Everywhere, pointedly abbreviated as HOPE VI and established by Congress in 1992, it was a direct response to the National Commission on Severely Distressed Public Housing. Over the next eight years, $4.5 billion in federal funds would support 165 HOPE VI "revitalization grants"; the old projects would be demolished but would also be replaced and on their own sites. From Boston to Atlanta to Chicago, a new formula would be tried, in a new search for public housing that would work. In some ways, HOPE VI projects harked back to the projects' modern housing roots and the goal of serving the working class. They would be specifically designed as "mixed-income housing"; the "concentrated poverty" of Atlanta's Techwood Homes would be replaced by Centennial Place, whose 195 apartments would include, as its marketing literature puts it, "both low-income and moderately affluent residents alike. The development sports tree-lined streets, pools, playgrounds, an early learning center and even an elementary school."[24] As in many HOPE VI projects, "town homes" replaced high-rises. The Atlanta Housing Authority (AHA) would lease the low-income units but contract with a private property management firm. Similarly, adjacent to the site of what had been the Cabrini-Green high-rises arose North Town Village, combining "market-rate" units (50 percent) and moderately subsidized "affordable" units (20 percent), with another 30 percent reserved for former Cabrini residents.[25]

HOPE VI was emblematic of an era of optimism and innovation early in the Bill Clinton administration, not unlike the experimentation of the New Deal; Vice President Al Gore especially embraced the idea of "reinventing government." HOPE VI would be, as HUD put it, "the most ambitious effort to date to address the problem of severely distressed public housing, . . . to decrease (or avoid) the concentration of very low-income households, and to build sustainable communities. To achieve these goals, the program combines physical revitalization with management improvements and supportive services for the public housing residents."[26] The shadow of the projects could be discerned here, as well: the goal of this new round of housing idealism was at least as much to correct previous sins as to house people in need.

Not only did HOPE VI represent a new generation of design, but it was based on a significant new group of assumptions. Its mixed-income model was not just a financial innovation; it was seen as a vehicle for social uplift, an antipoverty program in its own right. It was based on the assumption not only that day-to-day quality of life would improve as the concentration of poverty was diluted and services improved but also that the life trajectories of the poor—their aspirations and ambitions—would be improved through interaction with those who were better-off. It was not to be a mere housing program.

As a study commissioned by HUD put it, "One of the premises of the HOPE VI program is that deconcentrating poverty and creating mixed-income communities will benefit the poor. Low-income families will interact with neighbors in their new communities, forming new social networks. These networks are hypothesized to offer a range of benefits for original residents, including positive role models for adults and children, access to information about economic opportunities, and peer groups for children and youth that are less likely to support delinquent activity."[27] One might go so far to say that by housing the poor in residences indistinguishable from those of more affluent neighbors, their lives, too, would, through some social alchemy, also come to resemble each other's. Alexander von Hoffman of the Harvard Joint Center for Housing Studies has skeptically termed this idea "environmental determinism."[28] Similar doubts have been expressed by Robert Chaskin and Mark Joseph in their book *Integrating the Inner City: The Promise and Peril of Mixed-Income Public Housing Transformation*.[29]

Even those who applauded such an approach, as did the 2013 *Architect* magazine retrospective essay on Harbor Point, acknowledged how distinct it was from US norms: "Although Americans regularly pay lip service to the value of diversity, the truth is that people of different incomes generally choose—for a variety of reasons—to live apart. Nevertheless, since 1992, the federal government has spent more than $5 billion to encourage the rich and poor to live side by side. The so-called Hope VI program has awarded several hundred block grants to scores of cities around the country to replace the barracks-like public housing projects of the 1950s with a blend of subsidized and market housing."[30] The same essay noted, however, that managing this sort of housing would be no easy task. Indeed, Harbor Point not only was permitted to screen new tenants but had free rein to evict residents for drug and gun possession. It ran its own security force.

"We are able to relax some rules as the property matures, and in other properties we make them more strict as the resident population evolves," says Miles Byrne, who managed Harbor Point for seven years. "There is so much distrust in the early years of any mixed-income community, in large part because we inherit a resident population that has only known the public housing universe, where promises were broken, properties were neglected, and decisions were reached without resident input."[31]

It is one thing to maintain the buildings and ensure security but another to achieve the subtle social goals built into HOPE VI. In a place where many residents do not share the commonalities that characterize most US communities, hopes of uplifting via osmosis are ambitious. A HUD-commissioned evaluation of the program raises reasons for doubt. It observed that "survey respondents reported fairly low levels of social interaction with neighbors.... Relatively few respondents reported having more than limited interactions with their current neighbors." Notably, the affluent portion of the "mixed-income" developments chose to keep to themselves: "Unsubsidized households and voucher holders are less likely than public housing residents to report having friends and family in the area and reported the lowest levels of interaction with their neighbors. Our in-depth interviews suggest that the low levels of interaction are associated with a number of factors, including lack of opportunity (e.g., respondents or neighbors are not around during the day), language or cultural barriers, and personal preferences for keeping social distance from neighbors."[32]

There can be little doubt, of course, that there were households that moved from abject circumstances in the old projects to shiny new apartments with which they were pleased. As the 2002 HUD study tracking HOPE VI residents from the time they left since-demolished projects put it, "The findings from the HOPE VI Resident Tracking Study suggest that many relocated residents live in a new housing environment that is an improvement over their original distressed public housing. A majority of the original residents in our study sample are living in decent housing in neighborhoods that have lower poverty rates than their original public housing developments, and most are satisfied with their current living situation."[33]

Yet such improvement was not unmitigated among the people living in the HOPE VI complexes in eight cities surveyed. "A substantial proportion of public housing residents and voucher users reported problems with drug trafficking and violent crime in their neighborhood."[34] This despite the report noting that the low-rise "defensible space" approach had been incorporated into the new designs. Nor is it clear that the HOPE VI projects, themselves attractive like the original projects at the time of their ribbon-cuttings, will be well maintained over time; they, too, must rely on adequate rental income, whether from subsidized or nonsubsidized households.

There is no doubt that people with complaints are more likely to post them online, but it is nonetheless concerning to read some reviews of recent life in Harbor Point and Centennial Place. Many comments are upbeat and positive, such as this one about Harbor Point, but they also hint at issues: "The leasing staff are friendly and personable and the price is unbeatable. Other comments about fire alarms have been an issue in the past but have recently become less frequent. They just repaved all of the roads so that shows that they are keeping up with the property. Neighbors tend to be quiet and while there are some issues with crime, let's face it folks, while it might not seem like it, this is Dorchester!" Others are blunter:

> Beware.... Only 2 weeks ago a female was shot 250 ft. from my windows. This was an hour after I called security and told them there was a large crowd of people drinking and partying in the parking lot. This place is not as it appears. I have far too many complaints to list! Please think twice before moving your college kids here. This place is not safe. I am sorry I moved here and will be moving as soon as my lease is up. If you have questions regarding this place, please ask and I will tell you the truth.[35]

Anecdotes can be misleading, to be sure, but their prevalence is notable.

Indeed, by 2019, twenty years after Atlanta's Centennial Place opened, its managers reported plans for substantial rehabilitation of the complex. That, of course, might be viewed as good news, reflecting the sort of ongoing capital investment that responsible building managers make routinely. At the same time, tenant reviews posted on the consumer site Yelp were reminiscent of the old projects. One described Centennial place this way: "DANGEROUS, NO AMENITIES, HORRIBLE EXPERIENCE. . . . Homeless people constantly walk around and look in your windows. One actually stole my patio furniture! All of it :). The parking lot gate is ALWAYS open. No matter how many times you call to close it for security purposes. NOTHING changes! Ever! There were multiple shootings in my parking lot. The SWAT team even came and pulled Ak-47's out of the neighbor's backpack."[36]

There is more to ponder here, including additional assumptions implicit in the program, as well as, of course, the complex and persistent problems of the disorganized poor and family structure—subjects that transcend housing policy. The effect on cities themselves merits consideration, as well, however. Built into HOPE VI is the assumption that the best—indeed, the only—use of the sites of severely distressed housing to be considered was replacement housing of some sort. The side effects of public housing can be said to include a "frozen city." In contrast to the norm of urban real estate, housing project land cannot, as a rule, be sold for nonhousing purposes, even as cities and their economies change. In Brooklyn, for instance, the Ingersoll Houses near the East River waterfront were intended for shipyard workers. When the Brooklyn Naval Shipyard, busy during World War II, closed, the project remained. Urban economies thrive when land is put to its "best and highest use," which could include housing but might include a new manufacturing plant or retail complex. Reserving a site for housing precludes that dynamism.

It is sheer and perhaps unjustified speculation that private development might bid for a HOPE VI site—and might want to build something other than subsidized housing. But one cannot rule out the possibility. One can only wonder whether low-income households would not be worse off without replacement housing or even better off if inexpensive land were bought by start-up businesses, rebuilt with stores and streets or perhaps with small homes so modest as to be privately "affordable." But a path had been chosen. In contrast to the original modern housers—who sought to improve cities overall through a combination of new housing and slum clearance—the goal of building a better project had become an end in itself.

Yet we must also consider whether, in Richard Nixon's formulation, the new tenants are part of a group of a "favored few"—provided shiny new housing at a guaranteed low rent for as long as they choose to live in it. This complication points up what a long road had been traveled from the modern housing vision, which would have had a large percentage of the overall population housed in projects managed like public utilities. Saving what had become a small remnant of that vision inevitably serves a small number, even if a project per se is upgraded. Nor has there been any test of the novel theory of HOPE VI—that proximity to those who are better-off will inspire upward mobility among the former residents of projects. "All we have," says one former HUD HOPE VI official, "are anecdotes."[37]

Put another way, HOPE VI represented yet another form of housing utopianism—an artificial community envisioned by planners, not preferences. Cabrini-Green and Columbia Point residents may have successfully pressured housing officials to be able to be relocated in the completed HOPE VI project, but the overall blueprint was, once again, drawn from afar by public officials. This is not to say that HOPE VI was not ambitious—or that, as in the projects' early golden age, the living situations of some former public housing tenants has not been improved. "Over the course of 15 years, HOPE VI grants were used to demolish 96,200 public housing units and produce 107,800 new or renovated housing units, of which 56,800 were to be affordable to the lowest-income households."[38]

Critics of the program note, as per those numbers, that the number of housing units for the poorest declined as a result of it. This, of course, was a feature, not a bug; the goal was income mixing. More broadly, however, we are left to wonder whether a new generation of projects—planned communities designed to achieve social and economic goals—will work any better than their predecessors. As with Techwood Homes or Cabrini-Green, new projects, including and perhaps especially HOPE VI, are impressive when the ribbons are cut. It is unclear whether they can be well maintained, especially because maintenance revenues rely on a continuing stream of "market-rent" tenants. It is well worth keeping in mind that the strictures of income mixing are at odds with the demonstrated preferences of US households. Mandated mixed-income developments are at odds with what might be termed the unspoken rules of US housing markets—that moving to a "better" neighborhood requires good life decisions, whether thrift, employment, or marriage. Census data have shown, repeatedly, that US neighborhoods are characterized by residents with similar levels of income and education. As the Brown University sociologist Michael White has written, "Time and again it has been argued that socioeconomic status is the principal differentiator in the metropolis. Poor neighborhoods with residents who work in lower-status occupations and have lower levels of education are found to be separated from the high-status neighborhoods of the urban mosaic."[39] A sense of status and accomplishment matters in communities; thus, introducing new residents with lower levels of each is, inevitably, a recipe for tension. One may even wonder whether a combination of envy or feeling out of place may spur crime. Nonetheless, even as funding for HOPE VI declined, its approach would prove influential in a next wave of post-project projects.

8

Fixing What's Broken

The Future of Public Housing

Nearly a century after the Museum of Modern Art's housing exhibit made the case for public housing, its original principles have long been overtaken by events. The idea that government must finance housing for a third to two-thirds of the US population no longer guides US housing policy, if it ever really did, in practice. Nonetheless, the projects remain, as do their policy progeny.

What has not developed is an accepted theory of housing assistance. The HOPE VI program, discussed in chapter 7, proposed one idea: that the projects themselves could be saved and some of their former residents uplifted by mixing the poor and nonpoor. But it left standing significant numbers of "traditional" projects, and it has not shown definitive evidence that it provides a path out of poverty.

In the aftermath of the perceived failure of the original projects, ideas about how to save what is left of them and assist those who have lived in them or qualified to do so compete. They range from "contingent" assistance—such as housing tied to work or a time limit—to proposals to vastly increase the number of poor households that receive financial help through the vehicle initiated by Richard Nixon, the housing voucher. The assumption that an arm of local government—the housing authority—would own and manage its own housing has also been challenged, as management and maintenance of projects have been turned over to private firms, which rely on income from tenants receiving housing vouchers.

There is a commonality, however, to what appear to be widely differing post-project housing approaches. All are predicated on the idea

FIGURE 8.1. Cover of a HUD publication about HOPE VI. (HUD)

that they are fundamentally targeting not a large proportion of the US population but, rather, the poor or even very poor. In a sense, the projects—and their offshoots—have evolved to become a contemporary versions of a once-ubiquitous nineteenth-century institution, complete with debates similar to those that were historically waged about them. The contending worldviews were known as "indoor" and "outdoor" relief for the poor. Housing vouchers can be compared to outdoor relief: government-provided financial assistance meant to supplement income for people living in their own homes (not literally "outdoors"). In 1890, some 737,000 Americans received such aid. Indoor relief was literally provided inside: within a municipal institution known as the poorhouse. In 1890, there were an estimated sixty thousand poorhouses, sheltering some 3.1 million Americans.[1] Projects from Pruitt-Igoe to the Robert Taylor Homes and contemporary survivors have become poorhouses: shelter of last resort for the elderly poor and impoverished single parents. As this is written, in a far wealthier US, some 6.7 million Americans live in either the projects or a voucher household—a far smaller percentage of a much larger population. Nonetheless, in the twenty-first century, as in the nineteenth, the conditions of such relief have continued, in similar ways, to be debated.

Should residents receiving housing assistance be required to work or be subject to other conditions? Poorhouses, as an analogue, would double as places that either required labor or tested—as part of "scientific charity" methods—the capacity of residents to perform work, so as to discourage malingering. Indeed, Michael Katz, the premier historian of historical US antipoverty programs, writes that "the work ethic is what poorhouses were all about."[2] Housing vouchers, in contrast, reflect a belief that there are inevitably those who struggle to make ends meet in the US economy and that housing, like groceries (or, in cold climes, the cost of heating), is a special case: it should be provided to those who cannot pay the rent on their own. (Only 28 percent of voucher recipients report income from wages.)[3]

Nearly a century since the 1934 housing exhibition, public housing and its variations must be considered to have become a permanent part of US life. The thousands of local public housing authorities, creatures of the 1937 Housing Act, continue to manage properties or distribute housing vouchers.[4] Yet no consensus theory has emerged to replace that of the modern housing movement, even as it failed, as per Catherine Bauer, to put down deep roots in the United States. Instead, we support a series of competing theories. Each can be described in compelling ways, yet each has notable complications.

The approach that has grown the most since the time of Richard Nixon's public housing moratorium, however, is one that shares with Catherine Bauer and Edith Elmer Wood the belief that the cost of housing may be out of the reach of people of modest incomes—and that that shortfall is intrinsic to the US economic system. It would extend housing assistance—the vouchers first created by Richard Nixon—to as many Americans as might need them, based on their incomes. The heir to Bauer and Abbott, the intellectual leader of this perspective is the Princeton sociologist Matthew Desmond. Key to his concern is the prospect of people of limited means losing shelter altogether, as he dramatized in his 2016 book *Evicted*. In US Senate testimony, he has pushed for a no-strings-attached increase in the number of housing vouchers. "The idea is simple," he concludes. "Every family below a certain income level would be eligible for a housing voucher." In effect, Desmond would make available the public housing subsidy arrangement to all those who qualify. "The family would dedicate 30 percent of their income to housing costs, with the voucher paying the rest."[5]

This would constitute a vast change—effectively enshrining a version of the Bauer/Wood theory that government should serve all those who are paying too much in rent. The Census Bureau has estimated that some nineteen million "renter households" can be classified as "rent-burdened"; that is, they pay more than 30 percent of their income for rent. But housing authorities distribute just 2.7 million vouchers. Desmond, in his Senate testimony, endorsed legislation to increase that number by five hundred thousand—a down payment toward a much larger increase, it would seem.

For Desmond, such assistance would mitigate against "family insecurity, the threat of looming eviction and resulting moves from place to place, under desperate circumstances."[6] In his 2016 book, Desmond, in the Jacob Riis tradition, tells his own powerful stories of people struggling at the lower end of the housing market, whom he met during time spent with them in Milwaukee. The households whose stories Desmond returns to time and again, providing his narrative framework, struggle to find money to pay their rent—whether in a trailer park or in the Black ghetto of North Milwaukee. Desmond writes of "Arleen," raising two sons on her own: "The rent was $550 a month, utilities not included. The rent would take 88 percent of Arleen's $628-a-month welfare check." When the inevitable evictions do occur, the circumstances are poignant. "Larraine stood outside, silently looking on. The movers carried out her chair, her washing machine, her refrigerator, stove, dining table. . . . Her things were headed to Eagle Storage."[7]

Again, not unlike Bauer and Wood, their policy heirs—including Desmond and policy advocacy groups such as the National Low Income Housing Policy Center—clearly believe that housing is special, that the private housing market is so fundamentally flawed that assistance for housing must be provided, as it is, for instance, for food.

This is a policy progeny of "outdoor relief"—assistance without conditions other than need, as evidenced by low income or lack of shelter. Desmond makes a strong argument based on policy consistency. Why should only a small minority of those who qualify by income for a housing voucher receive one? It is an argument that is not inconsistent with Richard Nixon's skepticism about new public housing, which, because of its cost, would help only a "favored few." It is a view, however, that can be said to overlook what has long been the concern of "poorhouse" assistance: the danger that it dampens the incentive to earn or even encourages the formation of households that qualify for help. The apparent benefit of limiting a household's share of rent to 30 percent of income operates, as it has since the Brooke Amendment, as a tax on increased earnings—and a disincentive to increase work effort and to move up and out of the projects, broadly understood to include vouchers. The fact that people with higher incomes pay higher rent must be viewed as a prima facie work disincentive.

Just as data about the number of the "rent burdened" point toward one policy approach, so do other data point in another direction. In the nation's largest public housing authority, that of New York City, 78 percent of its 155,700 households have lived in its projects for ten years or more. Indeed, 32,678 of its households, or 21 percent, have lived in one for over forty years.[8] Nationally, a 2015 study for HUD found that the average "length of stay" in the housing voucher program was 6.6 years—which, statistically, means that a number of families, though not specified, stayed significantly longer.[9]

Per Desmond, this can be seen as a triumph of family "stability"; indeed, the legislation about which he spoke in favor was titled the Family Stability and Opportunity Voucher Act.[10] But it can just as easily be seen as evidence that the projects, and other versions of housing assistance, can be a fly trap of economic dependency.

The voucher approach—assistance without conditions—has been by far the sharpest-growing element of post-physical project housing assistance. By 2023, there were 2.4 million voucher households but only 907,000 households in public housing projects. But not all vouchers have been provided unconditionally. Experiments rooted in the tradition of "indoor relief"—help with conditions—have been under way, with limited fanfare, since 1996. It was then, during the Clinton administration and its zeal for "reinventing government," that HUD was authorized to include thirty-nine public housing authorities in an experimental program. In 1996, HUD launched the Moving to Work (MTW) demonstration program, whose objectives was to "give incentives to families with children where the head of household is working, is seeking work, or is preparing for work by participating in job training, educational programs, or programs that assist people to obtain employment and become economically self-sufficient; and increase housing choices for low-income families."[11] This can be viewed as a theory, or strategy, competing with that of universal entitlement advocated by Desmond.

Moving to Work quietly opened the door for making housing help contingent on behavior, as it were—for the first time since the early New York City Housing Authority required employment and good housekeeping, among much else, to screen potential tenants. Among the first Moving to Work authorities was one of the largest in the South, that of Atlanta. When the onetime corporate finance attorney Renee Glover took the helm of the Atlanta Housing Authority in 1994, that agency owned and managed fourteen thousand apartments in forty-three properties. Its total of fifty thousand tenants—98 percent of them African American—meant that the percentage of Atlanta's overall population living in projects was the highest in the US.[12] During Glover's twenty-plus-year tenure, that would change drastically. Over the course of those two decades, Glover did more than direct the demolition of notorious projects such as Techwood Homes—which Glover unsparingly described as "toxic." With the exception of a handful of apartment complexes for the elderly, the Housing Authority tore down not just a few but all of its "legacy" projects.

Some residents relocated to new, mixed-income developments erected on the sites of thirteen former projects, whose seven-thousand-plus rental units included thirty-six hundred set aside for former public housing tenants. That meant, of course, that the vast majority of former public housing tenants were "vouchered out": provided with a housing choice voucher to pay for the rent in a privately owned apartment. But there was more to what Glover branded as the "Atlanta Way." It included unusual conditions made possible by Moving to Work. To qualify for—and retain—the rental subsidy, the former project tenants had to do just what the program's name said: they faced a work requirement.

The requirement, however, was not imposed in a vacuum. It included, as well, what might be called a social work element. Under Glover, the Housing Authority would retain an outside counseling firm to work with individual former project tenants, in what can only be described as an effort to change their hopes, their habits, and, ultimately their lives, as I found when I visited.

The troops in the effort were employees of the Integral Youth and Family Project, a for-profit, private firm with which the Housing Authority contracted. Its president, Hope Bolden, told me that many of the households with which it dealt had not only not been employed but may have never paid bills for themselves. Utilities came with public housing, food stamps helped with groceries, and everything else was paid for in cash. Not surprisingly, the priority was to keep receiving benefits and, if possible, increase them. That meant keeping live-in boyfriends—even if one was the father of a child in the household—off the lease, lest the man's income lead to a rent increase. It also meant suggesting to school authorities that a child might have a learning disability: such a designation could bestow nearly $300 a month in Supplemental Security Income (SSI) on project households.

It was not uncommon, said Bolden, herself a Black Jamaican immigrant, for four generations to employ SSI and food stamps, along with housing assistance, to "get over." That originally was a church expression for overcoming obstacles, one derived from the biblical account of crossing Jordan: "You know my soul look back in wonder / How did I make it over?" In common parlance, this phrase from a Mahalia Jackson hymn has become synonymous with successful hustles.

Bolden's troops in the effort that Glover describes as "human transformation" are called "family support coordinators" (FSCs), and they are virtually all young African Americans in their twenties and early thirties. Some have made the journey out of public housing themselves. Kenya Tyson went from Atlanta's Harris Homes to Morehouse College and counseled families who lived in the now-demolished Harris Homes. Teaera Raines was raised by her grandparents in Macon, Georgia, after her parents succumbed to drug abuse; she went on to get a master's degree in management from Troy University.

The challenge of linking housing assistance to a path out of poverty was made clear by these idealistic young counselors. But so was the prospect of success. As adept as people in the public housing world have grown at maximizing government benefits, they are usually utterly unprepared to make their own way in life. As Raines puts it, "They basically say to us, 'You're trying to tell me to live a life I don't know anything about.'" She continued,

> Take a woman I'll call Darlene—a single mother of two teenage boys whom Pamela Elder, another Integral counselor, began to visit six months before tenants left the soon-to-be-demolished Bankhead Courts. Darlene, a longtime employee of the Checkers fast-food chain, had been fired recently because of attitude problems. She was not an irresponsible mother; she insisted that her boys stay inside their apartment to avoid gang life. But neither was she ambitious for them. Asked what future she envisioned for the boys, Darlene said that they would "work at McDonald's or someplace like that" and then added, tellingly, "That's what we do."

Two years after Elder first visited Darlene, that defeatism has vanished. Once she moved from public housing into a subsidized private apartment—and faced the requirement to work—Darlene did, indeed, start working again. In fact, she got a far better job than she ever had before: cleaning airplanes at Atlanta's Hartsfield-Jackson International Airport. ("I'd never even been on an airplane before," Darlene told Elder.) With her own circumstances and living situation improved, she has encouraged her sons, whom Elder describes as "smart" and "athletic," to stay in school, and the elder of the two was nominated for a selective Atlanta program for public school students displaying leadership qualities and academic promise.

The stories do not always have happy endings, of course. Kenya Tyson describes one that she said would stick with her for the rest of her life, involving a mother and her six children, formerly of the Hollywood Homes project. State officials took the children away from their mother because of her drug abuse.

The cost of the Integral Youth and Family Project is substantial. Over a seven-year period, the AHA has paid it $26.7 million to work with 14,281 people. But that is a substantial percentage of metropolitan Atlanta's 81,000 Black poor, meaning that the program has the potential not only to help individuals but also to change broader social norms. Over a seven-year period, between 2002 and 2009, the percentage of Atlanta Housing Authority households holding a job rose from 18.5 percent to 62 percent. The most recent figures show that 62 percent of AHA-supported household heads in Atlanta are employed. Before the 2019 recession, the figure had reached 70 percent.[13]

The statistical results are impressive, although it is impossible to determine which part of Glover's plan—the work requirement or the counseling—deserves more credit. Nor, as with HOPE VI, has a long-term study been undertaken to follow the post-project life trajectories of tenants. Glover, herself the daughter of Jim Crow–era northern Florida, thinks the combination of Black self-help and government effort that she is providing is welcome. As she puts it, "On so many occasions, people have said, 'Thank you for believing in us.' We were into a completely different planning process because we were not planning for poor people who were incapable, who could not be responsible. We were in the process of planning for God's children."

There will be inevitable concerns about the "Atlanta Way." It is far from inevitable that those who are displaced from the projects will be able to find somewhere within their means to live. The mixed-income replacement developments, to which a relatively small percentage of former project tenants have moved, are costly to build and maintain. During economic downturns, work requirements (although they are tempered by options such as enrollment in schools or training programs) may be unrealistic.

The Atlanta approach doubtless, however, reflects a key shift in the attitude of a public housing authority since its New Deal inception. As its population came to be dominated by low-income, single-parent households, its sense of mission changed, from that of simple provision of "safe and sanitary housing" to that of encouraging upward mobility—the "up and out" transition that many Americans had actually always seen as the implicit ideal of the projects but one that they failed, increasingly, to enable, over time.

Even Mathew Desmond, notwithstanding his endorsement of increased, unconditional housing assistance, expressed hope that housing vouchers, in their own way, could lead a way out of poverty. For Desmond and the Harvard economist Raj Chetty, that means moves to what have come to be called "opportunity neighborhoods." What can be called a third new theory of housing assistance is this: if assistance makes it possible for poor households to live in more affluent neighborhoods, they will be able to avail themselves of the better schools and overall better public services (clean and safe streets) associated with higher-income zip codes. As HUD itself puts it, "High opportunity neighborhoods often have attributes that, based on recent research, seem to have a positive effect on the economic mobility of residents."[14] The key research to which HUD refers has been that of Chetty, who reached his conclusion based on an analysis of a previous HUD program called Moving to Opportunity. In a 2016 paper, Chetty analyzed the effects of a so-called demonstration program run by HUD through housing authorities in five cities—Baltimore, Boston, Chicago, Los Angeles, and New York. The idea was to compare the lives of onetime public housing tenants who moved, through the use of housing vouchers, to "high opportunity" areas with those who moved to lower-income ones. Chetty's conclusion pointed to yet another means of the post-projects "life transformation" of which Atlanta's Rene Glover dreamed. The projects had served as a poverty magnet; a post-project response would undo their damage. Wrote Chetty and colleagues, "Offering families with young children living in high-poverty projects vouchers to move to lower-poverty neighborhoods may reduce the intergenerational persistence of poverty."[15] "Low-income children are most likely to succeed in counties that have less concentrated poverty, less income inequality, better schools, more two-parent families, and lower crime rates."[16]

As with work requirements and public housing time limits, the "moving to opportunity" idea raises a number of practical questions. Because rents are higher in high-income areas, the value of the vouchers must increase, something housing authorities may well do but at the expense of the overall number of persons assisted. One must wonder, as well, whether it is practical to relocate large numbers of the poor to more affluent areas, given the paucity of apartments in higher-income suburbs, for instance. Nor, given the sociology of residential patterns, can we be sure that relocating large numbers of the poor to middle-income areas will not inspire discomfort among those who are being moved and resistance among the incumbent residents, who may feel that others are being rewarded without having worked their way up, as it were. Moving to Opportunity, implies, moreover, that low-income neighborhoods—urban ports of entry as the Lower East Side once was—are antithetical to opportunity. Like public housing itself during the New Deal, however, there is no doubt that this is an idea with intellectual momentum.

The Atlanta model may appear to differ fundamentally from that of Moving to Opportunity. One provides conditional help; the other provides help based on need, as judged by income compared to the cost of housing. On closer inspection, surprising commonalties emerge between these two responses to a shared conclusion: that the projects, in practice, had failed; a utopian vision had devolved into concentrations of poverty. Both Moving to Work and Moving to Opportunity endorse a shared lesson: the poor must be dispersed. For both, low-income neighborhoods are inherently flawed. The effort to deconcentrate them shares a great deal with the early modern housers' aversion to "slums." For latter-day housing reformers, the fate of the projects has proved the point: too many poor households living in close quarters is a recipe for social ills.

That same idea animates, in part, another significant response to the shared viewed that the projects, in practice, harmed, rather than helped, the poor. In 2012, the Obama-administration HUD joined the question of how to stop the ongoing descent of projects around the US into severe distress, absent direct financial assistance from Washington to local housing authorities at levels that Congress had long resisted and that had not been contemplated when public housing began. The new initiative has an opaque, technical title: the Rental Assistance Demonstration (RAD) project. What can be viewed as a fourth new theory of housing assistance can, because of its scale, if nothing else, be seen as a watershed in the ongoing effort to learn lessons from the history of the projects.

Most dramatically, RAD turns its back on a core precept of modern housing: government management of the projects. The failure of bureaucrats to be effective property managers—one of the fears of the early modern housers—had continued to be sadly realized. Even in New York City—once celebrated for providing "public housing that worked"—the local housing authority had, in response to a federal suit initiated by a federal US attorney, been placed under the oversight of a federal monitor in 2019. The court responded specifically to the physical ills of the city's projects, as compared to the charge of the 1937 Housing Act and described by the federal prosecutor's office: "In fact, living conditions at NYCHA are far from 'decent, safe, and sanitary.' Mold grows unchecked at many NYCHA developments, often on a large scale. Across the city, residents are provided inadequate heat in winter, leading to frigid apartment temperatures. Pests and vermin infestations are common, and as senior New York City officials have acknowledged, NYCHA 'has no idea how to handle rats.' Elevators often fail, leaving elderly or disabled residents trapped in their apartments or sleeping in building lobbies because they cannot return to their homes. Leaks, peeling paint, and other deterioration are commonplace, but go unaddressed."[17]

The Rental Assistance Demonstration program—adopted in New York and at some six hundred local housing authorities around the US—would use some public finance jujitsu to repair and rebuild. In technical jargon, it works this way: "the RAD program allows [housing authorities] to leverage additional funding, in the form of debt and equity, to make vital improvements to units that would otherwise continue to fall into disrepair."[18] In plainer English, public housing tenants receive their aid in the form of that Nixon-era type of help, the housing voucher, which then provides a government-guaranteed stream of income that private developers can borrow against. They use the funds they borrow to fix up the projects and then become the managers, able to realize net operating income—profit—in doing so. In plainer English still, public housing gets a private landlord. There is irony here, given historical concern about private landlords' treatment of poor tenants. Nonetheless, this is a major new approach. These can be undertakings on a large scale.

HUD, for its part, expresses hope not just that the projects will be in better shape but that local housing authorities—in response to those fears about concentration of poverty that are so widely shared—will, in effect, move projects to opportunity, as Mathew Desmond might define it. As HUD itself puts it

> RAD provides a unique opportunity to transfer housing subsidy to neighborhoods that expand opportunities for low-income families. With this tool, known as a transfer of assistance, PHAs can replace public housing in impacted or isolated locations and place new project-based assistance contracts on homes in new neighborhoods, giving current and future residents access to better schools, jobs, infrastructure, and other local amenities.
>
> Across 140 RAD "transfers of assistance," PHAs have placed 8,300 affordable housing units in "better" neighborhoods, with a poverty rate that is on average 24% lower than the poverty rate of the original sites. Approximately 63% of [such] conversions also feature new construction, which means that residents can move into brand new, energy efficient units, with improved community facilities, access to broadband, and other amenities.[19]

This, in other words, is yet another post-project approach to poverty deconcentration.

In many cities, especially New York, the impulse to such deconcentration has also taken the form of "inclusionary zoning"—the requirement that larger new private apartment building developers set aside some units for people of specific income groups—so as to provide "permanently affordable" housing and avoid the dreaded concentration of poverty.[20]

The goal of such assumed "moving to opportunity" harks back to the Chicago Housing Authority's Elizabeth Wood in the early 1950s, when she set off a firestorm of controversy by urging that public housing be widely dispersed. "The logical conclusion is that it is most humane to develop a housing program which allows wide choice.... Housing should not be built to fit inflexibly into the existing pattern of transportation, utilities, or existing school and park plants. Frequently such patterns must be redesigned, relocated, and created anew in order to build communities that will not deteriorate."[21] Whether Wood in her day or

HUD, Matthew Desmond, or Raj Chetty in 2024, idealism, ambition, and a sense of expertise drive public housing.

One can think of Catherine Bauer, Elizabeth Wood, Rene Glover, Mathew Desmond, et al. as jointly engaged in a search for the alchemists' philosopher's stone—the approach to the projects and their successors that will provide safe, sanitary, and uplifting housing that will remain so for the long term. Their successors have suggested four post-project strategies reviewed here: making assistance contingent on work, making housing assistance an entitlement, using vouchers as a ticket to higher-income neighborhoods, and dispersing new subsidized, privately managed developments. It is sobering, however, to reflect on the fact that housing policy in every era described in this book has shared similar goals and in a variety of ways found them, not at first but over time, to be elusive.

Indeed, like the original projects and their successors, those that are newly renovated through private financing will not continue to be well maintained absent a reliable stream of income. That means both ongoing, uninterrupted federal rent subsidies for the tenants in projects, at a level high enough to maintain the structures. It means, too, that new-era "mixed-income" housing that relies on wealthier tenants to pay higher rents so that poorer tenants can pay lower ones will have to be able to continue to attract the affluent as the buildings age—lest they follow the same downward trajectory of the original projects. That will depend, in part, on the willingness of the better-off to share an apartment building with those who are poorer than they—a historically atypical American preference.

So it is that the US federal government—and municipalities across the country—struggle with how to salvage the projects and improve the lives of those who were served by them. As they do so, there is much that is unconsidered, including the founding principle of modern housing, that poor neighborhoods are both bad neighborhoods—slums—and likely to remain permanently so. We search for the right formula that will make either physical projects or their voucher progeny work, whether to ensure that low-income households do not pay too great a share of income in rent or that their income and life outcomes improve over time.

The wide range of approaches toward picking up the pieces of the modern housing movement underscore both its original ambition and the challenge it has left behind. Should housing assistance remain a core part of the social welfare safety net? If so, how?

9

The Projects Today

Five Snapshots

No story of any one public housing project today can stand for the projects as a whole. The high-rise "towers in the park" still stand, especially in New York City, but so too do new, much-smaller buildings in small southern towns and "mixed-income" replacements for the once-infamous projects of Chicago's lakefront.

But visits to the remaining projects do serve to reveal both the past and present of the projects. The descriptions that follow have been gathered through personal visits by the author to the housing developments discussed and interviews with principals. They have not been chosen through a social science prism but rather that of the journalist who feels it crucial to add to this volume a sense of what conditions are like at the time of this writing in a variety of public housing projects.

Andrew Jackson Houses, Melrose Section, Bronx, New York

If there were a mayor of the Jackson Houses in the Bronx—blocks away from Yankee Stadium but a world apart—that would be Danny Barber. He even holds a formal position, as the head of Jackson's tenant engagement committee (every New York City "development" has one) and the president of all such committees for the sprawling New York system. When he sits on a bench in the project's courtyard, he greets a steady stream of passersby personally. In many ways, his own life story overlaps with the story of public housing.

At age fifty-three, Barber has lived for fifty-one years in the Jackson Houses, an eight-hundred-unit set of brick midrise buildings, one of many in New York named for US presidents (including Grant, Jefferson, McKinley, and Washington), reflecting the national pride that accompanied their construction.

But even Barber's pre-project life reflects public housing history. His family was relocated to Jackson only after their walk-up apartment building on nearby Morris Avenue was demolished in a slum clearance project. His parents, he recalls, were in no way dissatisfied with their "tenement" life. "Nah, they loved it. It was an opportunity. Man, my godfather baptized in a church, a Sicilian. I was raised by Sicilians. Morris Avenue was Little Italy of the South Bronx. I remember the Feast of San Gennaro when you shut down the street, and they walking down with the statue, and everybody is singing and dancing, and all the food trucks, the zeppole, sausage and peppers, and everything is out there, and everybody knows everybody. That was family. They tore it down to modernize. To modernize. But never got insight from the community."

He recalls Jackson, in contrast to the racially and ethnically mixed nearby neighborhood in which his family had previously lived, as always having been predominantly African American. Project residents, he says, always understood the nearby Cross-Bronx Expressway, the highway project that took hundreds of homes by eminent domain, as a dividing line between Black and white projects. But he nonetheless recalls the early years in the relatively new Jackson Houses—built in 1960—positively. Maintenance was steady and prompt, in part, he says, because of a management office at the development itself.

> The grass was greener than the Great Lawn at Central Park. It was more of a family feel than public housing. People were fighting to get into public housing. If you lived in public housing, you cherished living in NYCHA. You cherished it because it was cool. It was beautiful.

> It was a family atmosphere. If [you] threw a piece of paper on the floor, somebody could yell at [you], "Pick that paper up and put it in the trash, young man." "Yes, ma'am." "Yes, sir." You did it. It wasn't just your parents that raised you. It was the village where you lived. It was family orientation. It was community.

Some of that spirit persists, as time next to Barber on his park bench makes clear. He reminds a tenant passing by about a nephew's birthday party that afternoon. He bursts with pride about the young woman he calls his "protégé," who has served on the wider neighborhood's community board and has married and lives with her husband at Jackson, at least for now. "She waited until she got married to have kids, and then she had triplets."

But he makes clear that the deterioration that has visited "public housing that worked" is found at Jackson. "We still have community, but no one in the community tries to assist or to lift up." The NYCHA website, which tracks "service outages," project by project, in New York, reveals hundreds of "unplanned outages"—some for such basics as heat and water, the majority for elevator failure, no small problem for the project's many elderly residents or for Barber himself, a onetime high-school football player disabled after two heart attacks and obese to the point that walking is an effort. Somewhat surprisingly, he blames not only an unresponsive bureaucracy for service issues but tenants, as well:

> The residents have to stop using the elevator as a bathroom. The elevator's not the restroom. When you get on the elevator, you can't hold the door, because it's like the brain. If you overwork the brain, the brain freezes. When you hold the door, you're throwing it off. When you're banging on the buttons thinking you're making it come quicker, all you doing is blowing the fuse in there, and now that mechanism don't work to call it now. And when you educate the residents, "Oh, shut up and mind your business." No, we're not going to talk to each other like that. Especially, you're not going to talk to me like that.

Whether due to poor maintenance or bad behavior, outages are extensive at Jackson. City records show that over a six-month period starting at the beginning of 2022 through mid-2023, the Jackson Houses experienced sixty-four elevator breakdowns, fourteen heat and hot water outages, six electricity blackouts, and sixty-three gas outages, in its seven buildings.[1]

Barber gets upset, as well, about many tenants he says simply throw bags of garbage out their windows, rather than placing them in the trash chutes that each building has. "Garbage out the windows. Urinating in the lobbies, the hallways. But the most common is throwing the garbage out the windows, because you could sit there—you could be sitting outside, and we'll hear 'boom.' Sound like a bomb went off. Somebody threw a whole bag of garbage out." He would like to see such "infractions" punished such that three violations might lead to eviction, but he says enforcement relies on his own initiative and position as a tenant leader.

Some maintenance problems, however, clearly have nothing to do with tenants' behavior. Unrepaired roofs that should be replaced invite leaks and not only cause mold and mildew in bathrooms below but also infiltrate the buildings' brick façades. As a result, the bricks can tumble down from the sides of the buildings. To guard against the lawsuits that would result, the Housing Authority has installed, not only at Jackson but across its system, so-called sidewalk sheds: tunnels over the walkways into the lobbies. These dark entryways, in turn, invite crime. At the same time, at Jackson, they also, sadly, serve their purpose. A local New York news site, *The City*, described the events of May 2023:

> Before dawn on Thursday, a big panel of bricks broke loose from up around the 15th floor of 3505 Park Avenue, one of the buildings flagged as "unsafe" in 2016, and plummeted toward the street below.
>
> The masonry crashed down onto the sidewalk shed, which collapsed into a heap of wood and metal. If anybody had been underneath that shed, they likely would have been severely injured, or even killed.

What is more, continued the article, the problem with potentially falling bricks could be found across the city, including 538 "façade violations" noted by city inspectors since 2003—but not corrected twenty years later.[2]

That Daniel Barber himself has lived virtually his whole life at Jackson is not atypical: more than thirty thousand New York public housing households have lived in their units for more than forty years. That he can do so reflects the sense of something akin to property rights that tenants feel they have. It is common, says Barber, for residents to add adult children to their lease, so that they can continue to live in the project even after a parent dies. Indeed, he continues, many deaths go unreported, although that leads, he notes, to squatters, who get wind of a death and simply move in and take over apartments. Nor is it uncommon for apartments to be sublet when the people on the lease move out, without informing the Housing Authority, or for additional tenants—boarders or boyfriends—to go unreported. Barber credits such rule avoidance to the effects of the income-based rent rule. What reformers viewed as the "lodger evil" persists—and helps project residents make ends meet, even as it strains building services, such as the trash compactors and dumpsters.

"How many people got people living in their houses, and their income isn't being recorded or turned in? And that's just the fact of the matter, that you're scared your rent going to go up. I've got my kids on my lease, and my kid's making $100,000 a year. I don't want you on my lease, because when it's time to pay the rent, you don't want to pay." Put another way, increased earnings are punished.

But by far the most sobering and concerning dimension of Danny Barber's description of life at the Jackson Houses is that of the lives of teenage and young adult males at the overwhelming Black and Hispanic project. (The presence of Mexican and Central American residents, in addition to Puerto Ricans, does reflect ethnic change in the Bronx over the past decades.)

Barber brings over a friend, longtime resident Eugene McCoy, to explain. "They trapped in their area. This is the furthest they can go is the pizza shop on 153rd. Once they pass 153rd Street, it's kind like a no-man's-land. They can't go and do anything. They can't leave their area. 'Cause of the gang activity. Gang activity is—it's killing the community. And a lot of the times, the reason why they all joining gang and violence is because it's nothing here for them. They think it's cool, and it's not."

Jackson residents, the two say, must take care only to visit projects and surrounding blocks where they have "allies" and avoid "ops," short for "opponents." This is what the Radiant City has been reduced to: projects with their own specific gang identities. Even those who are unaware of the gangs might, says Barber, be shot, for wearing the wrong color on the wrong block.

Barber traces the rise of gangs to the decline of the two-parent families that were once typical at Jackson, when his own family first moved in:

> You have situations where it's one mother raising her three, four children and might be helping someone else with their children. The demographics, it varies. It changes. But there are quite a few single households, majority predominantly women, where the young men, a lot of them, and this conversation was held last night, where a gentleman just came home from a penitentiary, how he had a lot of problems with the younger generation inside, behind the wall, because they were from no-father households. And they had a lot of anger issues, and anything from ten to twenty-four, they look at anything from twenty-five and older as old. They look at it as old and say, "This old man." And I'm like, "Wow." That they develop this anger towards their own father, that they take it out on the world. They take it out on the world.

The Jackson Houses residents include Treez Da Stoner, who regularly posts videos, including one about life at Jackson. He and a friend provide a revealing tour of Jackson. They walk unimpeded into one building lobby and down a staircase, as he narrates, along with a companion he identifies as Smoke:

> SMOKE: Actually both of these buildings are open on this side.
> TREEZ DA STONER: Yeah, 'cause we seen an opening building, you feel me? A nice opening.
> SMOKE: We can cut through the parking lot.
> TREEZ DA STONER: Oh, shit, yeah. We could go through the parking lot. We Gucci.

They do seem to be aware of gang turf, however.

> SMOKE: We're gonna have to go through this way.

Like tour guides, they discuss what is going on in the project as they walk and talk.

> TREEZ DA STONER: I see they got their sprinklers on and shit. I see niggas outside chillin', niggas smokin', drinkin', doin' whatever the fuck they wanna do. You feel me? With no care in the world, as they should.

The two take note of police presence around Jackson but evince little concern about it.

> TREEZ DA STONER: Yeah, they go to jakes right here. Jakes [slang for police] is heavy on this block.
> SMOKE: Yeah, don't give a fuck about the cops.
> TREEZ DA STONER: I don't give a fuck about the police. I still smoke my weed. What the fuck they gonna do, lock me up for smoking weed? Nigga, this ain't 2010.
> SMOKE: This ain't even 2012.
> SMOKE: Most of the time, we be high as hell.

TREEZ DA STONER: Yeah. We be coming out here, we be high. We be smack, bro.

Finally, Treez reflects on the larger neighborhood, not far from Yankee Stadium.

TREEZ DA STONER: I see a lot of construction being done in the keys, too. Not just—yo that shit everywhere. I think they trying to gentrify this shit, bro. I could be wrong, but I know I'm right. I know I'm right.[3]

Baychester Houses, Bronx, New York

The contrast, at least on the surface, between Baychester Houses and Jackson Houses, in the same New York City borough, could not be starker. Once plagued by the same problems of garbage and crime, Baychester—another housing project in the Bronx—has been physically transformed, thanks to a financing approach that enables housing authorities to call on private funding and property management. Specifically, the Rental Assistance Demonstration program—deployed at more than six hundred aging projects across the country—relies on a technical change in the status of tenants: as recipients of housing vouchers. The stream of guaranteed federal funds that become tied to the tenants, not the housing authority, becomes revenue against which private developer/managers can borrow, using the funds to renovate public housing projects. This financial instrument will allow a private developer to be assured of reliable funding, in contrast to the vagaries of direct federal "operating assistance" for housing authorities that developed once it became clear that tenant rents could not sustain a housing project. The assistance formula had its own quirks: were a housing authority to reduce costs by, for instance, reducing its heating costs, its level of assistance would decline because its costs were lower.

FIGURE 9.1. Baychester Houses, Cross-Bronx Preservation. (L&M Partners)

"Rebirth in the South Bronx" is how a *New York Times* architecture writer described the change at Baychester, a complex of eleven buildings and 441 apartments. The *Times* described the before and after:

> Built more than half a century ago, Baychester was never properly waterproofed, its buildings enduring a history of cracked and spalled masonry and deteriorated mortar joints. [One resident] would complain to housing officials about mold sickening neighbors. They suggested tenants try bleach, she said. A few years ago, NYCHA shut down its on-site management office, forcing residents, many of them seniors, to pony up for transportation to meet the people supposedly in charge of the property. Security was half a dozen cameras, frequently broken, sporadically manned.
>
> "Tenants used to throw garbage anywhere during NYCHA times," said Sandra Gross [president of the Baychester tenants' association]. "NYCHA didn't care, so residents didn't care."

Today the campus looks spotless, with refurbished playgrounds, fresh plantings and a new basketball court. The buildings have been reclad with a waterproof material and faux-wood paneling. The renovation is not Architecture with a capital A. But it is dignified and better than some market rate housing. Glassed-in entrances have replaced the old carceral doorways. There are new lobbies, new light fixtures in the hallways, new recycling rooms and compactors in the basements. Apartments have been outfitted with new bathroom fixtures, windows and kitchen appliances. The new managers, after consulting with tenants about their desires, brought in a GrowNYC farmers market. Staff now patrols the grounds 24/7, with hundreds of security cameras replacing the broken ones.[4]

The renovation was led by a group of developer/managers who have made RAD-style conversions a specialty and, at the time of my own 2023 visit to Baychester, were planning a similar renovation on a much larger scale: that of the Edenwald Houses, which adjoins Baychester but is far larger, comprising forty towers and some two thousand apartments. (Ironically, the task of the developers in renovating Edenwald, one of the largest public housing projects in the US, is complicated by the fact that it has been designated as a historic landmark; its dangerous brick façades must be preserved at significant cost, rather than being waterproofed by being "reclad," enveloped in a sort of exterior raincoat.)[5]

"Is this the way to save public housing?" the architecture critic Michael Kimmelman asks, rhetorically, about Baychester.[6] But beneath its well-kept surface, the complexities of the projects persist. "The daily operations are very technically challenging," says Joseph Ramlall, the head property manager at Baychester. He has built a career in public housing, starting out "sweeping floors" at the troubled Marcus Garvey Houses, a "defensible space" experiment that failed, its architect-designed "mews" having become gang havens because of their lack of outside visibility, he notes.

Ramlall regularly leads tours at Baychester and is proud of the physical change he helped lead, taking me through a "model unit," comparable to any private apartment, with up-to-date appliances and spiffy kitchen countertops. But he is candid, as is the tenant representative Sandy Gross, in saying that there are times that he feels that his role as property manager is akin to "law enforcement." He and Gross underscore the fact that the New York City Housing Authority continues to own Baychester—and to choose its tenants. A lumbering bureaucracy can leave up to thirty units vacant, as new tenancies await approval. Even more problematic, however, is the question of possible evictions.

Ramlall tells the story of a tenant plagued by mental illness who would "call 911 every five minutes. The police would respond to what he said was an emergency and break down doors." There are enough tenants with such problems that Ramlall's management firm contracts with a private social service provider; he understands himself to be in social work, as well as in the housing business, in other words. He is plagued, as well, by teenage tenants who keep back doors to the building open so that friends from elsewhere can freely enter, rather than going through the up-to-date lobby intercom systems. These residents, he points out, are those who had lived in Baychester prior to its renovation; some retain what he delicately calls a project psychology, still throwing trash out windows, along with breaking down doors. Ramlall and Sandy Gross work to stage events—such as a summer Family Day—to create, artificially, through the initiative of management a sense of community that the social clubs, churches, and even taverns of "slums" once did. One must wonder, moreover, whether the type of deeply committed management staff overseeing Baychester will be followed by others who are as motivated. New York City public housing was once, after all, broadly described as public housing that worked.

There is no doubt that, as this is written, the new Baychester is better than the old or that a renovated Edenwald Houses will be better, as well. But no elected official, whether Franklin Roosevelt or New York Mayor Fiorello LaGuardia, ever cut a ribbon or switched on the lights at a public housing project with the expectation that it would deteriorate to the point of needing costly, subsidized repairs. The Baychester renovation cost some $100,000 per apartment, notes L&M Partners cofounder Ron Moelis, in a conversation we had as we toured Baychester; he expects a similar renovation at another New York project, the Harlem River Houses, to cost $250,000 per unit—for apartments of just six hundred square feet. This at a time when the median home value in New York was $411,000 for homes of a median size of 1,556 square feet.[7] In other words, the cost of renovating a Harlem River House apartment is higher, on a per square foot basis ($416), than the cost of buying a home ($273). Renovation costs that high for those who live in specific projects again raise the question that Richard Nixon raised, whether, in the name of saving any one public housing project, benefits are flowing to a "favored few"—absent the sort of massive, new public housing projects that the original Museum of Modern Art housing exhibition envisioned.

But apart from initial cost, there remains the question of upkeep. Moelis notes the key: there must be enough revenue to provide for capital repairs as they inevitably become needed. Should revenue lag for any reason, the same downward trajectory that has plagued public housing for decades will be repeated; tenant rents are, by definition, inadequate. The essential idea of the projects is to provide tenants a "better" home than their incomes permit them to afford.

If the point is to save any individual project, at least for a time, Baychester and others like it must be deemed to be successes. But the projects, of course, were meant to be slum substitutes, not to become slums themselves that demanded their own replacement. With the projects now only tenuously connected to the original vision of their purpose, saving them has become an end in itself.

Craven Terrace and Trent Court, New Bern, North Carolina

The picturesque small city of New Bern on North Carolina's east coast might seem an unlikely place to find any public housing at all, let alone a public housing controversy. Yet hidden from the sight of tourists who come to see historic nineteenth-century homes and the imposing brick onetime seat of colonial British government are two sprawling low-rise brick projects; Trent Court (108 apartments) and Craven Terrace (361 units in forty-six buildings) date to the earliest days of public housing in 1942. In a city with a history of race relations both sordid and dramatic, the projects are, local officials both concede and lament, islands of concentrated Black poverty. Both their past and future stoke emotion.

The New Bern projects, it is important to note, are far from atypical in the South. Notwithstanding the indelible link in the public imagination between the image of the urban high-rise and public housing, both the big cities and small towns of the South saw their construction from the program's earliest days. In North Carolina, there are 124 local public housing authorities; in Alabama, 145; in Mississippi, 54. Small towns from West Point, Mississippi, to Gadsden, Alabama, to Mount Airy, North Carolina, all have their own housing authorities, overwhelmingly housing poor African Americans (78 percent in North Carolina; 87 percent in Mississippi; 69 percent in Alabama).[8] Recall that it was a Deep South congressman, Henry Steagall of Alabama, who cosponsored the crucial National Housing Act of 1937; it was Atlanta where Franklin Roosevelt himself spoke at the opening of the city's first project.

The question of why local officials in the Jim Crow South would have embraced public housing sparked animated discussion and debate on my visit in the late spring of 2023 to New Bern, where I spoke with local officials and residents, Black and white, from families rooted for generations in the onetime state capital. Their reflections quickly linked the two public housing projects—both designated as historic landmarks today—to early motives that can alternately be described as benevolent or paternalistic, public-spirited or self-interested, but without doubt, connected to and helping to perpetuate Jim Crow and racial segregation.

To understand the New Bern projects, I spoke with three New Bern residents whose roots in the city date back for many generations: the local historian Nelson McDaniel, white; the longtime city Land and

Community Development administrator Bernard George, Black; and Carol Becton of the city's African American Historical Association, Black. All agreed that to understand the full context of New Bern (and southern) public housing, one must actually go back to the post–Civil War nineteenth century and how an outpost of prosperous Black artisans, entrepreneurs, and institutions, including many the descendants of freed slaves, was transmuted into a birthplace for white supremacy. It is a story all its own, beyond this narrative but related to it. As historians writing for the New Bern Historic Preservation Commission have put it, "the state's largest concentration of free blacks [included] skilled . . . artisans [who] crafted the community's buildings, wharves and ships. . . . Black doctors, lawyers, businessmen and religious leaders influenced life. . . . The 1893 city directory counted some fifty black enterprises," including the state's first Black-owned bank.[9]

Such economic success was reflected in politics, as well. The Reconstruction era had led to the election of Black officials across North Carolina, especially including its eastern shore and the so-called Black Second (congressional district), which elected, thanks to a "fusion" ticket that appealed to Blacks and white populists, a series of Black Republicans, including George Wilson White, who, in 1898, defeated a white Democratic challenger, a former member of Congress, Furnifold Simmons.[10] Simmons warned whites of "Negro domination," as echoed by the state's major newspaper, the *Raleigh News and Observer*, which warned of "Black men running mad" in New Bern and "Negroes on top: in Craven County, the white men are not in it." Simmons proclaimed himself the "Chieftain of White Supremacy," moving to divide the interracial populist vote (which had supported improved public education and color-coded ballots to help the less-educated vote. He denounced "whites who vote for Negroes" and began a campaign, venal and successful, to strip Blacks of the vote. State constitutional amendments in 1900 disenfranchised Blacks through literacy tests and "grandfather clauses," denying the vote to those whose grandfathers had not had the right.[11] At the time of the Disenfranchisement

Amendment to the state constitution, no less than 65 percent of New Bern's population was African American.

Some four decades on, the advent New Bern's public housing in 1942 would be another chapter in the city's Jim Crow story, one of residential racial segregation. "The notion of a 'black neighborhood' or 'white neighborhood' is a relatively new thing in New Bern's long history. For the century and a half prior to the Civil War, slaves scattered like salt-and-pepper throughout town on the property of their masters. Many free blacks also lived in town, . . . [and] the habit of intermingling persisted for some years after the Civil War, even on important avenues in the heart of the city."[12]

Nelson McDaniel recalled in our interview that the working-class neighborhoods of Long Wharf, much of it providing housing for sawmill workers near the Neuse River waterfront, was racially mixed. Indeed, census records from 1920 show that, in the city's Ward 4, whites and Blacks were neighbors; the white bookbinder William Lausche lived immediately next door to Emily Porells, a Black seamstress, and her husband, Noah (not working at age seventy-three), who, in turn, lived adjacent to John Satchwell, a carpenter listed by the census as "mulatto." On neighboring Emid Street, Charlotte Lawrence, a Black cook, and her husband, James, a beer delivery "drayman," lived next door the white Water and Light plant engineer Walter Perry, whose other neighbor was the Black foundry worker Tom Middleton. Notably, of nine households on the Pollock Street section of the census district, the two white families were renters; all seven Black households owned their own homes.[13]

Public housing would help put an end to this sort of working-class racial integration in New Bern. Long Wharf would be cleared for Trent Courts, reserved for whites. McDaniel remembered, "Where Trent Court was built was a mixed-race neighborhood and had been for at least a hundred years, an area called Long Wharf. It was primarily working-class white and Black families. Many of them [were] employed originally as workers along the river, but then in the lumber mills. And they tore that down. And that was a mixed-race working-class neighborhood.

And that was all wiped out. Most of that area was wiped out in order to create public housing for whites. And then the public housing for Blacks followed after that." At the same time, parts of the Duffyfields neighborhood would be cleared for Craven Terrace, reserved for Blacks. For McDaniel, it is another part of a story of a heartbreaking "lost opportunity" for a nonracialist New Bern that flowered briefly and was lost.

McDaniel, however, is also quick to emphasize the complexities that lay behind the coming of public housing to New Bern and what it replaced. "There were dirt streets, very small, lofts, very small houses, some owned by the people who occupied them, some rentals that were owned by white families and Black families who rented to them. But you also had middle-class housing, primarily Black. Adds Bernard George, "In the area where Craven Terrace was built, there were many homes that were taken in that area. And there was a church there."

Carol Becton tells of the sort of strong, local Black culture in the area adjacent to or cleared for the Craven Terrace project, reserved for Blacks. "I was born in a house on Bloomfield Street. You can look from Bloomfield Street to Craven Terrace. My grandmother's house, like I said, is directly in front of Craven Terrace in that Black community, had about four churches, St. Steven Star Zion, Mount Cavalry, that's another one, West Street that were community. And we had that strong culture established there." There were Black owners of modest homes cleared for the projects, but there were, as well, shanty-like homes occupied by Blacks but owned by prominent New Bern whites, who collected weekly cash rents. Bernard George and Carol Becton, whose families lived there, recall dirt streets visited by agents for white owners in horse-drawn carts. Says George, "Some of them were so poor they needed to be knocked down: . . . clapboard houses, no paint, sitting up on blocks of hard pine as foundation pillars." Indeed, notes McDaniel, some New Bern whites opposed the projects as a threat to such income.

Such views did not prevail, however, in part, reflects McDaniel, because white racism was laced with paternalism and because of the white conceit that Blacks, notwithstanding their supposed inferiority, were well taken care of—and thus should be housed in what were, for 1942, modern brick homes a step up from shanties.

Observes Nelson McDaniel, "You have many white supremacists who may feel that they're being benevolent, which is the most [insidious] part about white supremacy. I mean, that's the scary underside is that they're not necessarily people who are trying to hurt their Black people. They may be trying to help their Black people, but they're still *their* Black people."

Architecturally, Craven Terrace was indistinguishable—separate but equal—from Trent Courts, although the white project was in a far more central locale, proximate to the downtown stores at which Blacks were not permitted to shop. Even more subtle white motives may have been in play. Tiffany Ortiz, the executive director of the New Bern Housing Authority in 2023—and a native of Rome, Georgia, where, she recalls, there was the "colored folks project"—speculates that southern whites may have seen the projects as a means to retain their Black population, even as the Great Migration to the North was under way. Indeed, New Bern Blacks had been fleeing the city for decades, notably since catastrophic fire in 1922 had destroyed large sections of the Black community, including areas on which public housing would later be built. Says Ortiz, "Maybe they wanted to make sure they'd have the maids and gardeners they needed." At the same, time, adds Nelson McDaniel, as the Depression lingered across the South, federal funding—a novel source of revenue for the most impoverished section of the US—translated into fees for local white lawyers, bankers, and construction contractors.

Formal race segregation may have characterized and distinguished southern public housing. But its trajectory from a golden age for the working class, remembered with nostalgia by the onetime Craven Terrace resident Carol Becton, to a reservation-like concentration of poverty and dependency follows the same path as big-city projects. "I lived in Craven Terrace. My parents moved to Craven Terrace. I guess maybe I was born in '52. I'm going to say maybe they moved there about '54.

But our house was well furnished. I know we ate. Craven Terrace was beautiful. It was neat. It was well-kept when it first opened up."

But as in New York and Chicago, Becton's family, and other working-class families, moved up and out of the projects, which, over time, became home to the Black poor—both at Craven and Trent—and fell into physical decline. As elsewhere, there is no doubt that New Bern's public housing has become a concentration of Black poverty in a city attracting both tourists and new residents. As per the latest data available at this writing, Trent Court and Craven Terrace were 97 percent Black in a city in which just a third of the population is African American; residents had lived in the projects an average of seven years; only 1 percent of households were two-parent families, while 44 percent were supported by public assistance.[14]

Just as the great fire of 1922 sparked dramatic change in the city, so did Hurricane Florence in 2018 do so for the city's public housing. Catastrophic hurricane-driven flooding ruined thirteen of Trent Court's buildings, sparking the need for New Bern to decide what it should do next with its projects.

Thus, an idea that was spawned in a combination of idealism and racism has left New Bern with decisions that remain fraught. At the time of my visit in 2023, debate simmered between the Housing Authority's director and a member of its board, Sabrina Bruegel, and New Bern's mayor, Jeffrey Odom. The key question was whether Trent Court should be rebuilt, albeit in a nonflood zone, with the same number of apartments for people of lowest income, as envisioned by the authority director or whether it should become, like an increasing number of project sites, a mixed-income development. The fact that Trent Court stands on a site overlooking the river for which it is named and could well attract high-paying residents, note Odom and Bruegel, makes the latter option plausible. Indeed, outright demolition, clearance, and repurposing of the site to a tax-producing higher and better use could even make sense, but the mayor is quick to say that such an option would be politically impossible. He has inherited real estate frozen in its use as housing, whether he likes it or not. Rebuilding the project as housing one way or another, however, is by far the most likely path for Trent Court—and at significant expense. The Federal Emergency Management Agency has indicated its willingness to provide $40 million for the purpose. Redevelopment may be funded as well by special tax credits for historic buildings—Trent Court, like Craven Terrace, is on the National Register of Historic Places as a landmark.

Like hundreds of other public housing authorities, New Bern could, to be sure, also choose the path of the Rental Assistance Demonstration program; RAD makes possible the advent of privately financed project restoration and subsequent management. Indeed, the New Bern Housing Authority has already used that vehicle to restore Craven Terrace, where the combination of housing voucher and historic tax credit revenues enabled restoration at a cost of $80,000 per apartment. City officials, however, have soured on the choice. A tour of Craven Terrace with the mayor finds him concerned about its overgrown grounds. He acknowledges, however, that the private firm, Preservation Management Corporation, that manages similar projects across the country faces a difficult challenge. It was forced to remove screen doors across the complex when tenants chose to keep inside glass doors open even as they ran air-conditioners. Like public housing tenants everywhere, they are not charged with paying their own utility bills. RAD, its promise in New York notwithstanding, has not turned out to be a silver bullet.

Nor has physical restoration proven to be an adequate path to a safe and sound community. Gangs and drugs are so common at Craven that the management has had to install a camera portal directly linked to the New Bern police. Such issues, as well as tax incentives that expire over time, prompt concern among New Bern officials that Craven Terrace may revert to the management of the New Bern Housing Authority.

As in Pittsburgh, Detroit, and St. Louis, public housing in this small southern town played a role in the demise of a thriving local Black community, which was also characterized by profoundly substandard housing. Judged sheerly on a physical basis, the advent of Craven Terrace and

Trend Court may have made sense. Over time, though, they have proven to be a solution that spawned a problem, one that continues to vex New Bern, North Carolina. No one locale can be fully representative, but there is no doubt that the New Bern public housing story is revealing.

In Carol Becton's view, "the federal government was trying to honestly provide better housing for people at an affordable price." At the same time, notes Bernard George, it helped perpetuate—indeed, even establish—racial segregation. "Public housing allows you to house people, but it's no threat to that status quo."

San Bernardino, California

The contrast between the public housing of San Bernardino, California, and the image of the big-city high-rise project could not be starker. As is often the case in the West, the buildings of the county Housing Authority are small, individual homes, single-family or duplex, built on concrete foundations and featuring their own yards and gardens, often located on wide streets lined with palm trees. With some eleven thousand units—either owned or leased—its high-desert, Inland Empire public housing portfolio is just 4 percent the size of New York City's.

The authority has adopted virtually all the innovations that have emerged in the nation's public housing system: private management through the Rental Assistance Demonstration program; demolition of older projects and their replacement with "mixed-income" developments aimed at "deconcentrating" poverty. But its most distinguishing feature, in place since 2012, is one that has moved it the greatest distance from the original public housing vision, which began as housing for the employed working class. In contrast, San Bernardino has embraced a different role—that of assisting people of lowest income in building or rebuilding their lives—and to do so with a stick, as well as carrots. In contrast to the lifetime subsidy that comes with public or assisted housing generally, new tenants here face a five-year "term limit." By comparison, the median stay in New York City public housing is twenty years.

What might look to be a draconian regulation, explains the authority's Nicole Beydler, was adopted for what officials saw in purely practical terms: housing assistance is limited, and waiting lists are long. "The only way for a new family from the waiting list to be served is for an existing family who's already receiving assistance to leave the program to open up that slot for the next person on the waiting list to have a shot.... Our goal was actually to help families who do receive their shot to use that as a stepping-stone ... so that when they eventually left affordable housing at the end of that time period, they would be more successful without housing assistance."

But what the authority's commissioners viewed as simple common sense has led to greater change: a new social work division of the Housing Authority aimed at helping new tenants adopt an attitude of self-improvement and to learn skills that enable them to rise. The term limit rule often comes as a shock to new tenants, says Kristan Alferez, the system's lead self-sufficiency specialist. "There are some that say, 'What's happening? What do I do?'"

Case workers assigned to tenants must, she says, convince new tenants that they can succeed. Her typical "customer," as she puts it, is a single mother of two to three children, in her early twenties, who has either never worked or worked sporadically at an Amazon warehouse or as a home health aide. Before getting her own housing voucher, she has "usually lived with Mom or Grandma." Employed, two-parent households, typical residents of public housing when it began in the 1930s, would probably not even qualify for admittance to San Bernardino or others of the thirty-two hundred US housing authorities today; they would be disqualified by incomes that would be too high. Nationally, households of two adults and children make up just 3 percent of public housing.[15]

Notably, in a county whose population is 9 percent Black, Alferez says that she most often sees young African American single parents. Observes Alferez, "It's possibly just generational. It's just that's what Mom did, that's what Grandma did. That's what they've seen. So they get on the wait list because they know how to apply. They know where to apply. And so they do. And that feels very normalized to them."

It is worth recalling that public housing projects nationwide were often built on the sites of Black neighborhoods, like Pittsburgh's Hill or Detroit's Black Bottom, which, though labeled as slums, were replete with mutual-aid institutions and owner-occupied small homes. It is hard to avoid the conclusion that the combination of urban renewal, public housing, and its policy progeny swept away once independent and self-reliant African American neighborhoods across the US, leaving behind a culture of dependency, which then requires social workers to provide help.

That need is dismaying, but at the same time, San Bernardino is showing positive results. The authority has retained nearby Loma Linda University to track the incomes of those who are subject to the term limit. (It applies only to the "career capable," not to the elderly and disabled who make up many of those it houses.) Its research shows an average increase in income of 145 percent between the first and last year of help and that residents probably move out before the five-year limit. Alferez tells stories of single mothers who have become truck drivers or welders, "making a ton of money." Some have even been able to buy their own homes, in part because their housing assistance continues, albeit at a lower level, as mortgage payment aid.

San Bernardino's success has attracted the attention of housing authorities from across the country, but only a handful would be able to adopt its approach if they chose to do so. It is one of a just a small number (thirty-nine) of so-called Moving to Work housing authorities, a Clinton administration initiative that allows San Bernardino to adopt its term limit, as well as a less-frequent "recertification" of income. The latter means that, in contrast to the typical public housing tenant, a Moving to Work resident's rent (set at 30 percent of income) will not go immediately go up when they earn more at work. In 2022, an additional one hundred Moving to Work housing authorities were authorized by HUD, but these lack San Bernardino's flexibility and must focus on a specific policy research goal.

Public housing began, as part of the New Deal, to house the working class. San Bernardino is showing that, nearly a century later, under the right conditions, it can help create one.

The Karl-Marx-Hof, Vienna, Austria

The organizers and authors of the Museum of Modern Art's housing exhibit of 1934 did not, surprisingly, mention what was then—and remains—the city of Vienna's Karl-Marx-Hof complex, which stretches three-quarters of a mile, spanning four stations on its subway line; it is considered the longest residential structure in the world, comprising more than twelve hundred apartments arrayed in a striking series of early modernist version of a medieval fortress, rendered in brick and stucco. Arrayed in the garden city style—with extensive open green space—it includes amenities ranging from laundry rooms to swimming pools, built on what was called, in a reference to Vienna's famous Ringstrasse of palaces and mansions, the "Ringstrasse for the proletariat." Its architecture is such that the complex is included among UNESCO World Heritage Sites. Built between 1927 and 1930, during the so-called Red Vienna period, the complex was so closely associated with socialist policy that it became a literal battleground between fascist and socialist armed groups in the 1934 Austrian civil war.[16]

In contrast to so many early US public housing projects, however, Karl-Marx-Hof not only still stands but remains, to this visitor's eyes, in good condition, providing small but clean apartments for a population of some five thousand, a mix of Austrian citizens and immigrants, the latter estimated by the city's mayor's office at 50 percent of the population.[17] To the extent that European precedents provided models for US promoters of slum clearance and replacement projects, Karl-Marx-Hof suggests the question, How has Vienna maintained public housing that works?

FIGURE 9.2. Karl-Marx-Hof, Vienna. (Ralph Deakin, RIBA Collections)

A close examination of its financing and residency rules is telling; they track in many ways those of the US public housing golden age. Notably, although set in a green space and built at a low density, Karl-Marx-Hof is not a high-rise, tower in the park. The six-story buildings each have their own lobby entrance, and most of the apartments have their own balconies.[18] If high-rises are inherently problematic—and, of course, many high-rise apartments continue to be built and attract tenants—Karl-Marx-Hof avoided that problem.

Notably, rents are set such that they are "sufficient to cover the operating costs and the costs of daily maintenance," says Christian Schantl of the city of Vienna's international relations division, who replied to inquiries to the city's deputy mayor.[19] Toward that end, households from a wide range of income levels, not just the poorest, are admitted to the complex. "We always try to offer apartments so that we can be quite sure that the prospective [tenant] will be able to afford the rent," says Schantl. Indeed, households earning more than €100,000 annually for a family of four can qualify for residency. "The relatively high income limits—75 percent of the Viennese population earn less—provide, that the 'middle class' also gets access to Vienna's subsidized housing stock."[20] This does not mean, however, that all potential residents qualify for similar apartments. Those with lower incomes, notes Schantl, are offered "less well-equipped apartments." Nonpayment of rent is grounds for eviction.

Moreover, rents are fixed; should incomes increase, the rent stays the same, in contrast to being linked to a percentage of income. "We control the income situation only when people apply for an apartment. So we do not know what our tenants earn afterwards," says Schantl.

Crucially, the city of Vienna has invested and continues to invest heavily in capital improvements to Karl-Marx-Hof. "The city of Vienna invests each year more than 350 million Euros in housing construction and the restoration of new buildings. . . . A complete retrofitting of the building with the installation of new elevators, new roofs, new windows would not be possible without subsidies of the city of Vienna," says Schantl, Indeed, he adds, just such investments have been made, including some meant to enlarge the units (some of which lacked private baths), in order to reflect current tenant preferences, as might a private real estate developer: "A base renovation was performed in the Karl-Marx-Hof in the years 1986 to 1992. Very small apartments were combined: windows, doors, and water lines were renewed, and fifty new elevators installed." That was followed by "another general renovation in the years from 2006 to 2015," with an eye toward the projects' historical significance, "under the artistic supervision of BWM Arhcitecten," a private firm. "As a result, architectural details and surfaces formerly ignored were analyzed and became an important part of the restoration."

There is much here on which to reflect for US public housing authorities. Vienna's middle class, notably, is willing to live in a public housing complex, and the city is willing to subsidize not only the poor but those who are significantly better off. It is worth noting that, in contrast to the Jackson Houses, tenants are said to be quite willing to criticize those who might drop garbage on the grounds. Nor is upward mobility—as reflected by increased household income—punished by higher rents tied to a percentage of income. That, along with the fact that a family of four may earn more than €100,000 and still be admitted as new tenants, helps ensure the rent revenue needed to operate Karl-Marx-Hof; it also means that a select group of the relatively affluent are subsidized, via both low rents and extensive public capital investments. So, too, does it reflect the fact that Austria is a small country with only one major city; Vienna, unlike US cities, is not surrounded by newer suburbs filled with small owner-occupied homes. Housing choices outside the main city are limited, as they are in Singapore, where government-built housing remains the norm, albeit with private apartment ownership. Thus, in Vienna, an older public housing complex, adjacent to mass transit and a major sports stadium, remains a desirable place to live (although the waiting list is just one and a half years).

So it is that public housing can, indeed, "work"—in an affluent nation willing to make significant ongoing investments in repairs and major renovations so as to ensure a reliable stream of relatively well-off, employed residents making regular rent payments. For the US and, for that matter, developing nations, the Vienna experience raises the question of not whether public housing can work, under specific conditions, but whether it should continue to serve as a guide to future housing policy.

10

Making Sense of the Projects

Looking Back and Ahead

The images of public housing—its high-rises and its superblocks—remain clear in the public mind. But the physical projects themselves have been gradually disappearing. In 1989, there were some 1.3 million public housing units in the US; as this is written, the total is estimated at less than nine hundred thousand. At the same time, the policy legacies of the projects remain with us, especially its central ideas, that private housing markets fail the poor, that housing is a special kind of good, as much a right as a product. From Catherine Bauer to Harry Truman to Richard Nixon to Matthew Desmond, that common thread can be followed.

In this chapter, I both try to take stock and offer recommendations.

We face choices: about the terms of receiving housing assistance, about where assisted housing should be located, about whether and how to renovate projects or to build new types. For this author, this can be viewed as a discussion about assisted housing as a latter-day poorhouse: how it should be run, what its goals should be.

But, in light of the complications and outright failures of nearly a century of projects, it is worth engaging the question of whether the ongoing, multibillion-dollar government involvement in providing or supporting housing for people of lower incomes should be revisited entirely, with fresh eyes.

In any retrospective of the projects and their progeny, it must be said that, at any given time, they have offered, as per their original legislative charge, "safe and sanitary" housing, which, by objective, physical criteria was better than what their tenants could have otherwise afforded. For poor Black southerners who had lived in literal shacks without indoor plumbing, the hundreds of projects scattered across small towns served as an upgrade in sheer shelter.

So, too, for those urban dwellers who may have had to share bathrooms with neighbors or whose apartments had limited light and air. It is ironic that, as this is written, similar upgrades are being provided for those who have lived not in shacks or slums but in the projects themselves. Nonetheless, if the goal of the National Housing Act is narrowly viewed as an initiative to provide better physical accommodations for people the government has served, its record can only be regarded as mixed: as one of providing such accommodations in some places and at some times but failing to do so at others, sometimes dramatically. Those failures can be seen as inherent in the idea of government ownership and management—as this author is inclined to do—or as evidence of a failure of Washington to provide, reliably over time, funds adequate to maintain and repair or replace the projects.

But it is also important to evaluate the record of the projects in relation to what is called "social policy," the ways in which it has affected the lives of people of very modest means who have come to be the dominant group of project and housing voucher residents. Recall that such was not the intent of those who organized the Museum of Modern Art housing exhibit in 1934; those acolytes of modern housing saw the projects as a new type of housing for working-class and even lower-middle-class tenants, for a large proportion of the population they believed were being ill served by private housing development. What is more, the project of the projects went well beyond housing toward the goal of a new type of city altogether—one "without streets" but of "campuses" set aside, of "towers in the park." As the US grew far more affluent after World War II, this vision proved unappealing to those with the means to choose, as single-family suburban homes proved far more attractive, even for New Yorkers long accustomed to apartment living. The projects gradually became magnets for the very poorest households, including single-parent families and the low-income elderly.

It is difficult, perhaps impossible, to determine with any precision whether the fact that making low-cost apartments available specifically to people of the lowest incomes played a role in encouraging the formation of such households in the first place. But once public housing rents were legally tied to one's income—through the Brooke Amendment, a key turning point in project history—it can be said with certainty that those households whose income might increase, whether through a better job or through marriage, adding an additional earner, were discouraged from doing either or both.

Put another way, as the projects and their progeny became the province of the poor, the terms on which their assistance have been provided have mattered more and more. The US, at this writing, devotes as much of the federal budget to housing voucher assistance ($30 billion) as it does to so-called cash welfare, a program known as Temporary Assistance to Needy Families. Yet the latter program comes with notable conditions: including a requirement that recipients be employed or in school and that assistance be limited to five years. This author is inclined to believe that both programs should be aligned, through similar conditions.

Thus, as the legacy of the projects is considered, one must ask whether the goals of housing assistance should, like cash assistance, go beyond sheer shelter and toward the encouragement of life-changing decisions that lead to upward mobility. For those who take a dim view of the US economy and believe that it will always leave behind a substantial proportion of the population who simply must not be left to live on the streets or in crowded quarters, concern about "dependency" wrought through housing assistance will seem misplaced. But the experiences of both the Atlanta and San Bernardino, California, housing authorities suggest that linking assistance to work—whether directly through a mandate or indirectly through a time limit—can encourage upward mobility from poverty to the working class. As this is written, the number of US housing authorities granted the flexibility to adopt such requirements has been significantly increased—from 37 to 126—and thus the chance to test such ideas more widely presents itself. It is true that the ideas of relocating the poor to so-called high opportunity neighborhoods or mixed-income replacement projects also seek to encourage upward mobility. By comparison, however, they are far less easy to evaluate with certainty because of the many complicating factors involved in a move to a new neighborhood.

The idea of the projects and their progeny serving as a form of temporary assistance makes even more sense in the context of the new generation of financial investments in the renovation, demolition, or replacement of an earlier generation of projects, as is happening through the Rental Assistance Demonstration program's mix of government incentives and drawing billions in private investment to project sites. Richard Nixon's observation that physical housing accommodations, provided by government, led to a program serving a "favored few" remains true. If one accepts the idea that households should pay no more than 30 percent of income for housing, far more Americans qualify for assistance than receive it. It can well be argued that the number receiving such assistance should be vastly increased. But such arguments have long failed to carry the day in Congress. It can, then, just as well—or more practically—be argued that a "transitional" form of housing assistance would make it possible to serve more households now languishing on waiting lists—and, more important, encourage work and resulting upward mobility. It is important to face squarely the probability that favoring people of lowest incomes in distributing housing assistance risks encouraging the formation of single-parent households, which are typically high poverty and whose children face statistically poor life prospects. Making housing assistance transitional—changing the terms of the de facto poorhouse that the projects have become—is a logical response. Imaginably, residents could even go from being tenants in HOPE VI affordable units to market-rate tenants in the same developments.

The logical rejoinder, to be sure, is concern as to what will become of households once their term of assistance runs out. Some may face hard choices, without doubt. But specific housing requirements—a bedroom for each child, a home for every parent, spending limited to 30 percent of income—suppress the range of choices available to those who are being assisted. We cannot and should not rule out the possibility that poorer households might prefer to "double up" to save for goals other than one's own apartment, that it might be desirable in many ways for people of modest means to pay their housing costs in an old-fashioned way: taking in lodgers or sharing bathrooms. Of course, this was once known as the "lodger evil" because of its potential for crowding or even introducing undesirables into a household. But it does potentially offer financial help to struggling households and is not currently an option in subsidized housing or even private homes in many municipalities.

Across the US, local laws limit the number of "unrelated persons" who may share quarters.[1] Yet such restrictions limit the elderly from taking in those who might help with chores and limit the poor from paying rent or even a mortgage by renting rooms. Children could benefit from the guidance provided by community members. Could overcrowding result? Perhaps. But in the projects as they work in practice today, many of the poor have gone from being overcrowded to "undercrowded" or "overhoused," in the jargon of HUD. Owing to the lack of a ceiling on "length of stay" in assisted housing, there are many subsidized tenants who no longer need apartments as large as those in which they live. The New York City Housing Authority has a multiyear waiting list, but nearly a third of its tenants live in units with empty bedrooms.

If the "length of stay" of tenants in assisted housing might be limited, it is also well worth revisiting the idea that the sites of projects themselves should continue to be the sites for assisted housing of one sort or another, in perpetuity. This should not be set in stone, as it were. In contrast to the views of Le Corbusier and the modern housing movement, vibrant cities put new uses to old sites all the time. A residential zone might be replaced by a commercial one: an apartment complex leveled for a laboratory. This has, in practice, begun to happen to public housing. In Newark, New Jersey—once known as "brick city" for its many brick-built projects—a film studio soundstage project is, as of this writing, scheduled to be built on the fifteen-acre former site of the Seth Boyden Terrace, built in 1939 and demolished in 2022. The city, notably, did not replace the 530 apartments that once stood on the site, instead permitting an entirely new use that is expected to attract investment and provide jobs.[2]

So, too, might remaining "superblocks"—still found particularly in their birthplace, New York City, in large numbers—be knitted into the surrounding neighborhood through the simple expedient of what might be called "restreeting," cutting new streets through the open, often crime-ridden courtyards. With these new streets would come new street corners and new streetscapes, potential sites for stores, homes, or, ideally, not what is designated by planners but whatever someone proposes to build. Should the new homes be designated as "affordable" for those who might qualify to live in the projects? Politically that might be necessary, but from the perspective of those who believe in living cities, it would seem to be appropriately an open question.

The question of what might replace the projects would be politically vexing, just as their original siting was a lightning rod for controversy. It is worth remembering that the dilemmas posed by such realities—and they are dilemmas—are only distant relations to the original vision of modern housing that fired up the advocates of the National Housing Act of 1937. But there is an important thread common to the projects and all the variations that they have spawned. From slum clearance to mixed-income development, from "towers in the park" to "moving to opportunity," urban renewal to defensible space, policy has been driven by expert views rather than the expressed views of people of low income themselves. Indeed, as we saw in the case of Pittsburgh's Hill District, those views were ignored. The onetime residents of the Hill, and of Detroit's Black Bottom and Brookline's Farm, continue to mourn their demolition, generations after the bulldozers.

That they do serves to impart a key and overlooked aspect of the projects and their ongoing variations. All view housing as shelter alone, rather than in the larger and crucial context of community. The slums cleared by Robert Moses were, no doubt, cramped and crowded. But they teemed with life: with apartments above stores, with churches and synagogues and newspapers and barber shops. They buzzed with what we call civil society: the social clubs and charitable groups born through the efforts of residents and neighbors. To view housing strictly in relation to income and bedrooms is a tragically blinkered approach that ignores a key idea: poor neighborhoods can be good neighborhoods (safe and clean, notably), and their replacements will not inevitably be better, especially for those who are uprooted.

No writer has ever reflected more deeply or cogently on the upheaval unleashed by slum clearance than Jane Jacobs, in *The Death and Life of Great American Cities*. Often viewed narrowly as a proponent of historic building preservation or an opponent of highways, Jacobs is far, far more: the sharpest critic of the projects at the very time they were being erected. Her underappreciated critiques deserve to be revisited at length, for their prescience and relevance to the topics of this book.

"It is fashionable to suppose that certain touchstones of the good life will create good neighborhoods—schools, parks, clean housing and the like. How easy life would be if this were so! How charming to control a complicated and ornery society by bestowing upon it rather simple physical goodies. In real life, cause and effect are not so simple." Jacobs cites a Pittsburgh study that, when comparing youth crime in a "slum" and its replacement, found crime to be higher in the "new housing projects." "Does this mean," she asked, "improved shelter increases delinquency? Not at all. It means other things may be more important than housing, however, and it also means that there is no direct relationship between good housing and good behavior, a fact which the whole tale of the Western world's history, the whole collection of our literature, and the whole fund of observation open to us has long since made evident. Good shelter is a useful good in itself, as shelter. When we try to justify good shelter instead on the pretentious grounds that it will work social or family miracles we fool ourselves."[3] Upgrading existing projects by introducing cross streets, shops, and institutions of civil society—integrating them into their surrounding cities—would probably gain Jacobs' approval.

If there is any sin that is common to the projects and their variations whose story this book has tried to tell, it is that of viewing housing in isolation—and failing to understand that good neighborhoods, that thriving residential communities, are much more than collections of housing. Instead, those who have planned the projects or proposed new versions of them—from Catherine Bauer to Matthew Desmond—have envisioned a long series of artificial communities, engineered for the asserted benefit of people of modest means but proposed and planned at a distance from them.

It is true, to be sure, that there have been many planned communities in the US, from Shaker Heights, Ohio, in the 1920s to Celebration, Florida, in the 1990s. But such communities have been predicated on the belief that they will attract residents, both buyers and tenants, that both will have the opportunity to express their preferences through their purchases or even disdain the communities altogether. The projects have been artificial in quite different ways. Slum clearance led to what amounted to the forcible relocation of low-income households that had lost their homes. Projects and their variations reflect the views of planners—that people of various incomes should be part of the same community, for instance—and incentivize prospective residents by offering low rents. One may well approve of such efforts and still acknowledge that they differ from communities formed and forged through the expressed preferences of residents, voting with their feet, as it is said. In this context, it is worthwhile to reflect on what Daniel Patrick Moynihan's proposed approach to race relations—benign neglect—could mean for people of modest means broadly when it comes to housing.

Much of this book has been devoted to ideas and policies predicated on having learned lessons from the problems of the projects. Might design have been the core problem? Might a concentration of the poor have doomed them? Might an income mix prove to be the antidote to previous ills? Might a support for rent in the private housing market be a better alternative?

To these questions and more, one must add another: Might refraining from intervening in the housing conditions of poor neighborhoods—aka "slums"—be an alternative worth considering? Might a housing equivalent of Moynihan's "benign neglect" be defensible?

In the preceding chapters, I have suggested a key reason that such an idea might not be anathema: that "slums," abhorrent from a distance to those who do not live in them, have historically been beehives of ambition and activity, places in which homes—including small homes in which one floor or even one room may be rented out—are characterized by dispersed ownership, landlords living on-site, small apartments above family-owned shops, and a range of community institutions, from churches to social clubs. In focusing on physical conditions, it is worth asking whether we have made a profound error in overlooking the value of these.

We have swept them away by demolition, to be sure. But it is reasonable to conclude that they have been undermined, as well, by the sheer advent of the projects, drawing tenants from community landlords through the lure of new buildings and cheap rents and better amenities, at least at first. Indeed, we have devalued the relationship between landlord and tenant as a positive aspect of social fabric, a relationship in which the contract between them requires one to provide services (heat and hot water, for instance) and the other to maintain the premises and pay rent, at the risk of eviction.

Housing assistance—whether in the projects or via a housing voucher—changes all of this. The expectation that each family unit of parents and children will have its own housing "unit" excludes the time-honored possibility of taking in lodgers and, more broadly, of extended families that are not viewed pejoratively as being "doubled up." All these relationships may be economic on one level but historically have helped to knit neighborhoods together, to create reasons for residents to know each other and rely on each other.

Put another way, one lesson of the projects can be that crowding and "substandard" conditions might not be as problematic as anomie and dependency. The modern housers and their legatees may have meant well, but they did not trust people of modest means to strive, to improve their conditions over time, to make choices as to how to spend their income and savings. They would get housing help first.

Robert Wood, the original HUD undersecretary, captured this attitude perfectly: "the tenement trail," readers will recall him saying, "was closed." The contemporary poor are trapped in "ghettoes," and the broader society simply must make them comfortable in their quarters. This is a profound policy pessimism masquerading as idealism.

Appearances to affluent observers aside, it is crucial to keep in mind that poor neighborhoods can be good neighborhoods. Concentrated poverty described the Lower East Side of 1900 and describes the crowded immigrant Asian neighborhoods of contemporary New York City. But their residents have shared ambition and hope, as surely as did those living in Detroit's Black Bottom and Pittsburgh's Hill District. To be sure, they are owed the public services that any healthy neighborhood needs.

FIGURE 10.1. A rendering of the National Public Housing Museum's main entrance. (Designed by Olalekan Jeyifous and Amanda Williams)

Parks, schools, and safe streets may not transform human behavior—per Jane Jacobs—but their importance should never be minimized. They do not create good communities inevitably, but neither, we have learned, do gleaming high-rise towers in the park.

The lessons of the projects are about much more, then, than housing policy. The failures and complications of the projects tell us that the visions of experts may not be wisdom, that the plans and preferences of ordinary citizens must be valued. So often, those choices have shaped great cities and made the world a better place. It is difficult to argue that the projects—launched with such idealism by the modern housing movement—have done the same.

ACKNOWLEDGMENTS

Thanks to Robert Doar of the American Enterprise Institute and Larry Mone of the Manhattan Institute for providing me the institutional homes and support that allowed me to research and write this book. Thanks also to Alex von Hoffman of Harvard's Joint Center for Housing Studies for our many helpful conversations about housing policy and history. Lastly, thanks to Brian Anderson and Paul Beston of *City Journal* and Yuval Levin of *National Affairs* for allowing me to conduct my public housing education in their pages.

NOTES

INTRODUCTION

1. Office of Policy Development and Research, "A Picture of Subsidized Households General Description of the Data and Bibliography," US Department of Housing and Urban Development, accessed October 4, 2024, www.huduser.gov.
2. New York City Housing Authority, "NYCHA 2023 Fact Sheet," April 2023, www.nyc.gov; Nicolas Dagen Bloom, *Public Housing That Worked: New York in the Twentieth Century* (Philadelphia: University of Pennsylvania Press, 2008).
3. New York City Housing Authority, "Monitor's First Quarterly Report," April–June 2019, https://nychamonitor.com.
4. Greg B. Smith, "How Shootings Spiked at NYCHA Complexes Targeted in de Blasio Crime Prevention Campaign," *The City*, January 31, 2021, www.thecity.nyc.
5. Office of Policy Development and Research, "Picture of Subsidized Households."
6. Office of Policy Development and Research.
7. New York City Housing Authority, "NYCHA 2023 Fact Sheet."
8. "Slum Surgery in St. Louis," *Architectural Forum*, April 1951, 128–36.
9. Visiting Vienna, "Karl-Marx-Hof Public Housing," February 5, 2024, www.visitingvienna.com.
10. Aaron Modica, "Robert R. Taylor Homes, Chicago, Illinois (1959–2005)," *Black Past*, December 19, 2009, www.blackpast.org.
11. National Public Housing Museum, "Mind to Grow," transcript, n.d., https://nphm.org.
12. "Human Story at Robert Taylor Homes," *Chicago Tribune*, September 7, 1987, www.chicagotribune.com.
13. New York City Housing Authority, Office of Performance Management and Analytics, Residents' Data Files as of October 1, 2022, provided at request of the author.
14. US Department of Housing and Urban Development, HOPE VI program, accessed October 9, 2024, www.hud.gov.
15. New York City Housing Authority, "About NYCHA," accessed October 4, 2024, www.nyc.gov.
16. Office of Policy Development and Research, "Picture of Subsidized Households."
17. Office of Policy Development and Research.
18. Office of Policy Development and Research, "63 Years of Federal Action in Housing and Urban Development," *Cityscape* (US Department of Housing and Urban Development) 1, no. 3 (September 1995), www.huduser.gov.

19 Harry S. Truman, "Statement by the President upon Signing the Housing Act of 1949," July 15, 1949, Harry S. Truman Library and Museum, www.trumanlibrary.gov.
20 Richard Nixon, "Special Message to the Congress Proposing Legislation and Outlining Administration Actions to Deal with Federal Housing Policy," September 19, 1973, American Presidency Project, www.presidency.ucsb.edu.
21 Christine Ferretti and George Hunter, "Detroit Mayor Cobo's Legacy Remains Divisive," *Detroit News*, October 10, 2017, www.detroitnews.com.
22 Frederick Wiseman, dir., *Public Housing* (Housing Films, 1997). See Bloom, *Public Housing That Worked*; Lawrence Vale, *Reclaiming Public Housing* (Cambridge, MA: Harvard University Press, 2002); Robert J. Chaskin and Mark L. Joseph, *Integrating the Inner City* (Chicago: University of Chicago Press, 2015).

CHAPTER 1. THE BIRTH OF A MOVEMENT
1 Carol Aronovici, foreword to *America Can't Have Housing*, ed. Carol Aronovici (New York: Museum of Modern Art, 1934), 7, www.moma.org.
2 Alfred H. Barr Jr., foreword to *Modern Architecture: International Exhibition, New York, Feb. 10 to March 23, 1932*, ed. Museum of Modern Art (New York: Museum of Modern Art, 1932), 17, www.moma.org.
3 Jake Blumgart, "Most Liveable City: How Vienna Earned Its Place in Housing History," *City Monitor*, June 22, 2023, https://citymonitor.ai.
4 Sarah Bean Apmann, "Landmarks of New York: First Houses," *Off the Grid: Village Preservation Blog*, December 3, 2015, www.villagepreservation.org.
5 Eleanor Roosevelt, "Eleanor Roosevelt Speeches: Speech for the New York City Housing Authority, December 3, 1936," Eleanor Roosevelt Papers Project, George Washington University, www2.gwu.edu.
6 National Association of Housing Officials, *Handbook for Housing Commissioners* (Chicago: National Association of Housing Officials, 1950). Quoted in Martin Meyerson and Edward C. Banfield, *Politics, Planning and the Public Interest: The Case of Public Housing in Chicago* (Glencoe, IL: Free Press, 1955), 19.
7 Richard Pommer, "The Architecture of Urban Housing in the United States in the Early 1930s," *Journal of the Society of Architectural Historians* 37, no. 4 (December 1978): 235.
8 United States v. Certain Lands in City of Louisville, 9 F. Supp. 137, 141, 139 (W.D. Ky. 1935), https://law.justia.com.
9 Joanna Merwood-Salisbury, "Lower East Side Siedlung," *Gotham* (blog), Gotham Center for New York History, September 3, 2015, www.gothamcenter.org. *Siedlung*, German for "settlement," refers to modernist housing in 1930s Berlin.
10 James Dunnett, "Le Corbusier and the City without Streets," in *The Modern City Revisited*, ed. Thomas Deckker (London: Spon, 2000), https://jamesdunnettarchitects.com.
11 Dunnett, 9.

12 "Housing Exhibit Scheduled by City," *New York Times*, October 11, 1934.
13 "Housing Exhibit Scheduled by City."
14 Thirteen PBS, "The Urban Log Cabin," accessed October 8, 2024, www.thirteen.org.
15 Museum of Modern Art, "Slum Flat Reassembled Second Floor," in *Housing Exhibition of the City of New York*, 1934, www.moma.org.
16 Victoria Campbell, "Catherine Bauer Wurster: Hero of American Affordable Housing," Urban Media Lab, February 28, 2021, https://labgov.city.
17 Edith Elmer Wood, "A Century of the Housing Problem," folder 5, box 67, Miscellaneous Papers, Papers of Edith Elmer Wood, Columbia University.
18 Catherine Bauer, *Modern Housing* (Minneapolis: University of Minnesota Press, 2020), 175.
19 Robert D. Kohn, "A National Programme for Housing in the United States," in Aronovici, *America Can't Have Housing*, 11.
20 Lewis Mumford, "The Social Imperatives in Housing," in Aronovici, *America Can't Have Housing*, 18.
21 Gili Merin, "AD Classics: Ville Radieuse / Le Corbusier," *Arch Daily*, August 11, 2013, www.archdaily.com.
22 Howard Husock, *The Poor Side of Town: And Why We Need It* (New York: Encounter Books, 2021), 21.
23 Robert A. Woods and Albert J. Kennedy, *The Zone of Emergence: Observations of the Lower Middle and Upper Working Class Communities of Boston, 1905–1914* (Cambridge, MA: MIT Press, 1969).
24 Edith Elmer, *Housing the Unskilled Wage Earner: America's Next Problem* (New York: Macmillan, 1919), 1.
25 Jacob A. Riis, *How the Other Half Lives: Studies among the Tenements of New York* (New York: Charles Scribner's Sons, 1890), 28.
26 R. L. Duffus, "What Modern Housing Means and Why It Is Delayed," *New York Times*, December 23, 1934, https://timesmachine.nytimes.com.
27 Alexander von Hoffman, "History Lessons for Today's Housing Policy: The Political Processes of Making Low-Income Housing Policy," Joint Center for Housing Studies, Harvard University, August 2012, www.jchs.harvard.edu.
28 Robert H. Bremmer, "The Big Flat: History of a New York Tenement House," RCC Honors History Project, March 15, 2009, https://rcchonorshistory.wordpress.com.
29 "Simkhovitch, Mary Kingsbury," Social Welfare History Project, VCU Libraries, Virginia Commonwealth University, accessed October 7, 2024, http://socialwelfare.library.vcu.edu.
30 "Isaac Newton Phelps Stokes," Wikipedia, accessed October 7, 2024, https://en.wikipedia.org.
31 James Ford, *Slums and Housing: History, Conditions, Policy* (Cambridge, MA: Harvard University Press, 1936), 266.
32 Ford, 267.

33 Ford, 375.
34 Ford, 394.
35 Ford, 414.
36 Ford, 377
37 Ford, 421. He cites a "Professor MacCunn," author of *Making of Character*. This is a reference to the 1900 book by the Oxford professor John MacCunn, *The Making of Character: Some Educational Aspects of Ethics* (London: Macmillan, 1900).
38 Ford, *Slums and Housing*, 611.
39 Ford, 466.
40 Ford, 466.
41 Aronovici, *America Can't Have Housing*, cover.
42 Otto Bartning, Fred Forbat, Walter Gropius, and Hans Scharoun, "Siemensstadt," *Architectuul*, September 20, 2019, https://architectuul.com.
43 Kurt Kohlstedt, "Ville Radieuse: Le Corbusier's Functionalist Plan for a Utopian 'Radiant City,'" *99% Invisible*, February 23, 2018, https://99percentinvisible.org.
44 Frederick Etchells, introduction to *The City of Tomorrow*, by Le Corbusier (Cambridge, MA: MIT Press, 1972), 7. The quotations are Etchells's summaries of Le Corbusier's concepts.
45 Catherine Bauer, "Housing: Paper Plans, or a Workers' Movement," in Aronovici, *America Can't Have Housing*, 21.
46 Walter Gropius, "Minimum Dwellings and Tall Buildings," in Aronovici, *America Can't Have Housing*, 41.
47 Gropius, 42.
48 Werner Hegemann, "Political Economy in German Housing Today," in Aronovici, *America Can't Have Housing*, 44.
49 Hegemann, 47.
50 Gavin Thompson, Oliver Hawkins, Aliyah Dar, and Mark Taylor, "Build It Up, Sell It Off: The Rise and Fall of Social Housing," in *Olympic Britain: Social and Economic Change since the 1908 and 1948 London Games* (London: House of Commons Library, UK Parliament, 2012), 29, www.parliament.uk.
51 Carol Aronovici, "The Outlook for Low-Cost Housing in America," in Aronovici, *America Can't Have Housing*, 74.
52 Bauer, *Modern Housing*, 165; Barbara Penner, introduction to Bauer, *Modern Housing*, 24.
53 Mumford, "Social Imperatives in Housing," 16–17.
54 Pommer, "Architecture," 238.
55 Ford, *Slums and Housing*, 837–38.
56 Bauer, "Housing," 20.
57 R. L. Duffus, "What Modern Housing Means and Why It Is Delayed," *New York Times*, December 23, 1934, https://timesmachine.nytimes.com.
58 Abraham Goldfeld, "The Management Problem in Public Housing," in Aronovici, *America Can't Have Housing*, 66.

59 Goldfeld, 67, 68.
60 Office of Policy Development and Research, "Rental Burdens: Rethinking Affordability Measures," Department of Housing and Urban Development, September 22, 2014, www.huduser.gov.
61 Goldfeld, 68.
62 Julia Selby, "Home Is Where the Harm Is: Corruption, Fraud and Abuse in NYC's Public Housing," *Cornell Policy Review*, December 2022, www.cornellpolicyreview.com.
63 Nora Caplan-Bricker, "The Depression-Era Book That Wanted to Cancel the Rent," *New Yorker*, July 18, 2020.
64 Center on Budget and Policy Priorities, "Policy Basics: Public Housing," June 16, 2021, www.cbpp.org.
65 John C. Weicher, *Housing Policy at a Crossroads: The Why, How, and Who of Assistance Programs* (Washington, DC: AEI Press, 2012), 57.
66 Mumford, "Social Imperatives in Housing," 15 (second emphasis added).

CHAPTER 2. BRINGING THE IDEA TO LIFE

1 Alexander von Hoffman, "History Lessons for Today's Housing Policy: The Political Processes of Making Low-Income Housing Policy," Harvard University Joint Center for Housing Studies, August 2012, www.jchs.harvard.edu.
2 US Census Bureau, "1940 Census of Housing: Volume 2. General Characteristics," 1943, table 75, www.census.gov.
3 Lillian Wald, *The House on Henry Street* (New York: Holt, 1915), 46.
4 US Census Bureau, "1940 Census of Housing."
5 US Census Bureau.
6 R. L. Duffus, "What Modern Housing Means and Why It Is Delayed," *New York Times*, December 23, 1934, https://timesmachine.nytimes.com.
7 Walter Hegemann to Edith Elmer Wood, September 18, 1934, folder 1, box 7, Edith Elmer Wood Papers, 1900–1943, Avery Library, Columbia University.
8 Carol Aronovici, "The Outlook for Low-Cost Housing in America," in *America Can't Have Housing*, ed. Carol Aronovici (New York: Museum of Modern Art, 1934), 72.
9 Robinson Newcomb, "The National Real Property Inventory," in Aronovici, *America Can't Have Housing*, 59 (emphasis added).
10 Folder 1, box 20, Catherine Bauer Archival Papers, Bancroft Library, University of California, Berkeley.
11 Leon Keyserling to Catherine Bauer, August 18, 1936, folder 22, box 20, Catherine Bauer Archival Papers.
12 J. Joseph Hutmacher, *Senator Robert F. Wagner and the Rise of Urban Liberalism* (New York: Atheneum 1968), 206–8.
13 President Roosevelt himself was slow to endorse the Wagner bill, in part because of his concerns about increasing federal debt. The US Housing Authority, under

the terms of the bill, was to advance $500 million in loans to local housing authorities, who would then repay the proceeds of the bonds. Roosevelt was wary about what he descried as a potentially sixty-year federal financial commitment. Hutmacher, 228.

14 The bill was formally the Wagner-Steagall Act, named for Wagner and Rep. Henry B. Steagall of Alabama.
15 Hutmacher, *Senator Robert F. Wagner*, 227.
16 US Department of Housing and Urban Development, "United States National Housing Act of 1937," accessed October 7, 2024, www.hud.gov.
17 "United States National Housing Act of 1937."
18 Robert Kohn to Edith Elmer Wood, November 1933, folder 4, box 5, Edith Elmer Wood Papers.
19 C. E. Pynchon, Public Works Administration, to Edith Elmer Wood, February 10, 1937, folders 1–4, box 14, Edith Elmer Wood Papers.
20 Abraham Goldfeld, "The Management Problem in Public Housing," in Aronovici, *America Can't Have Housing*, 66.
21 Michael Patrick MacDonald, *All Souls: A Family Story from Southie* (Boston: Beacon, 2007), 51.
22 US Department of Housing and Urban Development, "United States National Housing Act of 1937."
23 Dan Austin, "Brewster-Douglass Project," *Historic Detroit*, accessed October 7, 2014, https://historicdetroit.org.
24 New York City Housing Authority, "Developments," accessed October 7, 2024, www.nyc.gov; Nicholas Dagen Bloom, *Public Housing That Worked: New York in the Twentieth Century* (Philadelphia: University of Pennsylvania Press, 2008).
25 Folder 12, box 8, Edith Elmer Wood Papers. This refers to a Department of Interior conference in Washington, DC.

CHAPTER 3. CUTTING THE RIBBON

1 J. S. Fuerst, with D. Bradford Hunt, *When Public Housing Was Paradise: Building Community in Chicago* (Urbana: University of Illinois Press, 2005), 3.
2 Fuerst, 47.
3 National Public Housing Museum, "Mind to Grow," transcript, August 2021, https://open.spotify.com.
4 Chad Freidrichs, dir., *The Pruitt-Igoe Myth* (Paul Fehler, Chad Freidrichs, Jaime Freidrichs, and Brian Woodman, 2015).
5 Michigan Public NPR, "Motown Legend Says Brewster-Douglass Taught Her 'People Are People,'" March 18, 2015, www.michiganradio.org.
6 New York City Department of Parks and Recreation, "Pomonok Playground," accessed October 8, 2024, www.nycgovparks.org.
7 Terry Katz, dir., *Pomonok Dreams* (Pomonok Films, 2014).
8 Nicolas Dagen Bloom, *Public Housing That Worked: New York in the Twentieth Century* (Philadelphia: University of Pennsylvania Press, 2008), 176.

9. Terry Katz and Al Stark, "Pomonok Dreams," accessed October 7, 2024, www.pomonokdreams.com.
10. Dave Hoekstra, "Lauderdale Courts: Elvis Left the Building, *Chicago Sun Times*, March 7, 2005.
11. Katz, *Pomonok Dreams*.
12. Dave Hoekstra, "Lauderdale Courts: Elvis Left the Building," *Chicago Sun-Times*, March 7, 2005.
13. Linda Alvarez and Michael Wilson, "Up and Out of New York's Projects," *New York Times*, March 29, 2009; "Chicago Housing Authority," Wikipedia, accessed October 7, 2024, https://en.wikipedia.org.
14. Hutmacher, *Senator Robert F. Wagner*, 209.
15. Hutmacher, 214.
16. Adam Majendie, "Why Singapore Has One of the Highest Home Ownership Rates," *Bloomberg*, July 8, 2020, www.bloomberg.com. See also Beng-Huat Chua, "Race Relations and Housing Policy in Singapore," *Journal of Architectural and Planning Research* 8, no. 4 (Winter 1991): 343–54, www.jstor.org/stable/43029053.

CHAPTER 4. WHAT WAS DESTROYED

1. "Memorandum, April 4, 1938, from Wilfred Lewis, Secretary to Mr. H. A. Lagerquist, Engineer, Subject: Project Proposal for Continuation of Demolition Project for the Fiscal Year—July 1, 1938–June 30, 1930," New York City Housing Authority Archives, Wagner-LaGuardia Archives, LaGuardia Community College, New York.
2. "Correspondence, December 10 and June 29, 1934, Samuel C. Herriman, Counsellor at Law, 43 Cedar Street, New York, to Hon. Langdon Post, Tenement House Commissioner," New York City Housing Authority Archives.
3. Helen Harrison, "We Live Again," folder 16, box 0053A1, New York City Housing Authority Records, Wagner-LaGuardia Archives, LaGuardia Community College.
4. Harrison.
5. US Census Bureau, "1930 Census of Housing: New York Assembly District 001; Enumeration District 31-1," accessed October 7, 2024, www.archives.gov. An enumeration district, as used by the Bureau of the Census, was an area that could be covered by a single enumerator (census taker) in one census period (two to four weeks for the 1930 census). The full information from the 1930 census was made public in April 2022.
6. Zachary J. Violette, *The Decorated Tenement: How Immigrant Builders and Architects Transformed the Slum in the Gilded Age* (Minneapolis: University of Minnesota Press, 2019), 16–17.
7. Violette, 88.
8. Robert Moses to Board of Estimate, April 15, 1952, folder 0667E4, box 05, New York City Housing Authority Records.
9. Martin Anderson, *Federal Bulldozer: A Critical Analysis of Federal Urban Renewal, 1949–1962* (Cambridge, MA: Joint Center for Urban Studies, 1964), 1.

10 William J. Collins and Katharine L. Shester, "Slum Clearance and Urban Renewal in the United States," working paper, National Bureau of Economic Research, September 2011, 5 (emphasis added), www.nber.org.
11 Joint Committee on Housing in Baltimore, folder 1, box 6, Edith Elmer Wood Papers. See also Report of the Joint Committee on Housing in Baltimore, 1930s, P-4871, folder 81, box S3D-B5, American Civil Liberties Union of Maryland Records, R0002-ACLU, Baltimore Studies Archives, https://archivesspace.ubalt.edu.
12 Brian David Robick, "Blight: The Development of a Contested Concept" (PhD diss., Carnegie Mellon University, 2011), 16 (emphasis added), ProQuest Dissertations Publishing, 2011.3452459.
13 Historic Pittsburgh, "Bedford Dwellings," accessed October 7, 2024, https://historicpittsburgh.org; Matt Simmons, "On This Day: April 15, 1940, Construction of Bedford Dwellings Is Completed," WPXI, April 15, 2020, www.wpxi.com. Bedford Dwellings was built on the site of the baseball stadium used by the Pittsburgh Crawfords, one of the most successful teams of the so-called Negro League.
14 Robick, "Blight," 200.
15 Howard Husock, "Roanoke Atones for Urban Renewal—Artistically," *City Journal*, October 23, 2023.
16 US Census Bureau, "1940 Census of Housing: Volume 2, General Characteristics," 1943, table 4, www.census.gov.
17 Cheryl Finley, Laurence Glasco, and Joe W. Trotter, *Teenie Harris, Photographer: Image, Memory, History* (Pittsburgh: University of Pittsburgh Press, 2011), 63, 77.
18 US Census Bureau, "1940 Census of Housing: General Characteristics," table 6.
19 John L. Clark, "Wylie Ave.," *Pittsburgh Courier*, November 15, 1952.
20 August Wilson Education Project, "Hill District Map," accessed October 7, 2024, www.wqed.org.
21 John L. Dorman, "August Wilson's Pittsburgh," *New York Times*, August 15, 2017, www.nytimes.com.
22 Carnegie Library of Pittsburgh, "The Hill District: History." Quoted in "Hill District," Wikipedia, accessed October 7, 2024, https://en.wikipedia.org.
23 Jared N. Day and Joe William Trotter, *Race and Renaissance: African-Americans in Pittsburgh since World War II* (Pittsburgh: University of Pittsburgh Press, 2010).
24 Housing Authority, City of Pittsburgh, "HACP Managed Communities," accessed October 7, 2024, https://hacp.org.
25 Detroit Historical Society, "Encyclopedia of Detroit," accessed October 7, 2024, https://detroithistorical.org/learn/encyclopedia-of-detroit/franklin-clarence-lavaughn.
26 US Bureau of the Census, "Characteristics of Dwelling Units by Census Tracts," table 3, in "1950 Housing Census," 1950.
27 James Ford, *Slums and Housing: History, Conditions, Policy* (Cambridge, MA: Harvard University Press, 1936), 247.

28 US Census Bureau, "1940 Census of Housing: Volume 2. General Characteristics," 1943, table 1, www.census.gov.
29 Ashley Holder and Molly Calvo, "Extant Buildings in the Mill Creek Valley: Past, Present, and Future," *Decoding the City*, accessed October 8, 2024, www.decodingstl.org.
30 St. Louis Public Schools, "A History of Vashon High School," accessed October 7, 2024, www.slps.org.
31 "Slum Surgery in St. Louis," *Architectural Forum*, April 1951, 128–36.
32 Tim Arango, "Can Reparations Bring Black Residents Back to San Francisco?," *New York Times*, May 17, 2023, www.nytimes.com.
33 Bill Durette, "The Spirit of the Bunker Hill Projects Will Live On," *Charlestown Patriot-Bridge*, April 15, 2021, https://charlestownbridge.com.
34 I tell this story in greater detail in my book *The Poor Side of Town: And Why We Need It* (New York: Encounter Books, 2021).
35 Keith N. Morgan, *Brookline Comprehensive Plan, 2005–2015* (Brookline, MA: Department of Planning and Community Development Town of Brookline, 2015), www.brooklinema.gov.
36 "Mary Ellen McCormack Development (Old Harbor Village)," *SAH Archipedia* (Society of Architectural Historians), accessed October 7, 2024, https://sah-archipedia.org.
37 Over-the-Rhine is a historic Cincinnati neighborhood, still standing.
38 Alyssa Konerman, "25,737 People Lived in Kenyon-Barr When the City Razed It to the Ground," *Cincinnati Magazine*, February 10, 2017, www.cincinnatimagazine.com.
39 Deqah Hussein-Wetzel, "Urban Renewal in Cincinnati's Lower West End," Gray & Pape Heritage Management, June 17, 2020, https://storymaps.arcgis.com.
40 Konerman, "25,737 People Lived in Kenyon-Barr."
41 Ford, *Slums and Housing*, 267–68.
42 Tom Buk-Swienty, *The Other Half: The Life of Jacob Riis and the World of Immigrant America*, trans. Annette Buk-Swienty (New York: Norton, 2008), 143.
43 Eileen Latzman Moon, *Untold Tales, Unsung Heroes: An Oral History of Detroit's African-American Community, 1918–1967* (Detroit: Wayne State University Press, 1994), 46.
44 Author interview, in Howard Husock, "The Tragic Lessons of Urban Renewal at Brookline's Farm," *Boston Globe*, January 31, 2020.
45 Scott C. Davis, *The World of Patience Gomes: Making and Unmaking a Black Community* (Seattle: Cune, 2000), 21.
46 Davis, 47, 175.
47 Davis, 46, 22, 52.
48 Davis, 162–63, 214.
49 Davis, 166, 23.

CHAPTER 5. CRUMBLING FAÇADES

1. Office of Policy Development and Research, "Assisted Housing, National and Local," US Department of Housing and Urban Development, 2021, www.huduser.gov.
2. US Department of Housing and Urban Development, "Characteristics of HUD-Assisted Renters and Their Units in 1989," March 1992, 5.
3. US Department of Housing and Urban Development. See Howard Husock, "New York City Public Housing Fails the City's New Poor," Manhattan Institute for Policy Research, October 2017, 7, https://media4.manhattan-institute.org.
4. Office of Policy Development and Research, "Assisted Housing, National and Local."
5. Ken Coleman, "On This Day in 1935: Eleanor Roosevelt Helps Dedicate Detroit Housing Project," *Michigan Advance*, September 9, 2022, https://michiganadvance.com/blog/on-this-day-in-1935-eleanor-roosevelt-helps-dedicate-detroit-housing-project/.
6. Martin Meyerson and Edward C. Banfield, *Politics, Planning and the Public Interest: The Case of Public Housing in Chicago* (Glencoe, IL: Free Press, 1955), 100–101.
7. Meyerson and Banfield, 30.
8. Edith Elmer Wood, "The Negro in Public War Housing: National Housing Agency, Federal Public Housing Authority, Office of Racial Relations, a Statement Prepared for the FPHA Racial Relations Advisers Conference, May 8–16, 1942, Washington, DC," folder 20, box 1, Edith Elmer Wood Papers, 1900–1943, Avery Library, Columbia University.
9. Robert Kohn to Edith Elmer Wood, October 26, 1933, folder 4, box 5, Edith Elmer Wood Papers.
10. C. E. Pynchon to Edith Elmer Wood, February 10, 1937, folder 1, box 7, Edith Elmer Wood Papers.
11. Irene V. Holleman, "Techwood Homes," *New Georgia Encyclopedia*, accessed October 7, 2024, www.georgiaencyclopedia.org.
12. Elizabeth Anne Martin, *Detroit and the Great Migration, 1916–1929* (Ann Arbor: Bentley Historical Library, University of Michigan, 1993).
13. Nicholas Dagen Bloom, *Public Housing That Worked: New York in the Twentieth Century* (Philadelphia: University of Pennsylvania Press, 2008), 169.
14. Quoted in A. Scott Henderson, *Housing and the Democratic Ideal: The Life and Thought of Charles Abrams* (New York: Columbia University Press, 2008), 46.
15. Quoted in Bloom, *Public Housing That Worked*, 170.
16. Bloom, 170.
17. Holleman, "Techwood Homes" (emphasis added).
18. M. T. Cooke Jr., "Housing Site Problems: A Review of the Site Selection Experience of 12 Cities since 1949," *Journal of Housing* 9, no. 2 (February 1952): 46–50, 61, 64, 66, 67. Quoted in Meyerson and Banfield, *Politics, Planning and the Public Interest*, 24.

19. Meyerson and Banfield, *Politics, Planning and the Public Interest*, 24.
20. Meyerson and Banfield, 25.
21. Meyerson and Banfield, 156.
22. Meyerson and Banfield, 102.
23. Meyerson and Banfield, 155.
24. Meyerson and Banfield, 156.
25. Meyerson and Banfield, 159.
26. Meyerson and Banfield, 34.
27. Meyerson and Banfield, 25.
28. Meyerson and Banfield, 113.
29. Meyerson and Banfield, 110.
30. Meyerson and Banfield, 104.
31. Daniel P. Moynihan, Memorandum for the President, January 16, 1970, Richard M. Nixon Presidential Library and Museum, www.nixonlibrary.gov.
32. Federal Housing Administration, *Underwriting Manual* (Washington, DC: US Government Printing Office, 1947). Quoted in Charles Abrams, "Can We Plan for Democratic Neighborhoods?," *Commentary*, February 1949, www.commentary.org.
33. Arnold R. Hirsch, *Making the Second Ghetto: Race and Housing in Chicago, 1940–1960* (Cambridge: Cambridge University Press, 1983), 213.
34. Meyerson and Banfield, *Politics, Planning and the Public Interest*, 99.
35. Meyerson and Banfield, 154.
36. Kenneth Jackson, *Crabgrass Frontier: The Suburbanization of the United States* (New York: Oxford University Press, 1985), 190. The full Roosevelt quote is this: "A nation of homeowners, a nation of people who own a real share in their own land, is unconquerable."
37. National Housing Act, June 27, 1934, https://fraser.stlouisfed.org.
38. Meyerson and Banfield, *Politics, Planning and the Public Interest*, 22.
39. Jackson, *Crabgrass Frontier*, 190.
40. Elaine Tyler May, *Homeward Bound: American Families in the Cold War Era* (New York: Basic Books, 1999), 152.
41. Abrams, "Can We Plan for Democratic Neighborhoods?"
42. Legal Information Institute, Cornell Law School, "Shelley v. Kraemer," April 2021, www.law.cornell.edu.
43. Richard Rothstein, "Public Housing: Government-Sponsored Segregation," *American Prospect*, October 11, 2012, https://prospect.org.

CHAPTER 6. ABANDONING THE PROJECTS

1. Richard Nixon, "Special Message to the Congress Proposing Legislation and Outlining Administration Actions to Deal with Federal Housing Policy," September 19, 1973, American Presidency Project, www.presidency.ucsb.edu.
2. Caitlin Lee and Clark Randall, "Inside the St. Louis Rent Strike of 1969," *Belt Magazine*, June 4, 2019, https://beltmag.com; "Administration Housing

Moratorium Comes under Fire," in *CQ Almanac 1973*, 29th ed. (Washington, DC: Congressional Quarterly, 1974), 428–32.
3. Nixon, "Special Message to the Congress."
4. Lee Rainwater, *Behind Ghetto Walls: Black Families in a Federal Slum* (Chicago: Aldine, 1970), 10.
5. Rainwater, 12.
6. Rainwater, 11–12.
7. Michael Patrick Macdonald, *All Souls: A Family Story from Southie* (Boston: Beacon, 1999), 102, 160.
8. Catherine Bauer, *Modern Housing* (Minneapolis: University of Minnesota Press, 2020), 136.
9. Kenneth Jackson, *Crabgrass Frontier: The Suburbanization of the United States* (New York: Oxford University Press, 1985), 211.
10. Jackson, 218.
11. Jackson, 205.
12. Quinton McDonald, "A Brief History of Black Suburbanization," *BlackPast*, March 10, 2022, www.blackpast.org.
13. McDonald.
14. Lee and Randall, "Inside the St. Louis Rent Strike of 1969."
15. US Department of Housing and Urban Development, "Major Legislation on Housing and Urban Development Enacted since 1932," accessed October 7, 2024, www.hud.gov.
16. Office of Policy Development and Research, "Assisted Housing, National and Local," US Department of Housing and Urban Development, 2021, www.huduser.gov.
17. Roger Biles, "Public Housing and the Postwar Urban Renaissance, 1949–1973," in *From Tenements to the Taylor Homes: In Search of an Urban Policy in Twentieth-Century America*, ed. John F. Bauman, Roger Biles, and Kristin M. Szylvian (University Park: Pennsylvania State University Press, 2000), 153.
18. Richard Disney and Guannan Luo, "The Right to Buy Public Housing in Britain: A Welfare Analysis," *Journal of Housing Economics* 35 (March 2017): 53.
19. Cushing N. Dolbeare and Sheila Crowley, "Graph 13. Budget Authority for Public Housing," in *Changing Priorities: The Federal Budget and Housing Assistance, 1976–2007* (National Low Income Housing Coalition, August 2002), 10, https://nlihc.org.
20. Catherine Bauer, "The Dreary Deadlock of Public Housing," *Architectural Forum* 106, no. 5 (May 1957).
21. Bauer.
22. Bauer.
23. "Slum Clearance: 1932–1952," *CQ Researcher*, November 22, 1952, https://library.cqpress.com.
24. "Public Housing, 1955," *CQ Researcher*, April 20, 1955, https://library.cqpress.com.
25. Robert B. Semple Jr., "Johnson Submits $2.3 Billion Plan to Rebuild Slums," *New York Times*, January 27, 1966.

26 Jeanne R. Lowe, *Cities in a Race with Time: Progress and Poverty in America's Renewing Cities* (New York: Vintage Books, 1967).
27 Robert Wood, "Obligations of an Affluent Society," address to National Association of Social Workers, May 27, 1966.
28 Wood.
29 Daniel P. Moynihan, "Memorandum for the President," January 16, 1970, Nixon Library, www.nixonlibrary.gov.
30 Moynihan.
31 Quoted in John C. Weicher, *Housing Policy at a Crossroads: The Why, How, and Who of Assistance Programs* (Washington, DC: AEI Press, 2012), 82.
32 Roger Biles, "A Mormon in Babylon: George Romney as Secretary of HUD, 1969–1973," *Michigan Historical Review* 38, no. 2 (2012): 63–89, https://doi.org/10.1353/mhr.2012.0002.
33 Nixon, "Message to Congress."
34 Weicher, *Housing Policy at a Crossroads*, 98.
35 Robert Asen, "Nixon's Welfare Reform: Enacting Historical Contradictions of Poverty Discourses," *Rhetoric & Public Affairs* 4, no. 2 (2001): 262, https://doi.org/10.1353/rap.2001.0019.
36 Almaz Zelleke, "Fifty Years Later, Reflecting on the Defeat of Nixon's Family Assistance Plan," *Basic Income Today*, August 8, 2019, https://basicincometoday.com.

CHAPTER 7. DEALING WITH THE AFTERMATH

1 National Commission on Severely Distressed Public Housing, *The Final Report of the National Commission on Severely Distressed Public Housing: A Report to the Congress and the Secretary of Housing and Urban Development* (Washington, DC: National Commission on Severely Distressed Public Housing, August 1992), 1, www.hud.gov.
2 National Commission, 16.
3 National Commission, 16.
4 Ben Austen, "The Towers Came Down and with Them, the Promise of Public Housing," *New York Times*, February 6, 2018.
5 Austen.
6 Milena Almagro, Eric Chyn, and Bryan A. Stuart, "Urban Renewal and Inequality: Evidence from Chicago's Public Housing Demolitions," Becker Friedman Institute for Economics, January 5, 2023, https://bfi.uchicago.edu; Connie H. Casey, "Characteristics of HUD-Assisted Renters and Their Units, 1989," Housing and Demographic Analysis Division, Department of Housing and Urban Development, March 1992, www.huduser.gov.
7 Office of Policy Development and Research, "Assisted Housing: National and Local," US Department of Housing and Urban Development, accessed October 8, 2024, www.huduser.gov.

8. John C. Weicher, *Housing Policy at the Crossroads: The Why, How, and Who of Assistance Programs* (Washington, DC: AEI Press, 2012), 251.
9. Thomas P. Sullivan, "Independent Monitor's Report No. 5 to the Chicago Housing Authority and the Central Advisory Council," January 8, 2003.
10. Howard Husock, "Let's End Housing Vouchers," *City Journal*, Autumn 2000, www.city-journal.org. Based on author interviews.
11. Hannah Rosin, "American Murder Mystery: Why Is Crime Rising in So Many American Cities? The Answer Implicates One of the Most Celebrated Antipoverty Programs of Recent Decades," *The Atlantic*, July–August 2008, www.theatlantic.com.
12. Ingrid Gould Ellen, Michael C. Lens, and Katherine O'Regan, "American Murder Mystery Revisited: Do Housing Voucher Households Cause Crime?," NYU Wagner School and Furman Center for Real Estate & Urban Policy, March 2012, 1, https://furmancenter.org.
13. Austen, "Towers Came Down."
14. Xinhao Wang and David P. Varady, "Using Hot-Spot Analysis to Study the Clustering of Section 8 Housing Voucher Families," *Housing Studies* 20, no. 1 (2005): 29–48, https://doi.org/10.1080/0267303042000308714.
15. Weicher, *Housing Policy at the Crossroads*, 251.
16. Manpower Demonstration Research Corporation, "Rent Reform in Subsidized Housing: Launching the Stepped and Tiered Rent Demonstration," 5, accessed October 11, 2024, https://mdrc.org.
17. Weicher, *Housing Policy at the Crossroads*, 81.
18. Witold Rybczynski, "Looking Back at the Success of Harbor Point," *Architect*, August 16, 2013, www.architectmagazine.com.
19. Morgan v. Hennigan, 379 F. Supp. 410 (D. Mass.1974), https://law.justia.com.
20. Jane Roessner, *A Decent Place to Live: From Columbia Point to Harbor Point, A Community History* (Boston: Northeastern University Press, 2000), 186, https://archive.org.
21. J. E. Goody, "From Project to Community: The Redesign of Columbia Point [Place Profile: Harbor Point]," *Places* 8, no. 4 (1993): 23, https://escholarship.org.
22. Rybczynski, "Looking Back."
23. Rybczynski; Oscar Newman, *Defensible Space: Crime Prevention through Urban Design* (New York: Macmillan, 1972).
24. LCD Consulting, "America's First Public Housing Projects Are Converted to Mixed-Income Family Housing: Centennial Place Apartments (Phase IV), Scholars Landing (Phase III)," April 18, 2019, www.ldgconsulting.com.
25. Lawrence Vale, "Housing Chicago: Cabrini-Green to Parkside of Old Town," *Places*, February 2012, https://placesjournal.org.
26. Larry Buron, Susan Popkin, Diane Levy, Laura Harris, and Jill Khadduri, "The HOPE VI Resident Tracking Study," Department of Housing and Urban Development, November 2002, i, www.urban.org.

27 Buron et al., vi.
28 Alexander von Hoffman, "Calling upon the Genius: Housing Policy in the Great Society, Part Three," Harvard University Joint Center for Housing Studies, March 15, 2010, 3, www.jchs.harvard.edu.
29 Robert J. Chaskin and Mark L. Joseph, *Integrating the Inner City: The Promise and Perils of Mixed Income Public Housing Transformation* (Chicago: University of Chicago Press, 2015). Also in this interview: "Is Mixed-Income Public Housing the Answer?," *Institute for Housing Studies at De Paul University Blog*, May 9, 2016, www.housingstudies.org.
30 Rybczynski, "Harbor Point."
31 Rybczynski.
32 Buron et al., "HOPE VI Resident Tracking Study," vi.
33 Buron et al., viii.
34 Buron et al., viii.
35 Jennifer B, "Harbor Point on the Bay," Yelp, August 24, 2023, www.yelp.com.
36 Emil S, "Centennial Place Apartment Homes," Yelp, August 11, 2021, www.yelp.com.
37 Milan Ozdinec, correspondence with the author, April 25, 2023.
38 US Department of Housing and Urban Development, FY2010 Budget, June 20, 2010, https://archives.hud.gov.
39 Michael J. White, *American Neighborhoods and Residential Differentiation* (New York: Russell Sage Foundation, 1987), 27.

CHAPTER 8. FIXING WHAT'S BROKEN

1 Ellen Bassuk and Deborah Franklin, "Homelessness Past and Present: The Case of the United States, 1890–1925," *New England Journal of Public Policy* 8, no. 1 (March 1992): 67–85, https://scholarworks.umb.edu.
2 Michael Katz, *In the Shadow of the Poorhouse: A Social History of Welfare in the United States*, (New York: Basic Books, 1986), 37.
3 Office of Policy Development and Research, "Assisted Housing: National and Local," US Department of Housing and Urban Development, accessed October 8, 2024, www.huduser.gov.
4 Center on Budget and Policy Priorities, "Policy Basics: Public Housing," June 16, 2021, www.cbpp.org.
5 Matthew Desmond, *Evicted: Poverty and Profit in the American City* (New York: Crown, Penguin Random House, 2016), 3.
6 US Senate, Committee on Banking, Housing, and Urban Affairs, *"The Rent Eats First": How Renters and Communities Are Impacted by Today's Housing Market*, August 2, 2022, www.banking.senate.gov.
7 Desmond, *Evicted*, 3, 131.
8 New York City Housing Authority, "Annual Plan and Finance Information, Tenure Analysis," October 18, 2022, www.nyc.gov.

9 Kirk McClure, "Length of Stay in Assisted Housing," Office of Policy Development and Research, US Department of Housing and Urban Development, October 2017, www.huduser.gov.

10 Testimony by Matthew Desmond, in US Senate Committee on Banking, Housing, and Urban Affairs, *"The Rent Eats First": How Renters and Communities Are Impacted by Today's Housing Market*, August 2, 2022, www.banking.senate.gov.

11 US Department of Housing and Urban Development, "Moving to Work Demonstration Program," accessed October 8, 2024, www.hud.gov.

12 Stephanie Garlock, "By 2011, Atlanta Had Demolished All of Its Public Housing Projects. Where Did All Those People Go?," *Bloomberg*, May 8, 2014, www.bloomberg.com.

13 Howard Husock, "Atlanta's Public Housing Revolution," *City Journal*, Autumn 2010, www.city-journal.org.

14 US Department of Housing and Urban Development, "Areas of Opportunity," September 2020, www.hud.gov.

15 Raj Chetty, Nathaniel Hendren, and Lawrence F. Katz, "The Effects of Exposure to Better Neighborhoods on Children: New Evidence from the Moving to Opportunity Experiment," *American Economics Review* 106, no. 4 (April 2016): 860.

16 Raj Chetty and Nathaniel Hendren, "The Impacts of Neighborhoods on Intergenerational Mobility: Childhood Exposure Effects and County-Level Estimates," Harvard University and NBER, May 2015, 7.

17 United States of America vs. New York City Housing Authority, Complaint 18 civ. 523, filed June 11, 2018, www.justice.gov.

18 New York City Housing Authority, "NYCHA Fact Sheet: RAD (Rental Assistance Demonstration)," accessed October 8, 2024, www.nyc.gov.

19 US Department of Housing and Urban Development, "RAD Flyer, Rental Assistance Demonstration (RAD)," September 12, 2022, www.hud.gov.

20 "Mandatory Inclusionary Housing (MIH), enacted in March 2016, requires a share of new housing in medium- and high-density areas that are rezoned to promote new housing production—whether rezoned as part of a city neighborhood plan or a private rezoning application—to be permanently affordable." NYC Housing Preservation and Development, "Inclusionary Housing Program," accessed October 8, 2024, www.nyc.gov.

21 Meyerson and Banfield, *Politics, Planning and the Public Interest*, 161–62.

CHAPTER 9. THE PROJECTS TODAY

1 New York City Housing Authority, "Service Interruptions Overview," accessed October 8, 2024, https://my.nycha.info.

2 Greg B. Smith, "NYCHA Falling Facade in The Bronx Follows Years of Citations and No Action," *The City*, May 1, 2023, www.thecity.nyc.

3 Treez Da Stoner, "Inside Jackson Projects (Bronx)," YouTube, September 4, 2020, www.youtube.com/watch?v=HsVs4gZfM4M.
4 Michael Kimmelman, "Rebirth in the South Bronx: Is This the Way to Save Public Housing?," *New York Times*, August 19, 2021, www.nytimes.com.
5 The developers are Camber Property Group, MBD Community Housing Corporation, and L+M Development Partners.
6 Michael Kimmelman, "A Rebirth in the Bronx: Is This How to Save Public Housing?," *New York Times*, August 5, 2021.
7 FRED Economic Data, St. Louis Fed, "Housing Inventory: Median Home Size in Square Feet in New York-Newark-Jersey City, NY-NJ-PA," accessed October 8, 2024, https://fred.stlouisfed.org; Jack Caporal, "Average House Price by State in 2023," *The Ascent*, August 26, 2024, www.fool.com.
8 US Department of Housing and Urban Development, "PHA Contact Report by State and City: North Carolina," accessed October 8, 2024, www.hud.gov; US Department of Housing and Urban Development, "PHA Contact Report by State and City: Alabama," accessed October 8, 2024, www.hud.gov; US Department of Housing and Urban Development, "PHA Contact Report by State and City: Mississippi," accessed October 8, 2024, www.hud.gov.
9 Thomas W. Hatchett and Ruth M. Little, *The History and Architecture of Long Wharf and Greater Duffyfield: African American Neighborhoods in New Bern, North Carolina, City of New Bern* (New Bern, NC: Historic Preservation Commission, April 1994), 1, 12, https://digital.ncdcr.gov.
10 North Carolina History Project, "The 'Black Second' Congressional District, 1872–1901," accessed October 8, 2024, https://northcarolinahistory.org.
11 Hatchett and Little, *History and Architecture of Long Wharf and Greater Duffyfield*, 15.
12 Hatchett and Little, 25.
13 "US Census, 1920, Craven County, NC, City of New Bern, Ward 4, District 0025," Ancestry.com, accessed October 8, 2024, www.ancestry.com.
14 Office of Policy Development and Research, "Assisted Housing: National and Local," US Department of Housing and Urban Development, accessed October 8, 2024, www.huduser.gov.
15 Office of Policy Development and Research.
16 "Karl-Marx-Hof," Wien Geschichte Wiki, accessed October 8, 2024, www.geschichtewiki.wien.gv.at.
17 This and other data come from author's correspondence with Christian Schantl, Division of International Relations, City of Vienna, July 4, 2023.
18 Richard Conway, "Vienna Launched a Public Housing Revolution in the 1920s," Citylab, *Bloomberg*, November 8, 2023, www.bloomberg.com.
19 Conway.
20 City of Vienna, "Flat Allocation Criteria," accessed October 8, 2024, https://socialhousing.wien.

CHAPTER 10. MAKING SENSE OF THE PROJECTS

1 Howard Husock, "Household Size Limitations and Housing Costs," American Enterprise Institute, October 24, 2022, www.aei.org.
2 Tracey Tulley, "$100 Million Film Studio to Rise from Rubble of Ex-Housing Project Site," *New York Times*, May 17, 2022, www.nytimes.com.
3 Jane Jacobs, *The Death and Life of Great American Cities* (New York: Random House, 1993), 146–47.

SELECTED BIBLIOGRAPHY

Aronovici, Carol, ed. *America Can't Have Housing.* New York: Museum of Modern Art, 1934.

Bauer, Catherine. *Modern Housing.* Boston: Houghton Mifflin, 1934. Reprint, Minneapolis: University of Minnesota Press, 2020.

Bauman, John F., Roger Biles, and Kristin M. Szylvian, eds. *From Tenements to the Taylor Homes: In Search of an Urban Housing Policy in Twentieth-Century America.* University Park: Pennsylvania State University Press, 2000.

Bloom, Nicholas Dagen. *Public Housing That Worked: New York in the Twentieth Century.* Philadelphia: University of Pennsylvania Press, 2008.

Bloom, Nicholas Dagen, and Mathew Gordon Lasner, eds. *Affordable Housing in New York: The People, Places, and Policies That Transformed a City.* Princeton, NJ: Princeton University Press, 2016.

Bloom, Nicholas Dagen, Fritz Umbach, and Lawrence Vale. *Public Housing Myths: Perception, Reality, and Social Policy.* Ithaca, NY: Cornell University Press, 2015.

Caro, Robert A. *The Power Broker: Robert Moses and the Fall of New York.* New York: Knopf, 1974.

Davis, Scott C. *The World of Patience Gomes: Making and Unmaking a Black Community.* Seattle: Cune, 2000.

Finley, Cheryl, Laurence Glasco, and Joe W. Trotter. *Teenie Harris, Photographer: Image, Memory, History.* Pittsburgh: University of Pittsburgh Press, 2011.

Ford, James. *Slums and Housing: History, Conditions, Policy.* Cambridge, MA: Harvard University Press, 1936.

Friedman, Lawrence M. *Government and Slum Housing.* Chicago: Rand McNally, 1966.

Fuerst, J. S., with D. Bradford Hunt. *When Public Housing Was Paradise: Building Community in Chicago.* Urbana: University of Illinois Press, 2005.

Goetz, Edward C. *New Deal Ruins: Race, Economic Justice, and Public Housing Policy.* Ithaca, NY: Cornell University Press, 2013.

Henderson, A. Scott. *Housing and the Democratic Ideal: The Life and Thought of Charles Abrams.* New York: Columbia University Press, 2008.

Hirsch, Arnold R *Making the Second Ghetto: Race and Housing in Chicago, 1940–1960.* Cambridge: Cambridge University Press, 1983.

Hunt, D. Bradford. *Blueprint for Disaster: The Unravelling of Chicago Public Housing.* Chicago: University of Chicago Press, 2002.

Husock, Howard. *The Poor Side of Town: And Why We Need It.* New York: Encounter Books, 2021.

Jackson, Kenneth. *Crabgrass Frontier: The Suburbanization of the United States.* New York: Oxford University Press, 1985.

Jacobs, Jane. *The Death and Life of Great American Cities.* New York: Random House, 1993.

Kotlowitz, Alex. *There Are No Children Here: The Story of Two Boys Growing Up in the Other America.* New York: Random House, 1991.

Lubove, Roy. *The Progressives and the Slums: Tenement House Reform in New York City, 1890–1917.* Pittsburgh: University of Pittsburgh Press, 1962.

MacDonald, Michael Patrick. *All Souls: A Family Story from Southie.* Boston: Beacon, 2007.

Meyerson, Martin, and Edward Banfield. *Politics, Planning and the Public Interest: The Case of Public Housing in Chicago.* Glencoe, IL: Free Press, 1955.

Museum of Modern Art. *Architecture and Government Housing.* New York: Museum of Modern Art, 1936.

Newman, Oscar. *Defensible Space: Crime Prevention through Urban Design.* New York: Macmillan, 1972.

Rainwater, Lee. *Behind Ghetto Walls: Black Families in a Federal Slum.* Chicago: Aldine, 1970.

Riis, Jacob A. *How the Other Half Lives: Studies among the Tenements of New York.* New York: Charles Scribner's Sons, 1890.

Rossi, Peter H., and Robert Dentler. *The Politics of Urban Renewal: The Chicago Findings.* Glencoe, IL: Free Press, 1961.

Rothstein, Richard. *The Color of Law: A Forgotten History of How Government Segregated America.* New York: Norton, 2017.

Spewack, Bella. *Streets: A Memoir of the Lower East Side.* New York: Feminist Press at City University of New York, 1995.

Vale, Lawrence J. *After the Projects: Public Housing Redevelopment and the Governance of the Poorest Americans.* Oxford: Oxford University Press, 2019.

Violette, Zachary J. *The Decorated Tenement: How Immigrant Builders and Architects Transformed the Slum in the Gilded Age.* Minneapolis: University of Minnesota Press, 2019.

Wald, Lillian. *The House on Henry Street.* New York: Holt, 1915.

Weicher, John C. *Housing Policy at a Crossroads: The Why, How, and Who of Assistance Programs.* Washington, DC: AEI Press, 2012.

Williams, Jeremy. *Detroit: The Black Bottom Community.* Charleston, SC: Arcadia, 2009.

INDEX

Page numbers in italics indicate Figures

Abrams, Charles, 91, 101–2
Advisory Committee on Government Housing Policies, 115
Affluent Society, 116
affordable housing, 100, 133; in Chicago, 128; in HOPE VI, 142; in New York City, 128, 157; RAD and, 157
African Americans. *See* Blacks
Alabama, 6, 50, 172; Mobile, 84
Alferez, Kristan, 180–81
All Souls (MacDonald), 107–8
America Can't Have Housing, 11, 26, 28
American Association of University Women, 18
amortization, 41, 100
Anderson, Martin, 66, 70
Andrew Jackson Houses, in Bronx, 160–67
Architect (magazine), 133, 138
Architectural Forum, 2; Bauer at, 113–14; Pruitt-Igoe in, 76
Aronovici, Carol, 11, 30, 40–41
Astor, John Jacob, 47
Atlanta, 149–55; Blacks in, 90, 92, 152–53; Centennial Place in, 137, 140–41; demolition in, 126, 151; drugs in, 151, 152; Harris Homes in, 151; Hollywood Homes in, 152; HOPE VI in, 136–37; Jim Crow and, 90; MTW in, 149–50; pre-public housing, *83*; Roosevelt, F., in, 172; University Houses in, 90; upward mobility in, 153; Youth and Family Project in, 150, 152. *See also* Techwood Homes
The Atlantic (magazine), 130–31
Atlantic City, New Jersey, 88–89
Austria, 21

Ballard, Florence, 54
Baltimore: Blacks in, 68; demolition in, 126; Moving to Opportunity in, 154; slum clearance in, 67–68
Banfield, Edward, 86, 87, 93–94, 97, 102–3
Barber, Danny, 160–65
Barnes, Doug, 130–31
Baruch, Bernard, 47
bathtubs, 39
Bauer, Catherine: *America Can't Have Housing* and, 28; at *Architectural Forum*, 113–14; Blacks and, 94; on capitalism, 34, 109; as "Communist Catherine," 40; on Depression, 34; limited appeal of, 100; *Modern Housing* by, 19, 34, 40, 41, 59; Museum of Modern Art *Modern Housing Exhibition* and, 9, 18, 19–20, 25, 33, 132, 158; National Housing Act of 1937 and, 41–42, 44, 50, 113–14; on private housing market, 128; on public housing failure, 113–15, 146; slum clearance and, 65, 79; on specifics of building forms, 30
Baychester Houses, in Bronx, 167–71, *168*
Becton, Carol, 173, 175, 177, 179
Bedford Dwellings, in Pittsburgh, 69

219

Behind Ghetto Walls (Rainwater), 106
Belgium, 21
Berlin, 25–26
Beydler, Nicole, 180
Big Flat, in New York City, 21–22
Black, Ken, 57–58
"Black Flight," 110
Blacks (African Americans): in Andrew Jackson Houses, 161; in Atlanta, 90, 92, 152–53; in Atlantic City, New Jersey, 88–89; attitudes toward, 97–98; in Baltimore, 68; in Boston, 77, 78, 133–34; in Brooklyn, 84; in Charleston, South Carolina, 84; in Chicago, 84–85, 87, 93–99, 110; in Cleveland, 89; in Detroit, 9, 48–49, 74–75, 81–87, 92–93; FHA and, 98, 100, 101–3; Great Migration of, 90; in Harlem, 90; HUD and, 117–20, 122; immigrants and, 90, 99–100; Johnson, L., and, 116; migration of, 10, 90; in Mobile, Alabama, 84; Museum of Modern Art *Modern Housing Exhibition and*, 84; National Housing Act of 1937 and, 84, 92; in New Bern, North Carolina, 172–79; New Deal and, 89; New York Association for Improving the Condition of the Poor for, 21–22; in New York City, 91, 110; NYCHA and, 91; in Pittsburgh, 68–73; public housing and, 84–103; PWA and, 87, 89–90, 92; racial segregation of, 1, 48; restrictive covenants and, 98, 102; in Richmond, Virginia, 81–82, 88; in Roanoke, Virginia, 69–70, 93; in San Bernardino, California, 180–81; in San Francisco, 76–77; slum clearance and, 90–91, 102–3, 116; southern strategy and, 121–22; in Stamford, Connecticut, 89; in St. Louis, 75–76, 106–7; in suburbs, 109–10; in tenements, 80–81; tuberculosis of, 24; at Tuskegee Institute, 22; unemployment of, 120; upward mobility of, 98, 129–30; Wood, E. E., and, 88–90, 94
Blankfein, Lloyd, 58
Bloom, Nicholas Dagen, 54–55, 56, 91
Bolden, Hope, 150–51
Boston, 20, 36, 38, 46; Blacks in, 77, 78, 133–34; Columbia Point in, 133–35, *134*, 142; drugs in, 138; Harbor Point in, 136, 138–39, 140; HOPE VI in, 136–37; Moving to Opportunity in, 154; Old Colony in, 107–8; slum clearance in, 66–67, 77, 78; suburbs of, 77, 109
Boston Gas, 119
Boston Globe, 136
Brewster-Douglass Projects, in Detroit, 36, *48*, 48–50, 54, 75, 85–86
Bronx: Andrew Jackson Houses in, 160–67; Baychester Houses in, 167–71, *168*; Edenwald Houses in, 170
Brooke, Edward (Brooke Amendment), 9, 38, 111, 132, 148
Brooklyn, 20; Blacks in, 84; Ingersol Houses in, 36, 141; in pre-public housing era, 39; Rutland Towers in, 84; Williamsburg Houses in, 14–15
Bruegel, Sabrina, 177
Buffalo, 78
Bulger, James "Whitey," 108
Butler, Jerry, 58
Butler, Nicholas Murray, 15
Byrne, Miles, 139

Cabrini-Green Projects, in Chicago, 53–54, 95, 137; demolition of, 127–28
California, 20. *See also* Los Angeles; San Francisco
Campbell, Robert, 136
capitalism: Bauer on, 34, 109; Mumford on, 31
cash welfare, 188

Census Bureau, 34; on rents, 147
Centennial Place, in Atlanta, 137, 140–41
CHA. *See* Chicago Housing Authority
Charleston, South Carolina, 84
Chaskin, Robert, 138
Chetty, Raj, 153–54, 158
Chicago, 9, 20; affordable housing in, 128; Blacks in, 84–85, 87, 93–99, 110; demolition in, 127–28; drugs in, 131; HOPE VI in, 136–37; Housing Choice Vouchers in, 128–30; Moving to Opportunity in, 154; National Housing Act of 1937 and, 45; National Public Housing Museum in, 52–53, 99, *195*; North Town Village in, 137; politically influenced hiring in, 56; PWA in, 13; slum clearance in, 94–96; slums of, 80; Wentworth Gardens in, 126–27. *See also* Cabrini-Green Projects; Ida B. Welles Project; Robert Taylor Homes; Stateway Gardens
Chicago Housing Authority (CHA), 58, 98, 121, 127, 129; Wood, E., of, 94–95, 157–58
Christie-Forsythe project, 14
Cincinnati: Queensgate in, 79; slum clearance in, 77–78
Cities in a Race with Time, 116
"City of Green," 29
The City of Tomorrow (Le Corbusier), 27–28
Clark, John R., 71–72
Clark, Kenneth, 117
Cleveland, 13, 36; Blacks in, 89; home occupancy in, 80; National Housing Act of 1937 and, 45
Clinton, Bill, 137, 149, 181
Cobo, William, 9
Columbia Point, in Boston, 133–35, *134*, 142
Columbus, 126

Committee on Slum Clearance Plans, in New York City, 66
"Communist Catherine," Bauer as, 40
concentrated poverty, 10, 103, 112, 135; in Craven Terrace and Trent Court, 172; HOPE VI and, 137–38; in Techwood Homes in Atlanta, 137
Congress for Racial Equality, 91
contingent assistance, 144
corruption, 35–36
Craven Terrace, in New Bern, North Carolina, 171–79
Crazy Rich Asians (movie), 59
crime, 125; Black suburbanization and, 110; in Boston's Old Colony, 107–8; in slums, 63. *See also* gangs; violent crime
"Cross Out Slums" poster, 3
cross-ventilation, 28

dark ghetto, 117
Da Stoner, Treez, 165–67
The Death and Life of Great American Cities (Jacobs), 192–93
The Decorated Tenement (Violette), 64–65
defensible space, 169; in HOPE VI, 140
demolition, 2; in Atlanta, 126, 151; in Baltimore, 126; of Brewster-Douglass Projects, 49; of Cabrini-Green Projects, 127–28; in Chicago, 127–28; of Columbia Point in Boston, 135; in Columbus, 126; of Harris Homes, 151; of high-rise towers, 6; in HOPE VI, 142; in New Orleans, 126; in Philadelphia, 126; of Pomonok Houses, 54–55; of Pruitt-Igoe Project, 105, 106–8, *107*, 110–11, 126; of Robert Taylor Homes, 4, *124*, 127; of Stateway Gardens, 127; of Techwood Homes, 149–50; in Tucson, 126. *See also* slum clearance

Department of Housing and Urban Development (HUD), 112, 113, 116–17; Blacks and, 117–20, 122; Moving to Opportunity of, 154–55; MTW of, 149–50, 155, 181; on opportunity neighborhoods, 153–54; RAD of, 155–57, 167–68, 178, 179–80. *See also* Housing Choice Vouchers; Housing Opportunities for People Everywhere
Depression, 2, 3–4, 10; Bauer on, 34; housing starts in, 34; New Deal in, 12–13, 36
Desmond, Matthew, 147–49, 153–54, 156, 158
Detroit: Blacks in, 9, 48–49, 74–75, 81–87, 92–93; Brewster-Douglass Projects in, 36, 48, 48–49, 54, 75, 85–86; Model Cities in, 118; pre-public housing, 85; single-family homes in, 80; slum clearance in, 48–49, 74–75, 81–83, 86–87
Disalvo, Charles, 64
Disney, Richard, 112
domestic workers, slum clearance and, 68
Douglass, Frederick, 9, 48
drugs: addiction to, 9; in Atlanta, 151, 152; "Black Flight" and, 110; in Boston, 138; in Chicago, 131; at Craven Terrace, 178; dealing of, 4; HOPE VI and, 138; at Ida B. Welles, 53
Duggan, Moe, 108

Earned Income Tax Credit, 123
Edenwald Houses, in Bronx, 170
Eisenhower, Dwight, 115
"Eliminate Crime in the Slums through Housing" poster, of NYCHA, 5
Ellis, Bertrand, 53
England, 21, 112
environmental determinism, 138
Evans, Walker, 15

Evicted (Desmond), 147
Experimental Housing Allowance Program, 121

fair housing laws, 102–3
Family Assistance Plan, 123
Family Stability and Opportunity Voucher Act, 148–49
family support coordinators (FSCs), 151
Fannie Mae (Federal National Mortgage Association), 101
Father Coughlin, 40
Federal Emergency Administration of Public Works, 89
Federal Emergency Management Agency, 178
Federal Housing Administration (FHA), 98, 100, 101–3; suburbs and, 109
Federal National Mortgage Association (Fannie Mae), 101
FHA. *See* Federal Housing Administration
First Houses, of NYCHA, 13, 47–48
flush toilet, 39, 65, 71
Ford, James, 22–25, 33, 75, 79–80; Blacks and, 94
Franklin, Aretha, 75
Franklin, C. L., 75
FSCs. *See* family support coordinators
Fuerst, J. D., 52–53

Galbraith, John Kenneth, 116
gangs, 1; at Andrew Jackson Houses, 165; in Atlanta, 151; at Baychester Houses, 169; "Black Flight" and, 110; in Chicago, 131; at Craven Terrace and Trent Court, 178
garden apartments, 50
George Bernard, 173, 175, 179
Georgia, 6. *See also* Atlanta
Germany, 21; Nazi, 29–30
Glass, Carter, 43

Glover, Renee, 149–54, 158
Goldberg, Whoopi, 58, 110
Goldfeld, Abraham, 34–35, 46–47
Goldston, Eli, 119
Goody, Joan E., 135
Gore, Al, 137
gradualism, 99, 103, 119
Great Britain, Housing of the Working Classes Act in, 30
Great Migration, of Blacks, 90
Great Society, 113, 118
Gropius, Walter, 12, 25–26, 28–29
Gross, Sandra, 168–69, 170

Harbor Point, in Boston, 135–36, 138–39, 140
Harlem: Blacks in, 90; James Weldon Johnson Houses in, 90; riots in, 116; slum clearance in, 66
Harlem River Houses, 171
Harris, Teenie, 71, 72–74
Harris Homes, in Atlanta, 151
Harrison, Helen, 62–63
Hegemannn, Werner, 29; Wood, E. E., and, 40
Her Provincial Cousin (Wood, E. E.), 18
Herriman, Charles, 64
Herron Avenue at Intersection of Milwaukee Street, Hill District (Harris), 71, 72
Herter, Peter, 65
high-rise towers, 2, 4, 36, 50; demolition of, 6. *See also specific projects*
Hirsch, Arnold, 94, 98
Hispanics, 164
Hitler, Adolf, 29–30; Johnson, P., and, 40
Hoffman, Alexander von, 21, 38, 138
Holly, Bertha, 72
Holly, Seth, 72
Hollywood Homes, in Atlanta, 152
home ownership, 100–101
Homeowners Loan Corporation, 100

"Home Renovation and Modernization," in National Housing Act of 1937, 100–101
HOPE VI. *See* Housing Opportunities for People Everywhere
Houses at 6 and 8 Watt Street, Hill District, March-May, 1959 (Harris), 71
Housing and Home Finance Agency, 117
Housing and Urban Development Act of 1969, 111
Housing Census of 1940, 39, 70–71
Housing Choice Vouchers, 120–21, 122, 144, 146–47; cash value of, 131; in Chicago, 128–30; HUD and, 128–29; increases to, 147; length of stay with, 148
Housing Development Board, in Singapore, 59
Housing of the Working Classes Act, in Great Britain, 30
Housing Opportunities for People Everywhere (HOPE VI), 136–43, *145*, 189; mixed-income housing in, 137–38, 139, 143
housing stamps, 120
Housing the Unskilled Wage Earner (Wood, E. E.), 20
How the Other Half Lives (Riis), 21, 64, 80
HUD. *See* Department of Housing and Urban Development
Hughes, Langston, 48

Ickes, Harold, 13, 41–42, 50
Ida B. Welles Project, in Chicago, 84–85, 95; drugs at, 53; in *Public Housing* documentary, 9
immigrants: Blacks and, 90, 99–100; slum clearance and, 63–65, 80–81
inclusionary zoning, in New York City, 157
income, 1; rents as proportion of, 35, 111, 132, 147. *See also* Housing Choice Vouchers; mixed-income housing

indoor relief, 145, 149
industrial decentralization, 25, 79
Ingersol Houses, in Brooklyn, 36, 141
Integrating the Inner City (Chaskin and Joseph), 138
interest rate, 41
"International Style," 12, 14

Jackson, Kenneth, 109–10
Jackson, Mahalia, 151
Jacobs, Jane, 109–10, 192–93
James Weldon Johnson Houses, in Harlem, 90
Jeannere, Charles-Édouard. *See* Le Corbusier
Jim Crow, 87, 172; Atlanta and, 90; Boston and, 134
Jitney, 72
Joe Turner's Come and Gone, 72
Johnson, James Weldon, 48
Johnson, Lyndon, 113, 116, 118
Johnson, Phillip, 12, 15, 27; Hitler and, 40
Jones, Paul, 68–69, 72
Joseph, Mark, 138

Karl-Marx-Hoff, in Vienna, Austria, 182–85, *183*
Kastner, Alfred, 32
Katz, Michael, 146
Kennedy, Albert, 20, 38
Keyserling, Leon, 42
Kimmelman, Michael, 169
Klein, Joel, 57
Kohn, Robert, 19, 89
Kolokowsky, Betty, 64
Kolokowsky, Max, 64
Krieger, Louis, 64

labor unions, 32; National Housing Act of 1937 and, 47; National Labor Relations Act and, 41; Roosevelt, F., and, 118–19
LaGuardia, Fiorello, 13

Lauderdale Courts, in Memphis, 56–58
Lausche, William, 174
Le Corbusier, 12, 14, 20, 133, 135, 190; *The City of Tomorrow* by, 27–28
Lehman, Herbert, 13, 16
Lescaze, William, 14
Lewenberg Foundation, 34–35, 46
lighting, 29
Los Angeles: Moving to Opportunity in, 154; riots in, 116
Louisiana, 6
Louisville, Kentucky, slum clearance in, 14
Lower East Side, of New York City, 39, 45
low-rise projects, 52; Boston's Old Colony, 107–8
Lucas, Adolph, 64
Luo, Guannan, 112

MacDonald, Michael Patrick, 46, 107–8
Mackley Houses, in Philadelphia, 32
Making the Second Ghetto (Hirsch), 94
Malaysia, 59–60
"The Management Problem in Public Housing" (Goldfeld), 34–35, 46–47
Marine Drive, in Buffalo, 78
Marx, Karl, 3, 182–85, *183*
Mayfield, Curtis, 58
McCoy, Eugene, 165
McDaniel, Nelson, 172–75
McDonald, Quinton, 110
Memphis, 6; Lauderdale Courts in, 56–58; violent crime in, 130–31
Meyerson, Martin, 86, 87, 93–94, 97, 102–3
Middleton, Tom, 174
Mississippi, 6, 172
mixed-income housing, 150, 158, 193–94; in HOPE VI, 137–38, 139, 143
mixed-use projects, 25
Mobile, Alabama, 84
Model Cities, 118
Modern Housing (Bauer), 19, 34, 40, 41, 59

Modern Housing Exhibition. See Museum of Modern Art *Modern Housing Exhibition*
modernist architecture, 10, 27, 29; political and financial challenges of, 33
Moelis, Ron, 171
Moore, Edward Roberts, 15–16
Moore, Kevin, 130
moratorium, on public housing, 8, 104–24, 146, 148
Morgenthau, Henry, 55–56
Moroney, Frank, 81, 83
Moses, Robert, 9, 15, 192; Blacks and, 91; slum clearance and, 66
Moving to Opportunity, of HUD, 154–55
Moving to Work (MTW), 149–50, 155, 181
Moynihan, Daniel Patrick, 98, 104–5, 119–20, 193–94
Mr. T, 58
MTW. *See* Moving to Work
Mumford, Lewis, 9, 19, 25, 31, 37
Museum of Modern Art *Modern Housing Exhibition*, 1–37, *17*, *18*, *26*, 40–41, 50–51; Bauer and, 9, 18, 19–20, 25, 33, 132, 158; Blacks and, 84; Nixon's moratorium and, 105, 120; rents in, 55; Wood, E. E., and, 9, 18–21, 33, 36

NAACP, 88–89
National Action Plan, 126
National Association of Real Estate Boards, 115
National Bureau of Economic Research, 67
National Committee on Housing, 18
National Housing Act of 1937, 36, 38–51, 146, 191; Bauer and, 41–42, 44, 50, 113–14; Blacks and, 84, 92; "Home Renovation and Modernization" in, 100–101; labor unions and, 47; Nixon's moratorium and, 105; PWA and, 43–45; Roosevelt, F., and, 203n13; slum clearance in, 44–45, 48–49; United States Housing Authority from, 12, 42–43; Wagner and, 41, 42, 47, 58–59; Wood, E. E., and, 44, 45, 50
National Housing Act of 1949, 8, 43, 49–50, 115, 116; signing of, *51*; slum clearance in, 66–67, 77–78, 80, 118
National Industrial Recovery Act of 1932, 13
National Labor Relations Act, 41
National Low Income Housing Policy Center, 148
National Public Housing Museum, in Chicago, 52–53, 99, *195*
Nazi Germany, 29–30
the Netherlands, 21
Newark, New Jersey, 190–91
New Bern, North Carolina, Craven Terrace and Trent Court in, 171–79
Newcomb, Robinson, 41
New Deal: Blacks and, 89; in Depression, 12–13, 36; Nixon and, 104. *See also* National Housing Act of 1937
New Jersey: Atlantic City, 88–89; Newark, 190–91
new law tenements, in New York City, 21
New Orleans, demolition in, 126
New York (state): Buffalo, 78; State Commission Against Discrimination of, 91
New York Association for Improving the Condition of the Poor, 21–22
New York City: affordable housing in, 128, 157; Big Flat in, 21–22; Blacks in, 91, 110; Committee on Slum Clearance Plans in, 66; inclusionary zoning in, 157; Lower East Side of, 39, 45; maintenance in, 56; Moving to Opportunity in, 154; National Housing Act of 1937 and, 45; new law tenements in, 21; RAD in, 155–56; restreeting in, 191; settlement houses in, 22, 38, 39; slum clearance in, *49*, 55, 79–80; *Slums and Housing* and, 22–25, 75, 79–80; slums of, 80;

New York City (*cont.*)
suburbs in, 109; Tenement House Commission of, 22; Tenement House Law in, 65; tenements in, 21, 39, 46, 64–65, 132. *See also* Museum of Modern Art *Modern Housing Exhibition*

New York City (Bronx): Andrew Jackson Houses in, 160–67; Baychester Houses in, 167–71, *168*

New York City (Brooklyn), 20; Blacks in, 84; Ingersol Houses in, 36, 141; in pre-public housing era, 39; Rutland Towers in, 84; Williamsburg Houses in, 14–15

New York City (Harlem): Blacks in, 90; James Weldon Johnson Houses in, 90; riots in, 116; slum clearance in, 66

New York City (Queens), Pomonok Houses in, 54–55, 67, 91, 99, 117

New York City Housing Authority (NYCHA), 1; Andrew Jackson Houses and, 160–67; Baychester Houses and, 167–71, *168*; Blacks and, 91; corruption at, 35–36; as country's largest landlord, 6; "Eliminate Crime in the Slums through Housing" poster of, 5; First Houses of, 13, 47–48; in golden age, 56; Harlem River Houses and, 171; Museum of Modern Art *Modern Housing Exhibition* and, 16; notable residents of, 58; slum clearance by, 61–66; tenure in, 4; waiting list at, 7, 190

New York Times, 15–16, 74, 126–27

Nixon, Richard, 8–9, 98, 142, 189; Family Assistance Plan of, 123; Housing Choice Vouchers of, 120–21, 122, 128–30, 144, 146–47; moratorium by, 8, 104–24, 146, 148; southern strategy of, 121–22

no-bid contracting, 35–36

North Carolina, 6; New Bern, 171–79

North Town Village, in Chicago, 137
NYCHA. *See* New York City Housing Authority

Obama, Barack, 155
Odom, Jeffrey, 177
Ohio: Columbus, 126. *See also* Cincinnati; Cleveland
Old Colony, in Boston, 107–8
opportunity neighborhoods, HUD on, 153–54
Ortiz, Tiffany, 176
outdoor relief, 145, 148
overcrowding: in public housing, 95, 104, 190; in tenements, 19

Patrick, Deval, 50, 58, 110
pay as you go, 55–56
Pei, I. M., 136
Pennsylvania. *See* Philadelphia; Pittsburgh
Perez, Vikkey, 130
Perkins, Francis, 15
Perry, Walter, 174
pest infestation, 9
Phelps-Stokes, I. N. (Phelps-Stokes Fund), 22
Philadelphia, 13, 20, 23, 38; demolition in, 126; Mackley Houses in, 32; in pre-public housing era, 39; single-family homes in, 39, 80
Pittsburgh: Bedford Dwellings in, 69; Blacks in, 68–73; Model Cities in, 118; slum clearance in, 68–72, *72–74*
place-based subsidy, 120
Places (magazine), 135
playgrounds, 29
plumbing, 32, 68, 187; flush toilet, 39, 65, 71
Politics, Planning and the Public Interest (Meyerson and Banfield), 93–94
Pommer, Richard, 32

Modern Housing Exhibition. See Museum of Modern Art *Modern Housing Exhibition*
modernist architecture, 10, 27, 29; political and financial challenges of, 33
Moelis, Ron, 171
Moore, Edward Roberts, 15–16
Moore, Kevin, 130
moratorium, on public housing, 8, 104–24, 146, 148
Morgenthau, Henry, 55–56
Moroney, Frank, 81, 83
Moses, Robert, 9, 15, 192; Blacks and, 91; slum clearance and, 66
Moving to Opportunity, of HUD, 154–55
Moving to Work (MTW), 149–50, 155, 181
Moynihan, Daniel Patrick, 98, 104–5, 119–20, 193–94
Mr. T, 58
MTW. *See* Moving to Work
Mumford, Lewis, 9, 19, 25, 31, 37
Museum of Modern Art *Modern Housing Exhibition*, 1–37, *17*, *18*, *26*, 40–41, 50–51; Bauer and, 9, 18, 19–20, 25, 33, 132, 158; Blacks and, 84; Nixon's moratorium and, 105, 120; rents in, 55; Wood, E. E., and, 9, 18–21, 33, 36

NAACP, 88–89
National Action Plan, 126
National Association of Real Estate Boards, 115
National Bureau of Economic Research, 67
National Committee on Housing, 18
National Housing Act of 1937, 36, 38–51, 146, 191; Bauer and, 41–42, 44, 50, 113–14; Blacks and, 84, 92; "Home Renovation and Modernization" in, 100–101; labor unions and, 47; Nixon's moratorium and, 105; PWA and, 43–45; Roosevelt, F., and, 203n13; slum clearance in, 44–45, 48–49; United States Housing Authority from, 12, 42–43; Wagner and, 41, 42, 47, 58–59; Wood, E. E., and, 44, 45, 50
National Housing Act of 1949, 8, 43, 49–50, 115, 116; signing of, *51*; slum clearance in, 66–67, 77–78, 80, 118
National Industrial Recovery Act of 1932, 13
National Labor Relations Act, 41
National Low Income Housing Policy Center, 148
National Public Housing Museum, in Chicago, 52–53, 99, *195*
Nazi Germany, 29–30
the Netherlands, 21
Newark, New Jersey, 190–91
New Bern, North Carolina, Craven Terrace and Trent Court in, 171–79
Newcomb, Robinson, 41
New Deal: Blacks and, 89; in Depression, 12–13, 36; Nixon and, 104. *See also* National Housing Act of 1937
New Jersey: Atlantic City, 88–89; Newark, 190–91
new law tenements, in New York City, 21
New Orleans, demolition in, 126
New York (state): Buffalo, 78; State Commission Against Discrimination of, 91
New York Association for Improving the Condition of the Poor, 21–22
New York City: affordable housing in, 128, 157; Big Flat in, 21–22; Blacks in, 91, 110; Committee on Slum Clearance Plans in, 66; inclusionary zoning in, 157; Lower East Side of, 39, 45; maintenance in, 56; Moving to Opportunity in, 154; National Housing Act of 1937 and, 45; new law tenements in, 21; RAD in, 155–56; restreeting in, 191; settlement houses in, 22, 38, 39; slum clearance in, 49, 55, 79–80; *Slums and Housing* and, 22–25, 75, 79–80; slums of, 80;

New York City (*cont.*)
  suburbs in, 109; Tenement House Commission of, 22; Tenement House Law in, 65; tenements in, 21, 39, 46, 64–65, 132. *See also* Museum of Modern Art *Modern Housing Exhibition*
New York City (Bronx): Andrew Jackson Houses in, 160–67; Baychester Houses in, 167–71, *168*
New York City (Brooklyn), 20; Blacks in, 84; Ingersol Houses in, 36, 141; in pre-public housing era, 39; Rutland Towers in, 84; Williamsburg Houses in, 14–15
New York City (Harlem): Blacks in, 90; James Weldon Johnson Houses in, 90; riots in, 116; slum clearance in, 66
New York City (Queens), Pomonok Houses in, 54–55, 67, 91, 99, 117
New York City Housing Authority (NYCHA), 1; Andrew Jackson Houses and, 160–67; Baychester Houses and, 167–71, *168*; Blacks and, 91; corruption at, 35–36; as country's largest landlord, 6; "Eliminate Crime in the Slums through Housing" poster of, *5*; First Houses of, 13, 47–48; in golden age, 56; Harlem River Houses and, 171; Museum of Modern Art *Modern Housing Exhibition* and, 16; notable residents of, 58; slum clearance by, 61–66; tenure in, 4; waiting list at, 7, 190
New York Times, 15–16, 74, 126–27
Nixon, Richard, 8–9, 98, 142, 189; Family Assistance Plan of, 123; Housing Choice Vouchers of, 120–21, 122, 128–30, 144, 146–47; moratorium by, 8, 104–24, 146, 148; southern strategy of, 121–22
no-bid contracting, 35–36
North Carolina, 6; New Bern, 171–79

North Town Village, in Chicago, 137
NYCHA. *See* New York City Housing Authority

Obama, Barack, 155
Odom, Jeffrey, 177
Ohio: Columbus, 126. *See also* Cincinnati; Cleveland
Old Colony, in Boston, 107–8
opportunity neighborhoods, HUD on, 153–54
Ortiz, Tiffany, 176
outdoor relief, 145, 148
overcrowding: in public housing, 95, 104, 190; in tenements, 19

Patrick, Deval, 50, 58, 110
pay as you go, 55–56
Pei, I. M., 136
Pennsylvania. *See* Philadelphia; Pittsburgh
Perez, Vikkey, 130
Perkins, Francis, 15
Perry, Walter, 174
pest infestation, 9
Phelps-Stokes, I. N. (Phelps-Stokes Fund), 22
Philadelphia, 13, 20, 23, 38; demolition in, 126; Mackley Houses in, 32; in pre-public housing era, 39; single-family homes in, 39, 80
Pittsburgh: Bedford Dwellings in, 69; Blacks in, 68–73; Model Cities in, 118; slum clearance in, 68–72, 72–74
place-based subsidy, 120
Places (magazine), 135
playgrounds, 29
plumbing, 32, 68, 187; flush toilet, 39, 65, 71
Politics, Planning and the Public Interest (Meyerson and Banfield), 93–94
Pommer, Richard, 32

Pomonok Dreams (documentary), 54, 57
Pomonok Houses, in Queens, 54–55, 67, 91, 99, 117
"Poor Boys Done Good," 57–58
poorhouses, 1, 36, 103, 113, 125, 145–46, 148, 189
The Poor Side of Town (Husock), 10
Post, Langdon, 50, 62
Presley, Elvis, 6, 56–58, 117
private management, 33, 35; in National Housing Act of 1937, 44; with RAD, 179
protective (restrictive) covenants, 98, 102
Pruitt-Igoe Project, in St. Louis, 2, 54, 76; demolition of, 105, 106–8, *107*, 110–11, 126; rent strikes at, 111, 132
public housing: aftermath of, 125–43; average years of residence in, 112; birth of, 11–37; Blacks and, 84–103; current projects, 160–85; failure of, 104–24; future of, 144–59; golden age of, 52–60; limited appeal of, 100; making sense of, 186–96; moratorium on, 8, 104–24, 146, 148; overcrowding in, 95, 104, 190; as poorhouses, 1, 36, 103, 113, 125, 145–46, 148, 189; rules in, 136, 138–39; time limit for, 144, 154, 179–80, 188. *See also specific topics and projects*
Public Housing (documentary), 85
"Public Housing" (Rothstein), 102
Public Housing Conference, 22
Public Works Administration (PWA), 13; Blacks and, 87, 89–90, 92; at Museum of Modern Art *Modern Housing Exhibition*, 19; National Housing Act of 1937 and, 43–45; slum clearance and, 67, 75
Puckett, Kirby, 58
Puerto Ricans, 91, 164
Puerto Rico, 123
Pulitzer, Joseph, 15
PWA. *See* Public Works Administration
Pynchon, C. E., 89

Queens, Pomonok Houses in, 54–55, 67, 91, 99, 117
Queensgate, in Cincinnati, 79

racial segregation. *See* Blacks
RAD. *See* Rental Assistance Demonstration
Radiant City, 14, 20, 27; Andrew Jackson Houses and, 165; Columbia Point in Boston and, 133; National Housing Act of 1937 and, 47; Singapore and, 59
Raines, Teaera, 151–52
Rainwater, Lee, 106
Ramey, David, Jr., 69–70, 93
Ramlall, Joseph, 169–70
Reagan, Ronald, 120
Red Vienna, 3–4, 12
reformer's gaze, 23
Rental Assistance Demonstration (RAD), 155–57, 167–68, 178, 179–80
rent-burdened, 147, 148
rents: Census Bureau on, 147; employment *versus* welfare and, 125–26; for maintenance, 108; in Museum of Modern Art *Modern Housing Exhibition*, 55; in New York City, 56; as proportion of income, 35, 111, 132, 147; at Pruitt-Igoe Project in St. Louis, 111
rent strikes, 33; at Pruitt-Igoe Project, 111, 132
restreeting, in New York City, 191
restrictive (protective) covenants, 98, 102
Richmond, Virginia: Blacks in, 81–82, 88; slum clearance in, 81–82
Ricks, Annie, 126–27, 131
Riis, Jacob, 21, 64, 79–80, 147
Ring Estate, 26
Roanoke, Virginia: Blacks in, 93; slum clearance in, 69–70
Robert Taylor Homes, in Chicago, 50, *53*, 95, 110; demolition of, *124*, 127; waiting list at, 4

Robinson, Smokey, 49
Rockefelle, Abby Aldrich, 15
Romney, George, 121
Roosevelt, Eleanor, 13, 47–48, *48*, 85; NAACP and, 89
Roosevelt, Franklin, 12–13, 19, 36; in Atlanta, 172; labor unions and, 118–19; National Housing Act of 1937 and, 42, 203n13; at Techwood Homes, 90. *See also* New Deal
Rosin, Hannah, 130–31
Ross, Daniel, 54
Ross, Diana, 49, 54
Rothstein, Richard, 102
Russell, Ruby, 54
Rutland Towers, in Brooklyn, 84

San Bernardino, California, 179–82
San Francisco: National Housing Act of 1937 and, 45; slum clearance in, 76–77
Satchwell, John, 174
Schaeffer, Ben, 64
Schantl, Christian, 183–84
Schulz, Howard, 4–5, 58
Selby, Julia, 35–36
Seth Boyden Terrace, in Newark, New Jersey, 191
Severely Distressed Public Housing, 125–26; HOPE VI and, 136
settlement houses, in New York City, 22, 39
Shaw, George Bernard, 113
shootings, 1
Shoulder Straps and Sunbonnets (Wood, E. E.), 18
"Siemensstadt," 25–26
Simkhovitch, Mary, 22, 50
Simmons, Furnifold, 173
Singapore, Housing Development Board in, 59
single-family homes, 29, 109; in Philadelphia, 39, 80; in suburbs, 56

single-parent families, 1, 153; women in, 7, 125, 147, 151–52
slum clearance, 6, 13, 15; in Baltimore, 67–68; Bauer and, 65, 79; Blacks and, 90–91, 102–3, 116; in Boston, 66–67, 77, 78; in Buffalo, 78; central necessity of, 20; in Chicago, 94–96; in Cincinnati, 77–78; dark reality of, 61–83; in Detroit, 48–49, 74–75, 81–82, 83, 86–87; domestic workers and, 68; forced relocation from, 193; Ford for, 24–25; in Harlem, 66; immigrants and, 63–65, 80–81; losses from, 105; in Louisville, Kentucky, 14; in National Housing Act of 1937, 44–45, 48–49; in National Housing Act of 1949, 66–67, 77–78, 80, 118; neighborhood determinations for, 67–69; in New York City, 49, 55, 79–80; by NYCHA, 61–66; in Pittsburgh, 68–74, *72–74*; PWA and, 67, 75; in Richmond, Virginia, 81–82; in Roanoke, Virginia, 69–70; in San Francisco, 76–77; in St. Louis, 75–76; total of, 67
Slums and Housing (Ford), 22–25, 75, 79–80
Smith, Al, 16
"The Social Imperatives in Housing" (Mumford), 31
Sotomayor, Sonia, 4–5, 49, 58, 110
South Carolina, 84
southern strategy, 121–22
Spence, Harry, 134–35
SSI. *See* Supplemental Security Income
Stamford, Connecticut, Blacks in, 89
state-aided housing, 21
State Commission Against Discrimination, of New York (state), 91
Stateway Gardens, in Chicago, 95; demolition of, 127
Steagall, Henry, 172, 204n14

St. Louis: Blacks in, 106–7; National Housing Act of 1937 and, 45; politically influenced hiring in, 56; slum clearance in, 75–76; slums of, 80; suburbs in, 109. *See also* Pruitt-Igoe Project
Stonorov, Oskar, 32
Straus, Nathan, 50
Strech, George, 96
subletting, 154
suburbs: Blacks in, 109–10; of Boston, 77, 109; Fannie Mae and, 101; movement to, 109–10; in New York City, 109; population growth in, 101; single-family homes in, 56; in St. Louis, 109
Sulzberge, Arthur Ochs, 15
superblocks, 14, 27, 36, 94, 181, 186
Supplemental Security Income (SSI), 150–51
The Supremes, 54
swimming pools, 47
Swope, Herbert Bayard, 15

Taft, Robert, 57, 58
Techwood Homes, in Atlanta, 90, 92; concentrated poverty in, 137; demolition of, 149–50
Temporary Assistance to Needy Family, 188
Tenement House Commission, of New York City, 22
Tenement House Law, in New York City, 65
Tenement House Museum, 16
tenements: Blacks in, 80–81; of Lewenberg Foundation, 46; in New York City, 21, 39, 46, 64–65, 80–81, 132; overcrowding in, 19; in religious terms, 64–65
Tennessee. *See* Memphis
tenure, 1–2; in NYCHA, 4
transfer of assistance, 157

Trent Court, in New Bern, North Carolina, 171–79
Truman, Harry, 8–9, *51*
tuberculosis, 23–24
Tucson, demolition in, 126
Tuskegee Institute, Blacks at, 22
Tyson, Kenya, 151

Underwriting Manual (FHA), 98
unemployment: benefits, 112; of Blacks, 120
United States Housing Authority, 203n13; "Cross Out Slums" poster of, *3*; Keyserling of, 42; from National Housing Act of 1937, 12, 42–43
University Houses, in Atlanta, 90
upward mobility, 57; in Atlanta, 153; of Blacks, 98, 129–30; decline in, 112; in Richmond, Virginia, 81

Vandenberg, Arthur, 58
Vicari, George, 64
Vienna, Austria, 3–4; Karl-Marx-Hoff in, 182–85, *183*
violent crime, 1; with HOPE VI, 140; HOPE VI and, 138; in Memphis, 130–31
Violette, Zachary J., 64–65
Virginia. *See* Richmond, Virginia; Roanoke, Virginia
Virgin Islands, 123

Wagner, Robert, 41, 42, 47, 57, 58–59, 203n13, 204n14
waiting list: at Columbia Point, 134; at Karl-Marx-Hof, 185; at NYCHA, 7, 190; RAD and, 189; at Robert Taylor Project, 4; in San Bernardino, 180
Wald, Lillian, 38
Wales, 112
Weaver, Robert, 117
Weicher, John, 122, 129, 132

Welles, Ida B., 9, 53
Wentworth Gardens, in Chicago, 126–27
When Public Housing Was Paradise (Fuerst), 52–53
White, George Wilson, 173
White, Michael, 143
Williamsburg Houses, in Brooklyn, 14–15
Wilson, August, 72–74
Wilson, Mary, 54
Wiseman, Frederick, 53, 84–85
women, in single-parent families, 7, 125, 147, 151–52
Wood, Edith, of CHA, 94–95, 157–58
Wood, Edith Elmer, 38, 132, 146; Blacks and, 88–90; Hegemannn and, 40; home ownership and, 101; Museum of Modern Art *Modern Housing Exhibition* and, 9, 18–21, 33, 36; National Housing Act of 1937 and, 40, 43, 44, 45, 50; on private housing market, 128; slum clearance and, 65
Wood, Robert, 20, 117–18, 195
The World of Patience Gomes, 81, 88
Wright, Frank Lloyd, 40

Yamasaki, Minoru, 76
Youth and Family Project, in Atlanta, 150, 152

zone of emergence, 20
zoning laws, 28

ABOUT THE AUTHOR

Howard A. Husock is a Senior Fellow in Domestic Policy Studies at the American Enterprise Institute and the author of four previous books, including *America's Trillion-Dollar Housing Policy Mistake: The Failure of American Housing Policy* (2001), *The Poor Side of Town: And Why We Need It* (2021), *Who Killed Civil Society? The Rise of Big Government and Decline of Bourgeois Norms* (2019), and *Philanthropy under Fire* (2015). Previously, he served as the Director of Case Studies in Public Policy and Management at the Harvard Kennedy School of Government and as Vice President for Research and Publications at the Manhattan Institute for Policy Research. Awards for his work as a documentary film producer include the Robert F. Kennedy Journalism Award (for coverage of the disadvantaged), a National News and Documentary Emmy Award, and the Corporation for Public Broadcasting Local Programming Award. His writing has appeared in the *Wall Street Journal*, the *New York Times*, the *New York Times Magazine*, *City Journal*, *National Affairs*, *National Journal*, the *Washington Post*, and many other leading publications.